EMBARGO

ALSO BY PHILIP DELVES BROUGHTON

What They Teach You At Harvard Business School: My Two Years Inside the Cauldron of Capitalism

Life's a Pitch: What the World's Best Salespeople Can Teach Us All

How to Think Like an Entrepreneur

PHILIP DELVES BROUGHTON

EMBARGO

HOW THE 1973 OIL CRISIS CHANGED THE WORLD

HUTCHINSON
HEINEMANN

HUTCHINSON HEINEMANN

UK | USA | Canada | Ireland | Australia
India | New Zealand | South Africa

Hutchinson Heinemann is part of the Penguin Random House group of companies whose addresses can be found at global.penguinrandomhouse.com

Penguin Random House UK,
One Embassy Gardens, 8 Viaduct Gardens, London SW11 7BW

penguin.co.uk

Penguin Random House UK

First published 2026

001

Set in 12.8/16pt Dante MT Std
Typeset by Six Red Marbles UK, Thetford, Norfolk

Printed and bound in Great Britain by Clays Ltd, Elcograf S.p.A.

The authorised representative in the EEA is Penguin Random House Ireland, Morrison Chambers, 32 Nassau Street, Dublin D02 YH68

A CIP catalogue record for this book is available from the British Library

ISBN: 978-1-529-15466-5 (hardback)
ISBN: 978-1-529-15467-2 (trade paperback)

MIX Paper FSC® C018179 www.fsc.org

Penguin Random House is committed to a sustainable future for our business, our readers and our planet. This book is made from Forest Stewardship Council® certified paper. For more information on our environmental initiatives please visit penguin.co.uk

For the Emergency Contact

Contents

CONTENTS

PART III

'The foreigners spoke and inquired about places no one knew of or ever went to, so it was clear that they were not looking for water.'

From *Cities of Salt* by Abdelrahman Munif

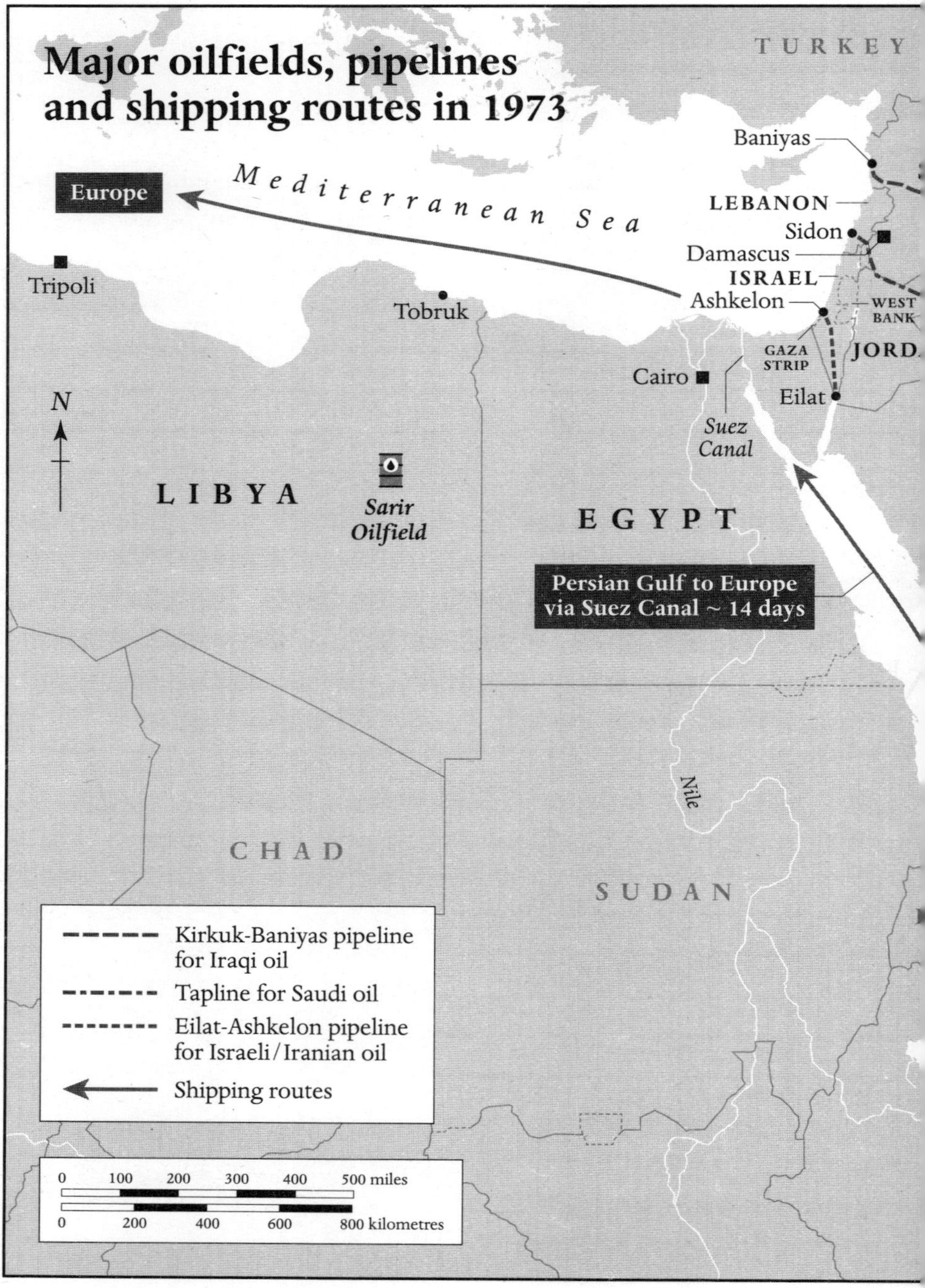
Major oilfields, pipelines and shipping routes in 1973
TURKEY
Baniyas
LEBANON
Sidon
Damascus
ISRAEL
Ashkelon
WEST BANK
GAZA STRIP
JORD.
Eilat
Mediterranean Sea
Europe
Tripoli
Tobruk
Cairo
Suez Canal
N
LIBYA
Sarir Oilfield
EGYPT
Persian Gulf to Europe via Suez Canal ~ 14 days
Nile
CHAD
SUDAN
Kirkuk-Baniyas pipeline for Iraqi oil
Tapline for Saudi oil
Eilat-Ashkelon pipeline for Israeli/Iranian oil
Shipping routes
0 100 200 300 400 500 miles
0 200 400 600 800 kilometres

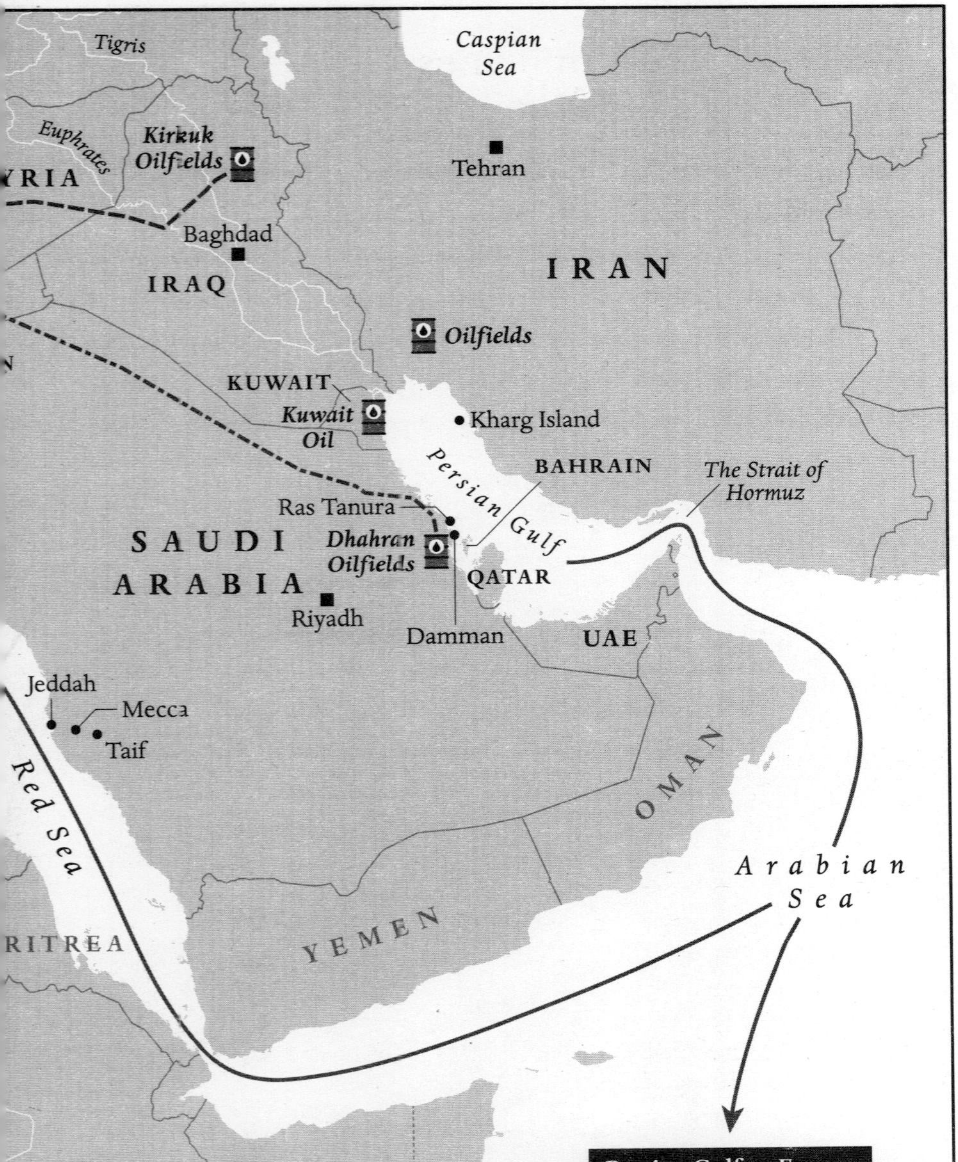

Tigris
Caspian Sea
Euphrates
Kirkuk Oilfields
RIA
Tehran
Baghdad
IRAN
IRAQ
Oilfields
KUWAIT
Kuwait Oil
Kharg Island
Persian Gulf
BAHRAIN
The Strait of Hormuz
Ras Tanura
SAUDI ARABIA
Dhahran Oilfields
QATAR
Riyadh
Damman
UAE
Jeddah
Mecca
Taif
OMAN
Red Sea
Arabian Sea
YEMEN
RITREA
Persian Gulf to Europe via Cape of Good Hope ~ 20–30 days

Israel's borders in 1949, after armistice agreements with its neighbours
LEBANON
Damascus
SYRIA
Haifa
Mediterranean Sea
Tel Aviv
JORDAN
Amman
Jerusalem
Occupied by Egypt
Dead Sea
ISRAEL
Suez Canal
Cairo
Sinai Peninsula
Eilat
Nile
Gulf of Suez
Gulf of Aqaba
EGYPT
SAUDI ARABIA
N
Red Sea
0 25 50 75 100 miles
0 50 100 150 kilometres

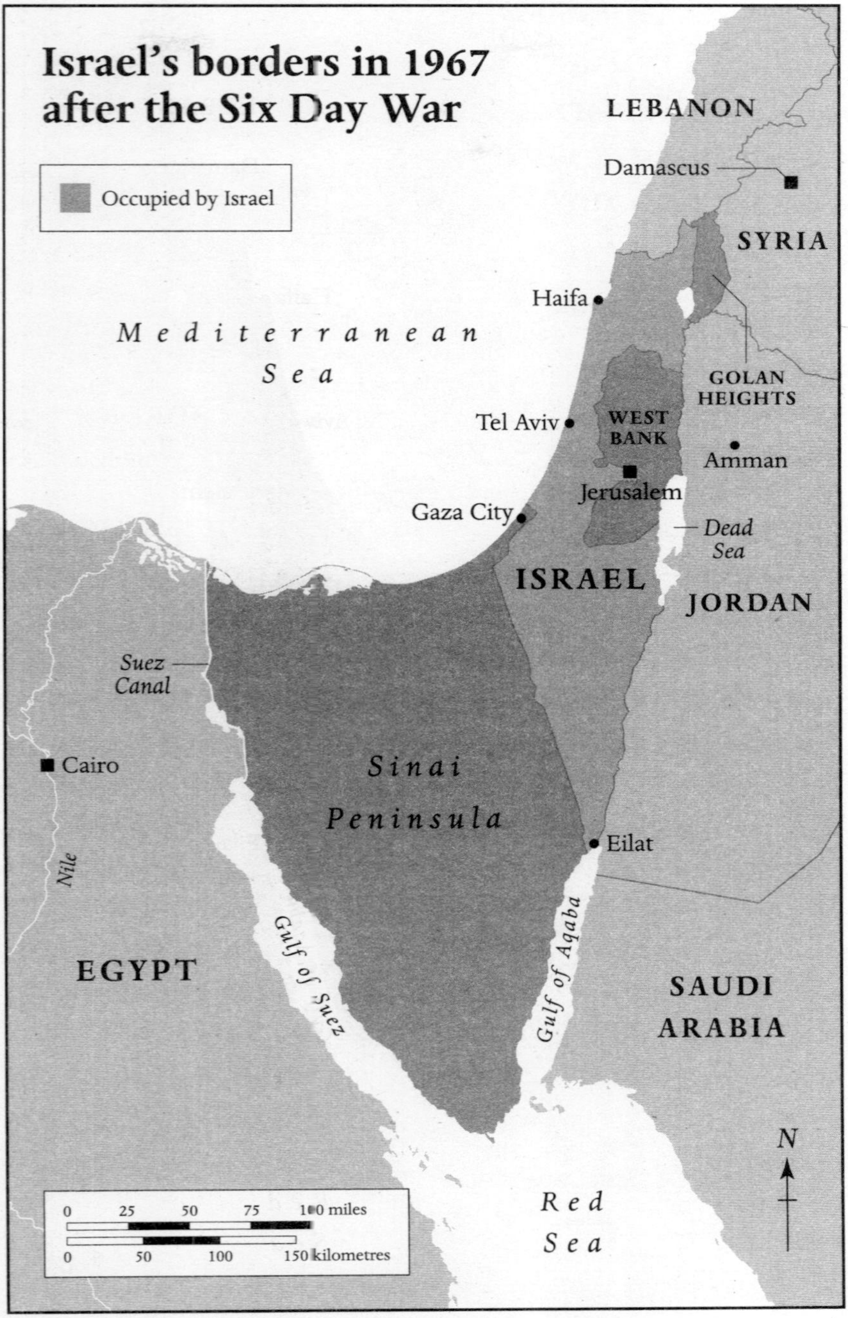
Israel's borders in 1967
after the Six Day War
Occupied by Israel
LEBANON
Damascus
SYRIA
Haifa
Mediterranean
Sea
GOLAN
HEIGHTS
Tel Aviv
WEST
BANK
Amman
Jerusalem
Gaza City
Dead
Sea
ISRAEL
JORDAN
Suez
Canal
Cairo
Sinai
Peninsula
Eilat
Nile
Gulf of Suez
Gulf of Aqaba
EGYPT
SAUDI
ARABIA
N
0 25 50 75 100 miles
0 50 100 150 kilometres
Red
Sea

Prologue

Hawking Season

In early October, falcons appeared in the sky above Saudi Arabia's northern border, flying south towards Africa for the winter. Hunters set up camps in the desert and waited. Early in the morning, immediately after dawn prayer, they set out to inspect their traps, to catch the birds of prey as they swooped down to eat. The hunters laid a dead bird out on the sand, luring the falcon with food. Once it landed and began tugging on the flesh, it yanked a cord which brought a net down on top of it. Sometimes, a hunter lay in a concealed hole dug next to the bait, waiting for hours. When the falcon was distracted and within reach, he closed his fist around its talons.

In Riyadh, King Faisal and his princes waited eagerly for the falconers to arrive, first with sakers and later in the month with peregrines. For a few weeks, the city filled with falcons, sitting in cars, and houses, on the arms of men as they walked through the airport and along the streets. The relationships between the ruling families and their falconers endured for generations. The falconers came to the royal majlis, the daily audience with the king, just like every other Saudi seeking favour. They presented their hawks, and the princes passed them around, lifting their leather hoods, and feeling around their necks and beneath their wings, to assess each bird's value and potential as a hunting companion. A few were chosen and three or four assigned to a falconer to be trained.

In England, it took fifty days to train a falcon. In Saudi Arabia, the falconers had them ready to hunt in fewer than twenty-five. The Arabs never left the birds alone in the initial period after capture. Wherever the falconer went, there were his falcons, sitting next to him on a stool during the day, sleeping beside him at night. The hood kept distractions to a minimum, allowing the falcon to get used to human company. To relax the birds, the falconer would stroke them firmly, starting around their necks, moving down to their legs, straightening their wings, lengthening out their muscles. The king liked to do this himself.

Faisal had been born long before the creation of the Kingdom of Saudi Arabia. He had known the harshness of desert life, and the brutality of tribal war. But the discovery of oil had made him the richest man in the world. His watchfulness, and silence, his hawkish face, frozen by years of physical pain, spoke of a man of boundless experience and emotional restraint. He had led armies on long campaigns of conquest, and exercised his judgement in every field of human affairs, from mundane disputes between herders, to the jostling of superpowers. To the unknowing, he could seem an ancient figure in a modern world, sweeping through in his gold-trimmed robes, flanked by tall Nubian guards with curving daggers thrust in their belts. But his mind whirred with the problems of his time, with war, trade, development, diplomacy, and the enrichment of his country at a speed and scale never known in history.

When he hosted private dinners, Faisal sometimes kept his latest falcon tethered on a stool beside him, stroking it through the meal. Every so often, he removed its hood, threw down a piece of meat and mimicked a falcon's piercing screech, the signal for the bird to attack the meat as if it were prey. The falcon responded with an even louder screech and lunged to the ground, jolting the entire party from their meal.[1]

Faisal had learned to hunt on the gravelly plains of the Nejd, but he now preferred the borderlands where the plains met the mountains of the Hijaz.[2] He hunted with sakers, which had better eyesight than the peregrines, and sought houbara bustards, birds the size of a female turkey, with long wings, powerful, loping and deceptively fast in flight. Hunters set off before light, walking their camels as they searched for a bustard's tracks. When they saw one take flight, they released a falcon in pursuit. Salukis, hunting dogs, took off after the falcon, to be ready to kill the prey when it landed. The bustard, despite being slower through the air, could evade a falcon's swoops with a languid turn and by squirting sticky stomach oil into its eyes. Once on the ground, it could stun its pursuer with a flap of its strong wings.[3]

October was a precious month for Faisal and his princes. The heat of summer began to ease and in the evenings they retreated to tents in their gardens and makeshift camps in the desert, to sip tea, eat and talk surrounded by falcons. But this October was unlike any other.

On 6 October 1973, Egyptian and Syrian forces had attacked Israel from the south and the north respectively. It was Yom Kippur, one of the holiest days in the Jewish year, and Israel was not prepared. Its intelligence services and military leaders had ignored reports of the imminent invasions. For several days the Israelis struggled to fight back, and lost thousands of soldiers. A week after the war began, their closest ally, the United States, began airlifting huge amounts of military supplies to Tel Aviv.

Since the discovery of oil in Saudi Arabia's Eastern Province in 1938, the country had grown into one of the largest oil producers in the world. Cheap, abundant Middle Eastern oil had fuelled the industrialised world's rapid growth since World War Two. But recently, the Arabs had begun to reverse what they saw as decades of economic exploitation. The Western companies which found, extracted, refined and shipped their oil had often treated them with colonial disdain. As the Arabs took control of their oil, they realised they had a weapon which could be held at the world's throat. If they shut off the flow of oil, they could stop their enemies' factories, close their schools and force them to spend their winters in darkness and cold. No country in the Middle East had more oil than Saudi Arabia.

King Faisal, who supported the Arabs, had warned the Americans that if they backed Israel he would deploy the oil weapon. But they ignored him, and doubled down. On 19 October, President Richard Nixon sent a request to Congress for a major increase in funding for Israel.

Nixon's secretary of state, Henry Kissinger, had decided that he would support the Israelis until they gained the upper hand in the fighting and then call for a ceasefire. He wanted both sides to be able to claim victory. If the Arab armies were crushed, Israel would have no reason to negotiate peace. If the Soviet-backed Arabs won, it would be a defeat for America and its major ally in the Middle East. A finely calibrated end to the fighting would create the conditions for talks.

Kissinger had recently acquired sweeping powers over American foreign policy. Barely a month earlier, he had added the position of secretary of state to his existing role as the president's national security adviser. Under Nixon, he had reinvigorated American diplomacy, initiating diplomatic relations with China, and negotiating nuclear arms control agreements with the Soviet Union. On 16 October, he was awarded the Nobel Peace Prize, along with the North Vietnamese diplomat Le Duc

Tho, for negotiating a fragile ceasefire in the Vietnam War. Le Duc Tho, whom Kissinger called 'Ducky' in private, refused the honour, as the ceasefire was not being respected. The war staggered on and thousands had since died. The less squeamish Kissinger accepted the prize on behalf of the 'quest for peace'. His admirers thought him the greatest diplomatic strategist of his time. His detractors found him bumptious, conniving and amoral. Nixon normally enjoyed the intellectual and political challenges of foreign policy. But as investigators homed in on his involvement in Watergate, the scandalous break-in to the Democratic National Headquarters months before the 1972 presidential election, he had become distracted and depressed. Kissinger enthusiastically filled the void.

But on the day Nixon sent his request to Congress, Kissinger had other business to attend to. He had constructed a busy social life alongside his political rise, and thrived on his access to the powerful networks of New York and Hollywood. Shortly before noon on 19 October, he interrupted his diplomatic machinating to take a call from Liza Minnelli, the wide-eyed, pixie-cut movie star then at the peak of her fame. She had just won the Best Actress Oscar for her vampish turn as Sally Bowles in *Cabaret*, hoofing and purring in Weimar Berlin.

'Excuse me for bothering you, I know you've got enough . . .' said Minnelli.

'I'm a great fan of yours,' said Kissinger.

Minnelli had been invited by the State Department to visit Israel, to 'say hello to the troops'. She had agreed, but was now having second thoughts. She did not want to appear to be endorsing one side or another in the conflict. She was due to travel the next day and worried she would be expected to make some kind of statement. She had brought her problem right to the top. The secretary of state paused and thought.

'Well, just say you're going, that you're an entertainer, you're not making any political judgments . . . You're doing this because of your friendship for the people you know there.'

'My personal friendships.'

'Your personal friendships.'

'Alrighty. O.K. I'd like to meet you sometime,' said Minnelli.

'I would enjoy that.'

'Me too.'

'Do you ever come to Washington?'

'Sure.'

'Well, when you do, when you can, will you let me know?'

'Yes I will, sir.'

'Good, I'd love to meet you,' said Kissinger. 'Call me when you get back.'

'O.K. I will. I love you, bye.'[4]

Barely an hour after Kissinger had put Minnelli's mind to rest, King Faisal received the news from Washington of Nixon's request to Congress. Two days earlier, Nixon had received the Saudi foreign minister in the Oval Office and promised him that America would negotiate an honourable end to the war, respecting Israel and guarding the Arabs' dignity. Faisal felt Nixon had betrayed him. The king summoned his long-serving oil minister, Zaki Yamani, to the palace in Riyadh. 'Write this down,' he said. 'In view of the increase of American military aid to Israel, the Kingdom of Saudi Arabia has decided to halt all oil exports to the United States of America.' The message was broadcast on the radio at 9 p.m. local time, picked up by the Americans listening in Amman, Jordan, and relayed back to Washington.

In Tripoli, on Lebanon's Mediterranean coast, Saudi oil which flowed hundreds of miles from the great oilfields of its Eastern Province, slowed to a trickle. At the terminal in Sidon, the storage tanks were full, but no tanker dared approach. Syria closed its terminals at Banias and Tartus. Egyptian planes had already bombed the Belayim oilfields on the Gulf of Suez, captured by Israel during the Six Day War. The last ship to leave for the West Coast of the United States, carrying 650,000 barrels of light crude, set out from Ras Tanura, the Saudis' great refinery on the Persian Gulf. For the next six months, at Faisal's instruction, no more would follow.

The embargo had begun.

PART I

I

Betrayal

As Ibn Saud, the founder and king of Saudi Arabia, grew older, his eyesight dimmed, and he needed the support of canes. But he assumed a kind of epic grandeur, a monument in motion, the embodiment of the country which bore his name. He towered over most men, six-foot-four at least, and over 250 pounds, his striking face and huge body scarred in battle, his virility the stuff of legend. He was rumoured to have married hundreds of women, many of them virgins taken to secure a tribal relationship. They had borne him scores of children. Over time, he limited himself to two new wives a year.[1] He kept a harem at his palace in Riyadh, which often travelled with him round the country. In the evening, he would end meetings around 9 p.m. and depart for his private quarters, where he would wash, put on a clean robe, and have a servant dab him with perfume. Then he would go to see his women and children, to sprawl on cushions in intricately decorated rooms, to drink coffee, gossip and escape the surly world of men.

At 3 p.m. on 12 February 1945, he ordered his household to 'strike the tents' in Jeddah, the port city on Saudi Arabia's Red Sea coast, and head to Mecca. He gave no reason, and no one thought anything of it. The king rarely shared his plans. He instructed his eldest son, Saud, to take charge of the country from Riyadh, and his second son, Faisal, to watch over the western province of Hijaz. He had arranged for a radio set to be installed in every village and town with over 300 people, and instructed an operator in Mecca to report even the slightest political flicker. Saud had to radio his father three times a day to assure him of peace in his kingdom. Instead of driving to Mecca, the king went straight to the docks of Jeddah where he boarded a US Navy destroyer. News of his departure on an American ship prompted several women in his harem to don mourning clothes and ashes. They went to Faisal wailing that the king had abandoned them. Others speculated that he had fled. They recalled how the Hashemite King Faisal had left Jeddah in 1921 aboard a British troopship to become king of Iraq.

What the king's son could not tell his father's despairing concubines was much more significant. President Franklin Roosevelt had asked to meet Ibn Saud during his return from the Yalta conference, where the Allied powers would be discussing the aftermath of World War Two. The Americans proposed the meeting take place on a US warship in the Great Bitter Lake, a salty bulge in the Suez Canal, where ships could pass. Roosevelt would sail in on the *Quincy*, escorted by a US Navy destroyer squadron. Ibn Saud would travel from Saudi Arabia on another destroyer, the *Murphy*.

When the captain of the *Murphy*, Commander Bernard Smith, received his assignment, he dug out an encyclopaedia. Ibn Saud seemed a wildly exotic figure. A direct descendant of Muhammad, a temporal and spiritual leader to hundreds of millions of Muslims. A man with strict religious, dietary and personal habits. The furthest he had ever travelled outside the Arabian Peninsula was Basra, in southern Iraq. The United States had not sent a resident envoy to Jeddah, the home of the kingdom's diplomatic community, until 1942. No

American more senior than a career diplomat had ever met the king.

A ship full of American sailors was not a place for a man averse to drinking, smoking and cursing. Smith feared he and his men would make a disastrous gaffe, and ruin Roosevelt's diplomatic ambitions. He went to see Ibn Saud's prime minister for advice, and invited him aboard the *Murphy*. The prime minister was appalled. Ibn Saud could not sleep in the commander's minuscule room, with its cramped bunk, desk and shower. The Americans would have to erect a more suitable tent on the deck. The prime minister would provide the canvas, along with rugs to protect the king's fragile legs, a suitable throne, and jugs of sweet water from the holy wells near Mecca, the only water the king would drink.

There was still the problem of the king's retinue. The State Department had authorised Smith to bring twelve Arabs. The prime minister said the king rarely travelled with fewer than 200 people, including members of his family and harem, the chiefs of the most important tribes, his cook, doctor, servants, strapping Nubian bodyguards armed with scimitars, and his personal astrologer. The harem was the easiest problem to solve. There was no way their dignity could be preserved in the narrow quarters of a navy ship where men were constantly jostling for space. As for the rest, the prime minister finally agreed to send just twenty of the king's usual retinue.

The king's panoply arrived on a barge loaded with equipment for the tents, boxes of gifts, special food and eighty-six sheep. The prime minister insisted that this was what the king ate: fresh lamb boiled in industrial quantities, spiced and served with rice. Smith agreed to ten sheep, and ordered a pen built at the rear of the deck. The king's cooks would have to use the flagstaff to hang the sheep, slit their throats and skin them for cooking, according to Muslim custom. Instead of twenty men, the king arrived with forty-seven.

In 1912, the year the *Titanic* and its colossal coal-powered steam engines sank to the bottom of the Atlantic, Faisal, Ibn Saud's third son, had turned six, the age for circumcision. He was slightly built compared to his brawny older brothers. But he had his father's hooded eyes and languid charm, which concealed a furious alertness. The cut was administered by Mahmoud of Mosul, a barber and teeth-puller, who treated the bleeding with cold ash.

From an early age, Faisal often sat beside his father at his daily majlis, an open audience where the emir received guests and supplicants. Anyone could come and raise an issue or ask a favour, from the lowliest herder arguing over a patch of land to the various tribes and foreign occupants of the Arabian Peninsula, Ottomans, British, French, Germans, Persians and Egyptians. It was democratic to the extent that the emir was accessible to anyone, but autocratic in that his decisions, and his largesse, were final. There was no bureaucracy, parliament or judiciary through which to challenge him.

Faisal's early life was defined by his father's conquests, and his subsequent search for legitimacy. In 1902, when Roosevelt was a sophomore at Harvard, Ibn Saud had led his family back from exile in Kuwait. They had been driven from their home in Riyadh by the Rashid family in 1891. Ibn Saud stole into the town at night, killed its Rashidi governor, and re-established the Al Sauds among the tribes of the Nejd, at the heart of Arabia. In 1919, he sent the fourteen-year-old Faisal as his representative on a visit to England. Faisal braved a cold winter to visit the king, the Houses of Parliament, a Welsh steelworks, the Bank of England and two Gilbert and Sullivan operettas. He was riveted by the stuffed gorilla at the Natural History Museum, and fed the seals at London zoo, though he fled when a sea lion crawled onto the rock where he was standing and flopped its way towards him.[2] His favourite thing of all was an escalator in the London Underground, which he rode up and down for most of a morning.[3] In Ireland, he was taken to the muddy North Slob in County Wexford to watch a shoot, and given a ride in a donkey cart.

Over the next decade, Ibn Saud and his sons fought and politicked their way across the Arabian Peninsula. When he was eighteen, Faisal led 5,000 men on a 700-mile trek over thirty days to establish a Saudi protectorate in the Asir, in the southern part of the Arabian Peninsula. He lived among his men like a desert warrior, barefoot, eating little, and waking long before dawn.[4] When he returned victorious to Riyadh, he rode back and forth before a reviewing stand shaking a spear, shouting the battle cries of the Ikhwan, his father's most feared warriors.[5] So impressed was Ibn Saud by his son's discipline, intelligence and authority, he said, 'I wish I had three Faisals'.[6] On 18 September 1932, thirty years after he had led the Al Sauds back from Kuwait, Ibn Saud announced the birth of a country named after his family: the Kingdom of Saudi Arabia.

Ibn Saud's main source of revenue in the early days of his Kingdom was pilgrims visiting the holy cities of Mecca and Medina. This was a scratchy existence. But prospectors who studied the rock formations in Saudi Arabia believed there was oil there. Perhaps even a lot of it. They had discovered it in Iran and Iraq, and more recently in Bahrain. The king sent Faisal to London to ask the British Foreign Office for a loan in return for his country's mineral rights. Sir Lancelot Oliphant, a senior civil servant, with thirty years of experience dealing with Persia and Arabia, told the Saudis that British firms were unlikely to 'sink capital in a little-known country at the present time'.[7] They already had extensive commitments in the Middle East. The French also passed, concerned that operating in Saudi Arabia would conflict with their activities in the regions to the west and north, once occupied by the Ottoman Empire. The door fell open for the Americans.

On 29 May 1933, the kingdom signed an agreement with Standard Oil of California (Socal) to search for oil in the Eastern Province, granting 'a concession for the exploitation of petroleum'. The deal promised Ibn Saud an immediate loan of £35,000, a further loan of £20,000 after eighteen months, and an annual rental payment of £5,000, all to be paid in gold, which Socal shipped from London on a steamer. There would be further loans totalling £100,000 if and when oil was found. Five years later, the American prospectors drilled 4,700 feet down into Well No. 7 of Dammam Dome. Within two weeks, it was producing nearly 4,000 barrels of oil a day. The great torrent of Saudi oil had begun to flow.

By the time the world went to war in 1939, access to this oil had become an urgent, practical matter for the United States. It was the only country in the Middle East where Americans had an exclusive oil concession. In 1940, Bert Fish, a Florida real estate operator then serving as US minister to Egypt, sailed into Jeddah as America's first diplomatic representative to the kingdom. Jeddah still felt like a medieval city, its houses facing inwards from the desert, its windows covered in lattices. But the camel pasturage outside Mecca had become a parking lot; the Zamzam Well near Mecca, which yielded the sweet water coveted by pilgrims, had a bottling plant; and Ibn Saud had amassed a fleet of thirty luxury cars.[8]

In February 1943, as domestic US oil production failed to keep up with the needs of World War Two, President Roosevelt designated Saudi Arabia a country of vital military interest, opening the spigot of lend-lease money, the millions of dollars which America paid to its allies to fund the war effort. Ibn Saud spent part of it on a huge palace in the heart of Riyadh, and smaller palaces for his adult children. Schools and hospitals were not his priorities.

By 1944, four American oil companies were operating in Saudi Arabia, Socal, Texaco, and Standard Oil of New Jersey, later Exxon, which each owned 30 per cent, and Socony Vacuum, later Mobil, which owned 10 per cent. They gave their joint venture a new name: the Arabian American Oil Company, Aramco. As the war dragged on, Aramco warned Washington that it needed to pay more attention to the Saudis or risk losing their concession. Now the oil was flowing, other countries would be eager to buy off the king.

The crew of the *Murphy* did their best to accommodate the king and his party. They allowed them to brew coffee on charcoal fires on deck, in breach of standard Navy rules. When it came time to pray, the ship's navigators established the direction of Mecca. The king sat in his throne looking towards his kingdom as they sailed past. He had never seen his own coastline like this. The first night aboard, the king invited the senior American officers to join him for dinner, sprawled on rugs. He spoke of hand-to-hand battles, and showed them where the shard of a Turkish cannon ball had immobilised one of his fingers. The officers brought him a gift of American apples, prepared *à la mode*, with vanilla ice cream. He liked the apples so much, he instructed that they be cultivated at his agricultural development centre in Saudi Arabia. The king seemed unperturbed by the gentle up and down of the ship, but the rest of his men spent that first night vomiting over the side.

The next day, the crew amused the king by firing the ship's guns and allowing him and his men to blast away with machine guns at target balloons. Three times that day, the *Murphy*'s radio operator radioed the king's station in Mecca to assure him of peace in his kingdom. Each time the conversation was the same. 'Murphy to Mecca. How is it?' 'Mecca to Murphy – okay.' During the evening, the king stayed on deck, but several of his men snuck downstairs to watch movies with the American sailors, including *Too Many Girls*, a racy comedy in which Lucille Ball plays an heiress who goes to college to seduce a man. The Arabs whistled and whooped at her japes, along with the crew.

The trip was such a success that the king gave every member of the crew a gift of cash. The officers received Arab costumes, daggers and watches. In return, the crew gave the king two Browning machine guns, with several thousand rounds of ammunition, and a pair of Navy binoculars. After some quick instruction, the Arab chieftains began blasting away with the machine guns, until they had to be stopped before any real damage was done.

On the morning of 14 February, the *Murphy* arrived at the Great Bitter Lake. The king was hoisted up in a bosun's chair so he could walk directly across to the *Quincy*'s higher deck. As the *Murphy* came alongside, Roosevelt saw a floating desert encampment, with a few sad-looking sheep, and there raised high up on his throne, a giant man with gold bands around his keffiyeh, surrounded by dark-skinned guards covered in enough swords and daggers to kill an army.

Ibn Saud told Roosevelt that he had not accepted his invitation in order to ask for money or military help. He had come to listen. In addition to securing the flow of Saudi oil, Roosevelt wanted to establish a Middle Eastern military base in Saudi Arabia, where they could operate without having to ask permission of the British and French. He was also concerned by the looming issue of where to settle Europe's Jews. Barely three weeks earlier, Soviet troops had arrived at Auschwitz to find around seven thousand emaciated prisoners and evidence of industrialised murder. The hideous truth of the Holocaust was emerging. If the United States were to help the Zionists achieve their dream of a new Jewish state in Palestine, Roosevelt said, it would rather do so with Arab support than without it.

Ibn Saud replied that the Axis powers had oppressed the Jews, so should pay the penalty with their land. The Palestinians were innocent bystanders. Why should Muslims pay for a crime committed by Christians? The question of Jewish settlement in Palestine would never be easy, Roosevelt acknowledged. But he promised the king that no decision would be made 'without full consultation with both Arabs and Jews', and no action taken 'which might prove hostile to the Arab people'.[9]

Ibn Saud said that he appreciated that the United States did not colonise other countries, unlike the British and French, who seemed to think that after the war they would have the Middle East to themselves again. Roosevelt said the old imperial spheres of influence were deflating. Soon the world would arrive at Saudi Arabia's door. All it needed to do was decide who had something to offer. The king did not have to defer to anyone.

Roosevelt's freewheeling vision had enormous appeal to Ibn Saud, and the president sealed the deal with a gift of a DC-3 passenger plane, tricked out with a rotating throne so the king could swivel and face Mecca while flying. He secured America's immediate future as Saudi Arabia's best friend in the oil business, and the right to expand its military presence in the country. When Ibn Saud admired his wheelchair, Roosevelt gave him his spare one. It was too small for the king, but he placed it prominently in his palace in Riyadh.

After the king had disembarked and the *Murphy* had sailed off, his personal physician begged to see Captain William Eddy, the US envoy to Jeddah. He had left the king's medicines on board. He produced six long sheets of paper listing some 240 different medicines, which Eddy gave to the chief medical officer of the US Army in the Near East, asking him to replicate them as best he could. The medical officer reported back that roughly 210 of the 240 treatments were aphrodisiacs, many either bogus or obsolete. There were enough for a regiment for a year. Fortunately for the king's doctor, the crew of the *Murphy* had found the medicine box and returned it by train to Cairo.[10]

When Winston Churchill heard that Roosevelt was meeting Ibn Saud, he bombarded his diplomats with demands for a similar meeting. Ibn Saud asked Roosevelt if he thought it worth his time. Roosevelt said he always enjoyed Churchill's company. The king agreed to meet the prime minister at a hotel in the Fayoum Oasis in Egypt, and then to take a British ship back to Saudi Arabia. Unlike the Americans, the British proved haughty and joyless. Out of respect for Ibn Saud's religion, Roosevelt refrained from chain-smoking. But Churchill would not be moved. He wrote: 'If it was the religion of His Majesty to deprive himself of smoking and alcohol, I must point out that my rule of life prescribed as an absolutely sacred rite smoking cigars, and also drinking alcohol before, after, and if need be during all meals and in the intervals between them.'

Ibn Saud believed that personal relationships were the foundation of relationships between tribes and nations. Roosevelt had been solicitous and direct even in areas of disagreement. But Churchill was evasive and arrogant. He told the king that he owed Britain for its financial and political support over the past two decades. Britain had defended Ibn Saud against his neighbours when Saudi Arabia was in its infancy. Once the war ended, he predicted, Britain would be the major world power in the region, its imperial swagger greater than ever. Britain wanted Ibn Saud to support the plan to settle Jews in Palestine by restraining the more fanatical Arab elements and finding common ground with the Zionists. It was the least he could do. The king did not take well to 'the big stick'.[11] There was no compromise to be made with the Zionists. The mass immigration of Jews to Palestine, he believed, would lead to decades of chaos and bloodshed. It was what he had told Roosevelt, and Roosevelt had heard him out. Churchill treated Ibn Saud like a customer with an unpaid bill.

Roosevelt died eight weeks after meeting Ibn Saud. The following year, 1946, Faisal flew to Washington to meet his successor, President Truman. On his way, his plane had to land in Lisbon due to engine trouble. America's diplomatic corps was alive to the Saudis' growing importance. The US ambassador summoned his staff from their weekend activities, and ordered them to dress up and greet Faisal at the Palacio Hotel. He hosted a dinner where Faisal sat in a high-backed canopied chair. After the dinner, the ambassador had it plated in gold and sent on to Riyadh as a gift.[12]

Dean Acheson, Truman's senior foreign policy adviser, described Faisal as a Hollywood stereotype of the 'dark and mysterious sheik'. 'Striking in white burnoose and golden circlet, which heightened his swarthy complexion, with black, pointed beard and mustache topped by a thin hooked nose and piercing dark eyes,' Faisal conveyed a 'sinister impression, relieved from time to time by a shy smile.' Acheson added: 'The Amir impressed me as a man who could be an implacable enemy and who should be taken very seriously.[13] But when they met, Faisal and Truman spoke at cross purposes, neither seeming to grasp the depth of the other's concerns.

Roosevelt had promised Ibn Saud that America would support no action on Palestine without consulting the Arabs. But Truman had domestic political considerations. He was concerned for the Jews now languishing in refugee camps in Europe. America was ready to accept 100,000 of them. The rest would have to go to their yet to be created state. The decision had been made, and Roosevelt's promise broken. The Arabs would be ignored.

At a United Nations summit in 1947, Israel was born with America's full support. Dean Rusk, a future secretary of state then handling US relations with the UN, remembered the sight of Faisal 'tall, erect, wounded pride, insulted honor,' speaking 'with great passion, with great clarity about this great injury that had been done to the Arab people. They were being forced by the West to pay for the crimes of Adolf Hitler.'[14]

Oil, Israel, and the fall and rise of foreign powers would occupy the rest of Faisal's life.

2

Aramcons

The Americans who came for the oil in the late 1930s first settled in Al-Khobar, a coastal town on the Persian Gulf, where most people lived in barastis – wooden houses with walls made of palm fronds, designed for ventilation. They built their own community apart from the local fishermen and pearl divers, a cluster of huts, some of insulated metal with air-conditioning, a few from limestone cut from the seabed, which turned damp and smelly in the wet heat. When they took delivery of a Ford Tri-Motor, a small three-engine passenger plane nicknamed the Tin Goose, they invited the local Bedouin to watch it make its first flight. The Goose rumbled along the beach, and took off, spraying sand. One of the Americans turned to the Bedouin's chief and said, '[I]sn't it amazing that a machine of this size can fly?' The sheikh, who had never seen a plane, said, '[I]sn't it supposed to?'

The world of the Americans and their search for oil, and the world of Ibn Saud and his emerging kingdom, barely touched. Their societies, cultures and politics were bound by a single economic thread, a long way from the thick ropes which would eventually bind them together. As the oil activity grew, Aramco operated three DC3s, the Camel, the Gazelle and the Oryx, on two flights a week from New York to Dhahran, stopping in Amsterdam, Rome and Beirut. The airport terminal in Dhahran was a shed with a bench, often barely visible in the violent swirl of heat and sand. Visitors were surprised to see so little obvious oil production going on. Unlike Texas, where it seemed drills and pumps cranked away in every ranch and backyard, there was only one landowner in Saudi Arabia. You could pop a drill down in one place, then another many miles away, and connect them with a pipeline, confident that no one would interfere with your production. Oil wells were not pumped in Saudi Arabia. Natural pressure forced the oil to the surface. The average Saudi well could produce thousands of barrels of oil per day compared to the average American well, which had to be vigorously pumped to yield just twenty or so barrels per day. If the oil map of Texas looked like a deranged scribble, with thousands of wells and battling owners, the oil map of Saudi Arabia resembled the most austere abstract art, the faintest of lines sketched on raw canvas. The pipelines converged on a loading facility on the Persian Gulf, and from there the oil disappeared across the sea, paid for with a deposit to Ibn Saud's treasury. To the Bedouin who still roamed the emptiness of eastern Arabia, the whole business seemed unreal.

The single men flown in to operate the rigs and build the plants lived in the 'sheepsheds' of Whiskey Gulch, rudimentary plywood barracks in a corner of the Aramco compound with basic rooms on either side of a dark corridor, stinking of clogged toilets. Many began their days soon after midnight, staggering out into damp, flare-lit nights, which turned into 120-degree, sand-whipped days. The single women, who worked as secretaries, nurses and teachers, lived in healthier quarters, which the slavering men called Petticoat Lane and Virgin Circle. Entertainment consisted of a pool hall and drinks at the Stag Club. The best food for miles was at a nearby oil camp run by morose Italians.[1]

The more adventurous 'Aramcons' drove out into the

desert in jeeps equipped with broad, soft-sand tyres.[2] They collected arrowheads and stone axes, and visited oasis settlements, visible across the blank desert with their soaring piles of camel dung built up over decades. Raiding parties from the desert and pirates from the sea still terrorised these communities. The 1942 edition of the *Persian Gulf Pilot*, a handbook for the captains guiding ships through the Gulf, warned that 'it is not safe to land unarmed on the mainland, on account of the Bedouin who may be occasionally met and who, for the sake of plunder, attack even their own townsfolk.' There was the equally mortal threat of malaria, carried by the swarms of mosquitoes which clustered around the scarce pools of water. The inhabitants of these settlements alleviated their existential worries with blazing colours: gowns and blankets as brilliant as the sun, bright yellow and searing red, embroidered saddle bags, striped tents and patterned trunks, breaking the harsh monotony of sand and rock.

The Aramcons who had grown up in the ranch lands and ranges of the American West now hunted in the desert. They raced after gazelles in their cars, shooting them from the back seats, lassoing them from the running boards. During the day, they prospected for oil. At night they studied geological maps and learned Arabic by lamplight in their tents.[3]

Aramco operated from three centres. Dhahran for administration and production, Abqaiq, close to the main production facilities, and Ras Tanura, for shipping. Drivers on the road from Abqaiq to Dhahran ran into swarms of locusts so thick they had to stop and scrape them off the windscreen. The Arabs skewered them on coat hangers to grill and eat later. On the road to Medina, a handful of sunburned Englishmen ran an outpost of the Locust Service, an international organisation which gathered information about locusts and killed them if they found them. They lived in a cluster of tents overshadowed by a giant stack of poison bait, which resembled a slag heap.[4]

Ibn Saud welcomed the money he was receiving on every barrel of oil, but he had trouble showing genuine interest in all of this strange activity. In January 1947, he visited Aramco's headquarters in Dhahran. It was only the second time he had bothered to do so since granting the company its concession in 1933. The first time, in 1939, he was driven for hours in a fleet of cars all the way from Riyadh. This time, he arrived in a convoy of six planes, an indication of his country's progress. On the second day of his visit, he was shown into the theatre at the Dhahran clubhouse to see a selection of short films about the oil industry. The first, *Deep Horizons*, dealt with the drilling of oil wells. The second, *Masters of Molecules*, was about refining. The final one, *Tanker*, described shipping. Ibn Saud sat in the centre of the theatre, while everyone else crowded into the hot, cramped space behind him. The king made it through *Deep Horizons*. But halfway through *Masters of Molecules*, he gestured that he had had enough.

The next day, when he was taken to visit the shipping terminal at Ras Tanura, he listened politely as he was taken around the machine shop, but perked up when he saw a group of men working a piece of hot metal under a drop hammer. He asked if these men could make a horseshoe. He was pleased to learn they could. At last, an activity he could relate to.

Aramco went to extraordinary lengths for the king's visit. An executive flew to Basra, Iraq, to buy an especially tall toilet for him, and returned with it on a chartered plane. They cleared space for the royal tents, including a private tent for the king, another for his daily majlis, and rigged up a flagpole with the round float from a flush tank welded to the top. The Saudis liked it so much, they took it with them when they left, concrete base and all.

The king's feasts were prodigious. A total of 782 sheep and 1,543 chickens were bought, killed and consumed over five days. The shopping list included 20,000 pounds of rice, American, Arab and Burmese, 4,000 pounds of Yemeni coffee, 1,200 pounds of cardamom and 9,500 pounds of sugar; thousands of pounds of fruit and vegetables, ghee and cheese, confectionery for the king's breakfast and saffron for the roasted meat. One evening, the king attended a banquet given by a local emir where the main course was a whole camel, legs, head, the works, surrounded by trays loaded with rice, each topped with a whole roasted sheep. The next day, he entertained a fellow Bedouin with a camel stuffed with sheep, the sheep stuffed with chickens, the chickens stuffed with eggs, and everything stuffed with rice, raisins and almonds.

But amidst the lavish displays of tradition, a new Saudi Arabia was flickering. At the end of his visit, after he listened to a laudatory Bedouin ode composed by a member of Aramco's Transportation Section, Ibn Saud attended a reception for the 185 women and fifty children living in the company town. The women, in long-sleeved dresses or suits, formed a line to greet the king, who shook hands with them all, even the children who were small enough to be held in their mothers' arms. He seemed delighted by the experience, particularly when he saw the children scrambling for juice and cookies. His sons and retinue were fascinated. Women had been excluded from the rest of the king's visit and he rarely received foreign women in Riyadh. They had never seen him in such company, let alone so relaxed and happy. When he had to leave, the American women and children gave him three cheers.

The Aramcons were running a grand experiment: to prove that a private-sector, Western company could develop a profitable industry in a far-flung country, crucial to the industrial growth of the entire world, to the satisfaction of a New York corporate boardroom and an Arab monarchy. This led to an unusually cosmopolitan culture in the desert. Aramco paid its Saudi employees in silver riyals minted in Mexico, and the government in 4-inch slugs of gold bullion minted and stamped in Philadelphia. The riyals were stacked up in crates in Aramco's offices, and driven out to the producing districts in unguarded trucks. Men lined up every other Thursday and filled their hats with coins. Paying the government in gold worked until the sums became so vast that Aramco's purchases began to move the entire global gold market. Aramco then stealthily bought British gold sovereigns from nearby countries, until the Saudis' paper currency evolved. In the late 1970s, Aramco was still moving millions of dollars of cash around the desert in bags, loaded into the back of a Volkswagen van.

Aramco's managers, engineers and geologists, became their own tribe within the kingdom. They were problem solvers, trained in the practical sciences of geology, seismology, and petrochemical engineering at schools in Texas, Oklahoma and Nebraska. They were blue-collar men for whom white-collar work was an extraordinary privilege, not a wearisome right. No one wore a suit and tie. Office hours were 6 a.m. to early afternoon, when the men returned home for pink gins – two jiggers of gin and a dash of angostura bitters in a tumbler full of ice. The days of Whiskey Gulch soon passed, and the area where the Aramcons lived came to resemble a new suburb in central California, tidy ranch houses with green lawns, yellow school buses, a cinema and soda fountain. During the summer, the rooftop water tanks heated up so much that if you wanted a cold bath, you had to fill the tub with ice cubes.[5] Unlike the oil companies in America, which had strict hierarchies, at Aramco, the most senior executives lived next to junior engineers, and everyone mixed with each other. The strict religious rules which applied in the rest of the country did not apply within the compound. Over time, the company added tennis courts, a bowling lane, and a nine-hole golf course, the Rolling Hills Golf Club, where the fairways were made of sand and rock, and the 'greens' of crushed nut husks mixed with sand and black oil. The ball rolled as if it were on clipped Bermuda grass. On Fridays, their days off, the ex-pats took fishing boats out before sunrise to catch hammour, a local grouper, to grill before long games of bridge.

The Saudi government was generally relaxed about allowing different rules for the Aramcons. American help came with American habits. Within the compound women could drive, you could buy pork in the supermarket, and alcohol was widely available. But the visitors took care to steer clear of the dreaded Committee for Public Morality, the religious police, and its notorious local boss, Sheikh No-Nose, nicknamed for his habit of smashing in the faces of anyone he suspected of immorality.[6] This could be anything from sexual profligacy to owning a record player. The editors of *Arabian Sun and Flare*, the Aramco employee newspaper, filled their articles with cautious euphemisms to duck the attentions of No-Nose. Dance was considered lewd, so parties where dancing broke out were 'shindigs'. The square dancing club was the 'Third Street Squares'. Card and board games were not permitted, so bridge parties were 'Culbertson-Lenz gatherings', and chess players 'Pawnpushers'. Photographs of women tennis players were unthinkable.[7] The thorniest issue was the most popular means of blurring the tedium and tension of these weeks in the desert: alcohol.

In 1952, a royal prince got drunk and shot and killed the British vice-consul in Jeddah. The government introduced a law banning the import, sale and transportation of alcohol. The royal decree stated that 'whoever violates our order shall be subject to severe consequences.' Citizens were given 100 lashes and imprisoned for a year. Non-citizens were deported. When the head of Aramco asked Faisal, then minister of foreign affairs, if the law also applied to the drinking and making of alcohol, Faisal said, '[T]here is nothing about manufacturing, but I can put it in in three seconds.' In his roundabout way, he was saying that as long as the Aramcons were discreet, the Saudis would turn the other way.

The chemical engineers made whisky that tasted more of charcoal than peat, a passable gin, and a spirit distilled from date sugar called *siddiki* – an Arabic word for friend. The embassies smuggled in alcohol in their diplomatic bags. Getting rid of the glass empties was another matter. One ambassador's wife put them into a sack and pounded them into splinters and dust in the embassy courtyard. She then smuggled the debris out on the embassy's boat during weekend picnics and, once far enough from shore, poured it into the sea.[8]

Every other year, the community staged a Christmas pageant. They brought in camels, sheep and donkeys, and turned the baseball field into Bethlehem. There was a game of donkey baseball. If the batter got a hit, he had to ride a donkey to first base. Santa Claus arrived by helicopter and was driven through town in a convertible. Even the Arabs loved to watch.

The curiosity went both ways. Aramco built a library in Dhahran and filled its shelves with books about Islam and the Middle East. Its research department invited Bedouin 'relators', travelling storytellers, and recorded stories that had been handed down orally since the birth of Islam. In the spring of 1957, a group of women living on the Aramco compound visited the company's research division in Dhahran to meet a group of these relators. A Bedouin poet composed a verse to welcome the 'honorable ladies and the chaste women, making their most amiable appearance, with eyes fluting with the eyes of gazelles, and with looks stirring the watchers to the so-far still feeling of yearning.' The poem, 'Worthy Gift', was translated by the Research Division.[9]

> Welcome to the ladies; this is the day of blessings;
> My dear friends, the chaste women are coming to visit you;
> They have arrived most and most welcome; a thousand welcomes to them;
> Verily they are the wives of men who are the lions of battles;
> They have allowed them to go around on a trip and watch things.

Ibn Saud died in November 1953. His eldest son and successor, Saud, promptly demolished his own gargantuan palace on the edge of Riyadh and replaced it with an even bigger one, a small city surrounded by a seven-mile-long wall, littered with swimming pools and fountains, illuminated with thousands of coloured lights, and teeming with concubines and Cadillacs. It sucked up half of Riyadh's entire supply of air-conditioning.[10] When Saud drove into the desert, he threw handfuls of gold and silver coins from his car window, which were gathered up by Bedouin children. Unlike his father, he invested in schools, hospitals and government ministries, but with no coherent plans or budgets. Within a few years, he turned Saudi Arabia into a regional laughing stock. The Arab socialists led by Egypt's President Nasser considered themselves the future of the Middle East, and the Saudi monarchy an anachronism, an unworthy beneficiary of the greatest treasure ever discovered in the Arab world.

When the oil first began to flow, the Saudis accepted a fixed royalty of thirty-four cents per barrel from Aramco. It was a simple deal which suited Ibn Saud's immediate financial needs. Over time, the Saudis had gained a better understanding of the economics of oil. They saw that as production costs fell and prices rose, the companies' profit margins increased while their royalty stayed the same. In the middle of World War Two, Venezuela, one of the largest suppliers of oil to the United States, tore up a similar deal and announced that it would be splitting its oil profits 50-50 with the companies. The more the companies made, the more the country made. In 1950, the Saudis demanded the same terms, and threatened to nationalise Aramco unless it agreed. Aramco turned to the US government for compensation on the grounds that their operations and good relations with the Saudis served the US national interest. The Treasury agreed to let them subtract any payments they made to the Saudis from their American tax obligations dollar for dollar. Aramco was effectively paying the Saudis with money it took from American taxpayers. For the US government, the credits to Aramco served as a stealthy subsidy to Saudi Arabia, which required no Congressional approval. For the companies it turned out to be such a valuable wheeze, they nicknamed it the 'golden gimmick'. It would not be the last time that the need for Arab oil muddied the lines between American private commercial interests and national strategic ambitions.

In 1955, the Saudis took a further step to try to ensure they were fairly and reliably compensated. They agreed on a system of 'posted prices', whereby the companies set a fixed price per barrel of oil to serve as a steady basis for royalty, tax and profit-sharing calculations. The advantage for the countries was a predictable stream of income whatever the market price of oil. Any variations in price were for the companies to absorb or take as profit. But in 1959, a glut of oil drove prices well below the posted price. Rather than consulting the producing countries, two of the largest companies, Standard of New Jersey and BP, cut their posted prices by fourteen cents a barrel. They said it was no longer fair to be making payments based on posted prices so much higher than the market price, regardless of the rights or needs of the countries. At a meeting of the Arab Oil Congress in Baghdad in September 1960, five oil producers, Saudi Arabia, Venezuela, Iran, Iraq and Kuwait, announced that they were joining forces to take on the oil majors. They called their new organisation the Organization of Petroleum Exporting Countries, OPEC. Between them, they produced about 82 per cent of the world's crude oil exports. A Saudi official said that the companies 'edged away from us as if we were lepers.'[11] They took three years just to recognise OPEC's existence.

Under King Saud, Faisal served as crown prince and at different times prime minister and minister of foreign affairs, depending on the sorry state of his brother's reign. In 1958, his brothers begged him to take over Saud's administrative powers. When he asked for the national accounts, he was said to have found just 317 riyals in cash, barely a hundred dollars, to meet the country's expenses. He quickly secured new loans from Saudi and American banks, the latter guaranteed by Aramco, and demanded a proper national budget. He slashed inflation and brought order to the state's finances. After eighteen months, Saud took back his powers and set about returning the country to penury. In 1964, the royal princes forced Saud to abdicate once and for all, exiled him to Beirut, and asked Faisal to be king on a permanent basis. Soon after his accession, Faisal said: 'The important thing about a regime is not what it is called but how it acts. There are corrupt republican regimes and sound monarchies and vice versa. The only true criterion of a regime – whether it be monarchical or republican – is the degree of reciprocity between the ruler and the ruled and the extent to which it symbolises prosperity, progress, and healthy initiative.'[12] He asked not to be called 'His Majesty' as it was a term reserved for God alone.[13]

Faisal introduced a five-year planning cycle to organise Saudi Arabia's development and modernisation. He banned the import of slaves, and eventually liberated those already in the country. He built the country's first schools for girls. His opponents resented the abandonment of a centuries old, pre-industrial pace of progress. They considered it an offence to their religion. But Faisal said modernisation was consistent with Islam. 'Our religion . . . requires us to progress and advance and to bear the burden of the highest tradition and best manners. What is called progressiveness in the world today, and what reformers are calling for, be it social, human or economic progress is all embodied in the Islamic religion and laws.'[14] The tension between progress and tradition would define his reign.

In his youth, Faisal had served as viceroy of the Hijaz, the western region of the Arabian Peninsula, which included Jeddah, and the holy cities of Mecca and Medina. It had been a formative experience. The Al Sauds were Nejdis from the eastern deserts, tough desert people. Like all Nejdis they despised the sophisticated, settled Hijazis, who lived along the Red Sea. They called the people of Jeddah the 'flotsam of the sea' and those from Mecca and Medina 'pilgrimage remnants', since they often married non-Arab Muslims. The Hijazis thought the Nejdis barbarians, crude nomads, capable of fighting but devoid of culture. The Nejdis prided themselves on their pure lineage and fighting spirit, while the Hijazis valued elegance and refinement.[15] Unlike the rest of the Arabian Peninsula, the Hijaz had a functioning administration, newspapers, libraries and schools. As a young man, Faisal had come to respect their education and liberalism. Decades later, he sought out Hijazis to help him rule.

As crown prince, he noticed a series of articles in a Jeddah newspaper explaining the evolution of Saudi law, as the traditional laws of Islam met the country's increasingly modern needs. He invited their author, a young lawyer, to his summer palace in Taif. After a brief exchange, he appointed him his legal adviser. Ahmed Zaki Yamani had been born in Mecca in 1930, two years before Saudi Arabia became a country, eight years before the discovery of oil. Not only did he come from a family of scholars and clerics, the kind of educated Hijazis the Nejdis loathed, his name, Yamani, indicated his family's origins in Yemen, Saudi Arabia's persistent enemy to the south. Saudis and Yemenis would fight three wars in Yamani's lifetime, in addition to frequent scuffles along their long border.

Yamani studied law at the University of Cairo in the early 1950s, when its campus thrummed with radicals, nationalists and communists, united in their loathing for the dissolute monarchy of Egypt's King Farouk. Yamani found the communists dishonest. How could they call for freedom from servitude and total fealty to their leaders? The religious fanatics of the Muslim Brotherhood reminded him of Saudi Arabia's worst religious conservatives. One of his fellow students was Yasser Arafat, the future leader of the Palestinian Liberation Organization (PLO), who became a lifelong friend.

After obtaining his degree, Yamani returned home to work for the Saudi Ministry of Finance. He soon realised that he needed a Western education to understand the Western technology and expertise underpinning Saudi Arabia's oil industry. The government sponsored him to spend two years studying in the United States. It was his first trip outside the Middle East. His friends shared all kinds of strange rumours and warnings about

America. One advised him to avoid men in red ties, as they were likely predatory homosexuals.

Yamani spent his first year at New York University studying comparative law, and a second at Harvard Law School, learning about capital investment and international disputes. His professors recalled a quiet student, often clicking his string of worry beads. In New York, he took a course in psychology at Columbia, which he later credited with influencing his approach to negotiations.[16] When he returned to Saudi Arabia, he split his time between the Ministry of Finance and the Office of Minerals and Petroleum, where he drafted and edited the detailed concession agreements with foreign oil companies. As he and his wife Laila started a family, he left government to set up a law firm, specialising in interpreting Saudi law for foreign companies. In the evenings he wrote the newspaper columns which caught Faisal's attention. With the foundation of OPEC, the pith-helmet era of Western companies treating the producers like colonial subjects was bound to end. The question was whether it would end in partnership or hostility.

Saudi Arabia's first minister of petroleum and minerals, Abdullah al-Tariki, was instrumental in creating OPEC, but he had gone further than merely standing up to the companies. He antagonised the concessionaires of Aramco by accusing them of being hostile, patriarchal, rapacious and riddled with CIA spies. If the chairman of Aramco wanted to see him, Tariki made him wait. In 1962, while prime minister, Faisal decided the country should have a less fraught relationship with the oilmen. He fired Tariki and replaced him with the more emollient Yamani, who told the head of Aramco he could see him whenever he wanted.[17] Yamani was thirty-one years old, and Saudi Arabia accounted for 5 per cent of the world's oil output, and rising.

A year after his appointment, Yamani invited an Aramco team to a villa in Broummana, a summer resort in the hills overlooking Beirut, for talks on the company's production for the coming year. He hired a consultant to fly in a planeload of computers. Whenever Aramco made a proposal, Yamani disappeared to run the numbers through these huge new machines, then return with a list of objections. The Aramco team were astonished by the Saudis' sophistication.[18]

That spring, Yamani concluded a number of favourable updates to the Saudis' arrangements with Aramco. Faisal was so delighted that, on the day of their signing, he invited the wives of the senior Aramco executives for tea at his palace in Riyadh. It was already noon, and the invitation was for 4 p.m. The harried members of Aramco's government affairs division scampered around Dhahran looking for wives. They found them on the golf course, in the supermarket, shopping in the commissary, and playing bridge in each other's houses. At 12.30 p.m., thirty women boarded a plane at the local airstrip. During the flight, they did their hair and make-up, and changed out of golf slacks and shorts into dresses more suitable for meeting the king. The country's religious leaders were upset, but Faisal had a wonderful time.

Yamani made the 'Saudization' of Aramco a priority. In 1963, he opened the College of Petroleum and Minerals in Dhahran, to educate new generations of Saudis about oil. The curriculum and teaching were in English. In the early days of Aramco, young Saudi men gathered at the company's gates each morning, pleading to be hired. Legally, they had to be eighteen to work, but many were unsure of their exact age. Part of the confusion came from the fact that the Hijri calendar was about eleven days shorter than the Gregorian calendar. So instead of lying, the men shouted through the gates 'Yimkin eighteen' – 'Maybe eighteen'. The Yimkin 18s were men close enough to eighteen, who seemed bright enough and healthy enough to start as coffee boys and receive an Aramco education. Now they had a real institution to attend.

Yamani also encouraged Saudis to study abroad, especially in America. The first wave, including him, had gone in the 1950s. Soon, hundreds were travelling to American prep schools and universities, many on Aramco bursaries.[19] Aramco's organisational chart underwent a constant process of 'greening', green being the colour of the Saudi flag. If a position was already held by a Saudi, its box was coloured green. If a Saudi was going to be ready for a position in two years, it was striped green. If a Saudi might be ready for a job at some undefined time in the future, it was outlined in green.[20] The goal was for the whole chart to be green.

To his friends, there were two Faisals. The suave, relaxed Faisal could hold his own among the most powerful of Washington or London, and the diplomatic salons of the Middle East. When Richard Nixon first met Faisal in New York in 1958, he recalled a man in a Western suit speaking impeccable English.[21] Soon after Faisal replaced Saud, he went for dinner at the residence of the American ambassador in Jeddah. Afterwards, the guests set up a game of Pocket Golf on the living room carpet. The king enthusiastically joined in.

The other Faisal was the austere warlord who could live like a Bedouin, ride bareback, speak tribal dialects, and squat beside a fire to eat rice and meat with his hands.[22] Faisal's gaunt face reflected an instinctive watchfulness. He suffered from ulcers for much of his adult life, which required long periods of recuperation, a plain diet with plenty of stewed fruit, and a daily habit of long walks. The constant pain partially explained his often gloomy demeanour. When his family built him a lavish new palace in Jeddah, he refused to move in. He preferred his more modest, traditional house, which was kept cool only by thick walls and breezes.

Faisal said little in public. He preferred to give hints rather than explicit opinions or instructions. The large reception room at his palace had a beige carpet, chandeliers, and blue and white pilasters. During his public audiences, Faisal sat at one end, while visitors occupied chairs along the walls in silence. Every so often, someone would whisper in his ear, or hand him a folded piece of paper and he might nod or murmur an instruction. He had learned good English, and encouraged his children to do the same. But he only ever spoke Arabic in public. At family gatherings, he would invite one of his sons to sit cross-legged in front of him and for an hour or so swap improvised lines of poetry. The challenge was to outdo each other in style, language, rhythm, and mastery of Arabic verse.[23] In the evenings, he drove out of the city to say his sunset prayers under the desert sky.[24] He also liked to pray by the sea. On Thursday evenings he attended a mosque service and invited everyone there for a meal.

Faisal embodied his country, having lived through its short, but extraordinary evolution. He had traipsed around a freezing London as a fourteen-year-old, been welcomed to the White House as an adult, and watched as his father went from being a tribal chief on the make, to one of the richest and most sought after rulers in the world. As minister of foreign affairs, Faisal summed up his approach: 'Avoid evil insofar as possible, but if evil appears, spare no force in combating it.'[25]

Yamani was a charmer and a sensualist. He liked elaborate meals and travelled with a couple of small bags containing bottles of flower essences, which he mixed for scents to match his mood. He carried a roll-on dispenser in his pocket, which he applied to his beard and head several times a day. He gave off a strong, musky smell. Visitors who accepted his persistent offers to try one of his essences found they stayed on their skin for days.

He was fluent in English, loquacious, his speech riddled with elaborate and playful courtesies. He had a couple of small, yapping Pomeranians, more suited to a pampered duchess. In the Middle East, Yamani wore a traditional dark thobe and ghutra, a long gown and a headdress secured with a black cord. Elsewhere, he wore fashionable Western suits, and travelled with a single aide. He eventually owned homes wherever the king did: in Riyadh, the capital; on the sea in Jeddah; and in the mountains, in Taif, where he grew grapes and liked to talk about love, poetry and psychology, anything but oil. Faisal's Nejdi relatives may have resented the influence of this dandyish Hijazi commoner. But Zaki Yamani would become the only man Faisal trusted to safeguard his country's treasure.

3
Jerusalem Syndrome

When Faisal visited London in May 1967, the Queen honoured him with the rare show of a Gallop Past of the King's Troop of the Royal Horse Artillery. It was a far cry from his first visit to London, when he was entertained by the seals at the zoo and the escalator at an Underground station. Oil wealth had changed everything.[1]

While he was away, Saudi Arabia's military forces were put on alert. The Soviets had told Nasser that an Israeli attack on Egypt was imminent. Nasser closed the Gulf of Aqaba to Israeli shipping, and began to mass his forces on the Sinai Peninsula. On 2 June, Palestinians set off three bombs in Jeddah. The targets were all American: the embassy, the Military Mission and a firm of contractors. It was a warning to Israel's friends. On 5 June, sensing the pressure on its eastern and southern borders, Israel made a pre-emptive attack.

In Dhahran, a ramshackle crowd led by Palestinians gathered at the Ras Tanura terminal and made its way to the Aramco compound. They burst in, overturned cars in the main parking lot and swept towards the houses. The Americans locked their doors, waiting for the worst. The local police chief arrived just in time and fired his gun into the air, dispersing the crowd, which marched downtown to attack the US consulate. Sand had drifted into piles against the consulate walls, so the protestors could walk up and over into the compound.[2] A couple of them reached the roof, where they took down the American flag. Another crowd broke into the US military mission at the airbase and smashed a few windows.[3] The US ambassador prepared to evacuate the Americans in Jeddah and the Eastern Province. The government sent National Guardsmen, the dishevelled, menacing Bedouin tribesmen loyal to the royal family, to reassure and protect them. If the Aramcons fled, Saudi Arabia's oil industry would collapse.

Saudi Arabia and Egypt had been scuffling for years in North Yemen, where the Saudis supported the royalists, and the Egyptians backed the republicans trying to topple them. Faisal despised Nasser's nationalist, revolutionary socialism, and resented his constant attacks on the region's monarchies. He considered Nasser the Soviets' channel into the Arab world. But across the Middle East, old rivalries and ideologies were now being overshadowed by the entanglement of oil and Israel. The infant state of 1948, which had seemed sometimes even to its creators like an improbable experiment, was emerging into young adulthood more confident of its rights and borders. Saudi Arabia was only sixteen years older, but its oil earned Faisal special treatment from heads of state around the world. It was unclear to him how that translated into leadership. His fellow Arabs, including the conservatives within his own country, had an answer. They wanted him to use his oil as a weapon against Israel.

For Faisal, it was not so simple. Much as he resented Israel, he owed his wealth to its greatest ally, the Americans, who discovered and produced his oil. Sustaining this paradox required subtlety, feints and wilful blindness. But now that war had broken out, the Iraqis pushed for an embargo on oil sales to Israel's allies, the United States, Britain and West Germany. Faisal hated the idea. It was nothing but theatre. The oil industry was too large and complex for Saudi Arabia alone to police. He saw no way to coordinate a complete shutdown of supplies to the United States, which had all the oil it needed in the western hemisphere, from its domestic suppliers, Venezuela and Canada. The only victims would be the producers. But on the second day of the war, Faisal gave in, and the first, stuttering embargo began.

The Saudi palace stopped all public mentions of visits by American or British diplomats to see the king.[4] But behind the scenes, he kept his relationships with the West alive. In the spring of 1967, the Americans had deployed two destroyers to the southern part of the Red Sea to put pressure on the Egyptians fighting in Yemen. During the embargo, the Saudis sent an oil barge in the middle of the night to refuel them. They also maintained their surreptitious flow of oil to the American military in Vietnam.

For Israel, the Six Day War was a military, political and psychological triumph. It took the Gaza Strip and the Sinai Peninsula from Egypt, the Golan Heights from Syria, and the West Bank and the holy sites of East Jerusalem from Jordan. It doubled in size and showed the world how quickly it had grown into an assertive and inevitable regional power. Its soldiers roamed wide-eyed through the Old City of Jerusalem and prayed at the Wailing Wall. Two thousand years of history appeared to have been reversed. The day after the end of the war, Israel's foreign minister, Abba Eban, spoke to a special assembly of the United Nations. He cited the long history of Arab countries vowing to attack and liquidate Israel. Egypt, Syria and Jordan had brought defeat on themselves. It would be easier 'to reconstruct a broken egg' than to return to the situation before the war.

The Arabs' armies and air forces were humbled, and their rhetoric exposed. The oil embargo lasted until September. Saudi oil production fell by 40 per cent in June, shredding Faisal's domestic spending plans just as he was finishing cleaning up the mess left by Saud. Venezuela and Iran kept on pumping and shipping oil, profiting at the Arabs' expense, while Libya increased its exports to Europe. Arab oil still found its way to the United States and Britain via the shadowy network of brokers and tankers.

Twelve days after the end of the war, the US ambassador to Saudi Arabia, Hermann Eilts, visited the king in Riyadh. 'He looked like death warmed over most of the time,' Eilts reported. 'He was a cadaverous figure, and always remained that no matter how much he might eat. He always looked emaciated.' But this time he seemed especially glum. Eilts respected Faisal for wanting to maintain good relations with the United States. He appreciated that he was a devout and traditional Muslim, but also modern in his understanding of the world. He made balanced, deliberate and considered decisions, and usually listened before he spoke. But this time, he spoke first, urgently and at length. He was angry that the United States government had not condemned 'Israeli aggression'. The Arab world was full of 'irrational people', 'crazy people', driven by 'mob psychology'. He was talking about the hardcore Muslim conservatives, who resented any forms of social progress, and accommodations with the West and Israel; the radical communists who supported Nasser; and the Palestinian nationalists who believed their cause trumped all others in the region. This was not a time for policy planners in Washington to tread gingerly between warring sides. 'Those of us who are trying to stand up for you are being let down,' said the king. 'Your actions . . . are intensifying pressures on me and other moderate Arab leaders.'

While the United States stood back from the conflict, he said, it was allowing communist influence to grow. If Faisal was to defend the US government to the Arab public, he needed something to sell them. He needed President Johnson to insist Israel return to its 1949 borders.[5] But nothing was forthcoming. At a meeting in Khartoum in September 1967, the Arab League made its stand. It adopted the Policy of Three No's. From now on, no peace, no recognition, and no negotiations with Israel.

By the spring of 1969, Faisal was tired, irritable and overwhelmed by the problems besetting him. His ongoing stomach pain meant he was easily exhausted, and the Hajj pilgrimage season at the end of February had worn him out. His brothers were feuding, Palestine was unresolved, and the friendship of the United States, he sensed, was not something he could count on. Despite his unchanging demeanour, he could veer manically between depression and elation.[6] A visiting group of British newspaper reporters found him drawn and unhappy. The man from *The Times* said he reminded him of his dying mother.

Modernising a country so ambivalent about change was proving an immense and fraught task. Faisal had promised a constitution and never delivered it. The jealousies between the insular Nejdi tribes and the cosmopolitan Hijazis simmered away. Faisal kept power, and the distribution of Saudi Arabia's growing oil wealth, firmly in his own hands. He was reluctant to delegate, even as the availability of highly educated advisers and ministers grew each year. He welcomed argument, but not criticism, so few dared to raise their voice. His habitual silence could inspire confidence and strength, or leave everyone uncertain of his intentions, and reluctant to assume responsibility. The result was executive and administrative paralysis.[7] [8] To ensure order, Faisal's palace guards prowled the streets of Riyadh and Jeddah in their scarlet Nissan jeeps mounted with machine guns. The National Guard, the Bedouin White Army, a primitive, brutal force, loyal to the king, camped outside the gates of the major cities, spoiling for the chance to beat down his opponents.[9]

At the end of May, the security forces arrested scores of men suspected of plotting against him. They included groups connected to Arab nationalists in Lebanon and anti-royalists in Yemen; communists plotting violent industrial sabotage at an oil refinery and steel mill; and army and air force officers suspected of collaborating with the Egyptians. Faisal worried that he had been too cautious with Nasser. The Egyptian leader's lectures on Arab nationalism, and criticisms of the Saudi government, were constantly broadcast into Saudi homes over the radio, despite the fact that Saudi Arabia provided Egypt with a handsome stipend. Faisal thought the Americans should have let the French and the British take Nasser out after he nationalised the Suez Canal in 1956. Or the Israelis should have pushed all the way to Cairo in 1967 and insisted on a new government.[10] Instead, Nasser remained in power constantly criticising the Saudis.

Estimates of the total arrested over the summer ranged between 160 and 300. Gruesome stories circulated that Faisal had ordered the conspirators to be flown out in helicopters over the sea and pushed out, though many of those assumed dead were found to be living happily years later. The false rumours were more evidence of a combustible mood than genuine threats.[11] Every wave of arrests and detentions in the country's gruesome jails generated more resentment to Faisal's rule.[12] Now, the king's paranoia was to take an even stranger turn.

An Australian farmhand confined to a hospital for the mentally ill in New South Wales, Australia, saw Israel's victory in the Six Day War as proof that God would soon return to Jerusalem.

Denis Michael Rohan suffered from depression and schizophrenia. From his window looking out onto the hospital's landscaped grounds, he could see a rowan tree, its bark silvery grey. In the autumn, its leaves turned from green to fire orange, and its white flowers to red berries, a magical colour thought to ward off witches and evil. Rohan, Rowan. Like Jesus Christ, he thought, I too must be the Branch of the Lord.

In hospital, Rohan had listened to *The World Tomorrow*, produced by the Radio Church of God, an American evangelical group based in Los Angeles. Four times a week, the church's founder, Herbert Armstrong, preached with a deranged confidence, offering his listeners 'divine solutions' to their problems. He said that evolution was a lie, masturbation an evil, and that Christ would soon return to earth in Jerusalem. Hitler and Mussolini were the Beast and the False Prophet described in the Book of Revelation, and the Second Coming was nigh.

Released from psychiatric care, Rohan arrived in Israel in March 1969 on a visit organised by the Jewish Agency, an Israeli state body which encouraged people to travel to Israel, especially Jews considering moving there. That spring and early summer, he worked on a kibbutz, and tended the orange groves and gladioli fields. He fell in love with his Hebrew teacher, an attractive young Israeli woman, Zipporah Danino. He sent her flowers and notes, but she never reciprocated. On 20 July, Rohan checked into a hotel in East Jerusalem. Over the next month, he frequented the area around the Dome of the Rock, a site sacred to Muslims, Jews and Christians. For Muslims, the Al-Aqsa mosque covers the rock where the Prophet Muhammad was said to have risen to heaven. For Jews it was the site of the First and Second Temples, and the Holy of Holies, the sacred room where they kept the Ark of the Covenant. For Christians it was thought to be one of the possible places for Christ's crucifixion.

Rohan had decided that God wanted him to destroy the mosque, one of 'Satan's temples', and pave the way for Christ's return. As a reward, God would bring all the maidens of Israel to bear his children, and make the elusive Zipporah his Queen. Just as David had been a shepherd when he was chosen to be king of Israel, so Rohan, the former sheep shearer, would be God's next king. He had a severe case of what psychologists later termed 'Jerusalem Syndrome', an emotional derangement caused by visiting a city drenched in religious significance.

Rohan's first attempt to burn down the Dome of the Rock failed. He shoved a kerosene-soaked cord into the keyhole of the mosque's south-east door and set fire to it. As he ran away, the cord fizzled and scorched the keyhole. The Second Coming needed a better arsonist. Ten days later, on 21 August, he tried again. He arrived at the mosque early in the morning with a rucksack containing three containers full of benzene and kerosene. When he saw the elderly guard at the gate of Bani Ghanim leave his post to go to the bathroom, Rohan slipped inside. He went to the pulpit, one of the most beautiful in the Muslim world, made of Lebanese cedar, inlaid with ivory and mother of pearl, given by Sultan Saladin in the mid-twelfth century to mark the liberation of Jerusalem from the crusaders. He crawled under its steps, poured kerosene on a woollen scarf, placed one end in a fuel container, the other on the pulpit steps, and set light to it. As the fire caught, he ran out and back towards the old city, shouting, 'Fire, fire!'

When the fire department arrived, comprised of Jewish, Arab and Christian firemen, the crowd which had gathered for morning prayers attacked them. People scrambling to remove treasures from the mosque before they were destroyed obstructed the firemen trying to get in, shoving them and standing on their hoses. The fire crept up to the windows just below the vast golden dome. By early afternoon, the firemen had saved the dome, but the mood in the city had turned. Crowds of young Arabs jammed the Via Dolorosa, the street taken by Christ as he staggered to his crucifixion, shouting 'Death to Israel'. One of the huge timbers in the ceiling of the mosque's nave crashed to the floor. Minutes later, Prime Minister Golda Meir arrived on the scene promising an official investigation and help to restore the building.

King Hussein of Jordan sent a telegram to King Faisal calling for a new Arab Summit to discuss Israel's aggression, and cabled the president of the United Nations Security Council deploring a 'new Israeli grave act of lawlessness.' Nasser told a gathering of Arab armed forces in Egypt that the burning of Al-Aqsa was a 'historical, Israeli crime' and that the only proper retribution was victory in war. 'In the coming battle, the Arab soldiers will not be soldiers of the Arab nations alone but soldiers of God and protectors of His religions, houses of worship and holy books.' In a communique released after a Cabinet meeting, Meir's government rejected the rumours that Israel was behind the arson. 'This vicious libel, which is designed to exploit the fire for purposes of political and religious incitement, merits the unqualified condemnation of all enlightened mankind.'

Faisal heard about the fire on the radio. As the custodian of the mosques at Mecca and Medina, he took a special interest in the Al-Aqsa mosque, the third holiest site in Islam. If a Muslim said a prayer beneath the Dome of the Rock, it was worth 500 prayers elsewhere. The Israelis had taken control of it in 1967, and now it seemed to Faisal they wanted to compound the humiliation by destroying it.

The young Australian, who had seen his destiny in the changing colours of a rowan tree, did not clear the way for the Second Coming. But the fire he started confirmed Faisal's darkest suspicion, that Israel had no desire to live alongside the Arabs, but wanted them and their religion eradicated. Faisal appealed to 'Muslim leaders and peoples throughout the world to hasten to the liberation of the Islamic shrines in beloved Jerusalem.' He repeated the call he had made during the most recent Hajj, to 'declare a holy war, now that all methods for settlement by peaceful means had been exhausted.' As he grew more despondent, he resolved to use every weapon against Israel's friends. One day, he would cut off their oil, and this time make it hurt.

4

The Gaddafi Effect

'Your armed forces have toppled the reactionary, backward and corrupt regime. With one strike, your heroic Army has toppled idols and destroyed them in one of Providence's fateful moments.' Libya's King Idris was out of the country for medical treatment. The voice now coming over the radio from Benghazi belonged to an unknown military officer from the Signals Corps. It was 1 September 1969 and Colonel Muammar Gaddafi, aged twenty-seven, had ambled into power. He and a young group of fellow officers renamed the Kingdom of Libya the Libyan Arab Republic.

George Lane, an American consular official in Benghazi, heard that the revolutionary council was meeting at the local television station to plan its next moves. Gaddafi and his Free Officers had seized the country's key military, political and broadcasting centres with little opposition. The streets were now teeming with teenaged boys brandishing Kalashnikovs. In front of the television station, an officer was directing traffic. Lane explained that he needed to get into the building, as he was trying to ensure that all the Americans working in the oil-fields of eastern Libya were safe. The officer said he could not help. Lane tried again, sounding more desperate, but again the officer rebuffed him. Finally, Lane asked the officer for his name.

It turned out it was Gaddafi himself, directing traffic as cover for watching the streets in case of a counter-coup.

Gaddafi had grown up in a goat hair tent, the son of a Bedouin herder. He had shown intellectual promise, risen through the army, and spent part of the year before the coup in England, on a signals course in Buckinghamshire. During his time off, he roamed the English country in his traditional Libyan cloak, pinballing between admiration for quiet, holy village churches and contempt for this land of snivelling imperialists. He developed his own brand alternative to capitalism and Marxism called the Third Universal Theory. It was Libyan ethnic supremacism lashed to Bedouin and Islamic primitivism, and gilded with oil wealth: 'All feebleminded individuals must be weeded out of society by taking appropriate measures towards perverts and deviants . . . A cultural revolution must be staged to rid Libya of all imported poisonous ideas and to fuse the people's genuine moral and material potentialities.'[1] He was, in the State Department's view, a man with 'the virtues and vices of a fundamentalist prophet,' and a 'strong sense of mission.'[2]

Once in power at the head of the Revolutionary Command Council, Gaddafi imposed his particular morality. When the police saw a woman in a mini skirt, they arrested her and sprayed her legs with oil paint. Gaddafi himself appeared with jeeps full of armed guards to close down nightclubs he deemed indecent, and to round up their patrons. When he thought government workers were slacking on the job, he took away their chairs, forcing them to spend their days standing up, or squatting on the floor. He instructed that all signs in English be scratched out, painted over or taken down. He confiscated property belonging to Jews, kicked the Anglicans out of their church in Tripoli and turned the Catholic cathedral into a mosque.[3] The large Italian community left Tripoli for Rome, abandoning homes and businesses which they had owned for years. Gaddafi sent fighter jets to jostle the American surveillance planes which flew 50 miles off the Libyan coast, hoping to provoke a reaction. The Americans complied by shooting several of them down.[4]

Gaddafi was rumoured to suffer from frequent nervous breakdowns, and under stress to lock himself away and scream until his doctors calmed him down with drugs.[5] He slept barely three hours a night, and would sometimes climb aboard a helicopter and disappear for weeks at a time into the wilds of Tripolitania. At Nasser's funeral in September 1970, he seemed so removed from the ceremony that a visiting American diplomat thought he was the first truly deranged Middle East head of state.[6]

American prospectors struck the first commercial volumes of oil in Libya in 1959. Hume Horan, one of the US State Department's leading Arabists, who would later serve in Riyadh during the embargo of 1973–4, said the Libyans were far from ideal recipients of such fortune. 'We're dealing with the traumatization of the disadvantaged, the ultimate vacuity, settled at the last moment by the loser tribes kicked out of Egypt and Tunisia, who were then colonized by the Italians – rulers as nasty as they come.' With the battles of World War Two, 'the rape is complete. Afterwards, it is the poorest country in the world, its biggest export, scrap metal from the war.' Libyans were 'passive, suspicious, dour and troubled,' and instant wealth did nothing to change that.[7]

Under King Idris, Libya had taken an unusual approach with the international oil companies. When they issued their concessions, the government had favoured independent companies over the majors. The cynical view was that the independents were more willing to pay bribes, and offer more flexible terms to the government than the more law-abiding majors. Libya's ruler at the time, King Idris, appeared pious and conservative, but ran a notoriously corrupt court. A more generous interpretation was that the Libyans did not want to be at the mercy of the majors, which had operations around the world, and could source oil from elsewhere if the Libyans caused trouble. They preferred companies who would be dependent on Libyan oil for their survival. Nelson Bunker Hunt was more than happy with the Libyans' arrangement.

Hunt loved cheeseburgers, ice cream and chocolate milk, and it showed. He wore ill-fitting suits with trousers that had to be gathered in the back with a safety pin. He drove his Oldsmobiles for years, and flew economy if he had to buy the ticket. He hunted for change beneath the cushions of his sofas, and hated paying for other people in restaurants so much that he waited until the waiters were stacking chairs and getting ready to go home, if he had to, for the other person to ask for the bill.[8]

Once he had finished work in his office in downtown Dallas, he drove home to his nearby ranch, the Circle T, where he had filled his bookshelves with porcelain birds, and applied his sharp, mathematical mind to the breeding possibilities among his stable of nearly 500 race horses and 2,000 purebred Charolais cattle.[9] He came off as a bumbler to some, but he enjoyed putting on a top hat and morning coat to watch one of his horses race in England, and chat to his fellow owner, Queen Elizabeth II.

Hunt's father, H. L. Hunt, had made his fortune in the oilfields of East Texas, and raised his family in a mansion modelled on George Washington's home, Mount Vernon. He was a grand Texan eccentric with multiple families, who lived on yogurt, bouillon, dates, pecans and vegetables, and believed in the health benefits of crawling on all fours. The Hunt family's wealth was as immeasurable as the Rockefellers', with no discernible end to their oilfields, cattle ranches, company stakes and ventures.

Bunker was keen to emerge from his father's shadow, and in his twenties spent millions looking for oil, and finding none, in Pakistan and Greece. But in 1957, when he turned thirty, he secured a concession to drill for oil deep in the Calanscio Sand Sea, a desert stretching south from Tobruk along Libya's border with Egypt. As the costs of prospecting mounted, he split the rights with BP, which had the resources to transport and market the oil, leaving him the task of finding it. His engineers ranged across the desert for four years, until the autumn of 1961 when they found what turned out to be the largest field yet found in Africa. As the BP construction teams marked out trucking routes through the 200-foot dunes, they discovered the bodies and wallets of the crew of the *Lady Be Good*, a B-24 bomber that crashed during World War Two. The men had parachuted out of the plane, and died staggering through the desert. BP and Hunt drilled eighty-nine wells in the Sarir field, built a terminal on the Mediterranean, and a 320-mile-long pipeline wide enough to move a million barrels of oil per day. Hunt's timing could not have been better.

Of the Middle Eastern producers, Libya had two major advantages. The first was the high quality of its oil, light, low in sulphur and easily refined into gasoline – 'sweet' in oil parlance. The second was the country's position on the Mediterranean. To reach the markets of Europe, oil from the Gulf had to travel through contested and often damaged pipelines, the Suez Canal, or the long way around the Horn of Africa. Libya's oil only had to cross the short, uninterrupted distance from North Africa across the Mediterranean.

In December 1966, the Syrian government stopped the flow of 900,000 barrels per day of Iraqi oil through the pipeline connecting the oilfields of Kirkuk to Mediterranean ports in Syria and Lebanon in a dispute over fees. Then, in June 1967, at the start of the Six Day War, Egypt closed the Suez Canal by scuttling boats at each end. It did not want Israel to capture the canal in working order. Tankers from the Gulf now had to sail around Africa to reach Europe and the United States. Demand for Libya's easily accessible oil shot up.

When King Idris came to open the new BP–Hunt oil terminal at Marsa al-Hariga near Tobruk in February 1967, he seemed a figure from another age, with small round glasses, a white beard, swirling black robe, head covered in a white shawl, and carrying a walking stick which reached up to his shoulder. A tanker named *British Confidence* blasted its horn in welcome. Twelve sheep were slaughtered and Hunt presented Idris with a golden key.[10] By the end of the 1960s, Libya was supplying Europe with one third of its oil. Operating from a hotel suite in Tripoli decorated 'like a Texas bordello',[11] Hunt was soon earning $30 million a year, after tax, from his Libyan investment. On top of his already large fortune, Libya had made him the richest man in the world.

The average age of Gaddafi's eleven-man Revolutionary Command Council was twenty-eight, but they had known each other for a decade. They fought and made up like any group of rough-housing young soldiers. But when it came to Libya's oil, they were clear-thinking and determined. They said they had no need for huge sums of money to develop their country, nor any desire to sit at the high table of civilised nations. They were not restrained by diplomatic niceties. As Gaddafi said: 'Libya has lived 5,000 years without oil and we can live without oil again.'[12] It was a strong bargaining position, which he would exploit within a year of his coup.

On 3 May 1970, a Syrian bulldozer crashed into the Tapline, the pipeline which carried Aramco's oil 850 miles from Eastern Saudi Arabia to the Mediterranean. The Tapline ran through the desert above and beneath ground. It was forged and restrained so that as hot oil flowed through, it barely expanded or moved. The crash stopped the flow of half a million barrels per day of Saudi oil to the Mediterranean. It would take nine months for the Syrians to repair it. Gulf producers and European consumers scrambled for scarce and expensive tankers to ship their oil all the way south around Africa. Eight days later, Gaddafi seized the opportunity for Libyan oil. He demanded a 20 per cent increase in the posted price of Libyan crude, retroactive to 1961.[13] Any company that refused would be nationalised.

Deep inside the State Department, the Economic Bureau of the Office of Fuels and Energy did the arithmetic. They divided European demand for oil by the number of tankers available to bring oil quickly enough from the Persian Gulf around Africa to the refineries at Rotterdam.[14] It was not even close. If Gaddafi shut down Libyan production, the Europeans would immediately have to draw down their stocks and soon resort to rationing. Libya had enough foreign reserves to pay for three years of imports and could easily outlast them. The State Department's advice to the companies was to accept the Libyans' terms.[15] It was important to maintain good relations if they wanted the oil to keep flowing.

In September, the American company Occidental became the first to surrender, agreeing to a thirty-cent increase per barrel. Unlike the majors, it had no other sources of oil besides Libya, and without it, it would go bankrupt. Within two weeks, three more of the independents had followed, Continental, Marathon and Amerada-Hess. 'The Libyans are not bluffing,' warned the US ambassador in Tripoli. If the oil companies did not comply,

Libya would not hesitate to shut off production, crippling the economies of Europe and Japan, with knock-on effects for the United States.[16] BP, Texaco and Chevron accepted Gaddafi's demands, and the other majors and independents, including Hunt, followed. They agreed to rises in royalties and taxes, and in Libya's share in profits from 50 to 55 per cent. In just a few months, the young colonels of Libya had outflanked the richest corporations and the most powerful country in the world. They had tilted the balance from the oil companies to the producing countries. By October, all had given in and Gaddafi could say 'we have won back our rights.'

In December, OPEC met in Caracas and did what the oil companies had feared. They followed Libya's lead and increased tax rates and prices to eliminate disparities between the organisation's members. Libya then made even greater demands, another 27 per cent price increase, to stay ahead of its peers. The colonels showed no deference as they became OPEC's battering ram. The rest of the organisation's members charged in happily behind, lepers no more.[17]

5
Tehran

In Iran's capital, Shah Mohammed Reza Pahlavi's new rich danced in nightclubs, and drove out at dawn to smoke hashish in abandoned caravanserai. Still in their party dresses and black tie, they prowled the countryside in their Range Rovers, their hunting dogs poised on the roofs, ready to tear off in pursuit if they saw a pack of gazelles. They snorted masses of cocaine provided by a Colombian who visited Iran so often he was nicknamed Concorde.[1] The growing middle class discovered middle-class pastimes like hiking in the mountains above Tehran, much as Los Angelenos hike the canyons of the Santa Monica mountains.[2] But most of the city's residents scraped by without clean water or a proper sewage system.

Iran was the second largest oil producer in OPEC, after Venezuela, and over the previous decade, the shah had used oil revenues to fund his 'White Revolution', a programme of economic and social modernisation. He had weakened the religious authorities and liberalised society. Women could now vote and run for political office. He forced the powerful landowners to sell land to smallholders, so more farmers could work their own land. Yet for all the cosmetic changes, the country was hostage to his authoritarian plans, whims and moods. His family and friends exacted bribes and kickbacks. His secret police, the SAVAK, had spies everywhere, to catch the merest flickers of subversion. Their torture methods ran from raping women in front of their husbands and pouring boiling water into their victims' rectums, to placing them naked on a metal plate and heating it until it burned their skin.

The shah had turned Iran's ruling class into peons. In 1967, he staged his own coronation, with a crown studded with 10,400 carats of rubies and diamonds. When he invited his ministers and business leaders to his palace, they had to line up like the emissaries carved into the friezes of Persepolis, waiting for a moment with their emperor.[3] In the evenings he dressed in jewelled robes at formal events, while courtiers in gold-braided jackets lined up to kiss his hand.[4] Staff minutes referred to him as HIM, short for His Imperial Majesty, Aryamehr Shahanshah, King of Kings, Light of the Aryans, Shadow of the Almighty and Vice Regent of God. His ambassador to Washington DC addressed him in correspondence as 'The Shadow of my God' and signed off offering to 'kiss Your Royal Feet a thousand times.'[5] One story had him delaying his arrival in Isfahan while he made love to one of his ministers' daughters in a helicopter hovering over the city.[6] Everything and everyone in Iran was at his service.

Like all the major oil producers, the shah had been watching the Libyans closely. No leader in the region had more experience of the relationship of oil to power. During the early twentieth century, Britain controlled Iran's oil through the Anglo-Persian and later Anglo-Iranian oil companies. In 1953, after Iran's prime minister, Mohammad Mossadegh, dared to nationalise his country's oil, the American and British security services deposed him and consolidated his powers in the young shah. Iran's oil went back under the control of a consortium of American and European companies. But like his neighbours, the shah had grown unhappy at having so little authority over the production and pricing of his own oil.

Between 1945 and 1970, the price of a barrel of crude oil had ranged between $1.50 and $3.50. Adjusted for inflation, it had fallen by around a third. The West's post-war growth and industrialisation had been powered and funded by cheap oil. As the producing countries grew richer and more confident, they realised they could challenge the Western companies which found, extracted and sold their oil. They were developing the scientific and financial expertise, and a fuller understanding of their political power. They controlled a commodity the world needed. They did not have to meekly accept the terms they were given. The Libyans had just given a virtuoso display of standing up for themselves. In January 1971, the companies and OPEC prepared to meet in Tehran to negotiate a new set of rules on pricing. The city, with all of its oil-fuelled contrasts, made the ideal setting for the Middle Eastern producers to confront the Western companies en masse.

Fearing what was coming, the oil companies turned to a familiar figure for help. John McCloy had been a successful corporate lawyer when he joined the War Department during World War Two. He served as the second president of the World Bank, high commissioner to Germany, chairman of the Chase Manhattan Bank and the Council on Foreign Relations, and an adviser to a series of presidents. He had the bouncy vim of a country club tennis player, and the selfless cheer and good sense essential for consiglieri. Kissinger compared him to a 'jovial gnome', but he kept the establishment's sharpest blades in his vest pocket. After he returned to corporate work in Manhattan, his clients included the West's major oil companies. When President Kennedy asked McCloy for his views on US oil interests in the Middle East, McCloy suggested that the companies operating there act together against the producers, who were beginning to realise their power. He had then spoken to Robert Kennedy, the attorney general, about the risk of breaching antitrust laws if the oil companies acted as a bloc. He visited every subsequent attorney general to raise the issue in case he ever needed a formal opinion. By the end of 1970, the moment had come.[7]

Representatives from twenty-three oil companies gathered in New York to agree on a common negotiating position for the Tehran talks. An official from the Justice Department's antitrust division attended to show the government's support. McCloy set up meetings in the offices of Chase Manhattan bank and Mobil Oil, and the establishment bastion of the University Club. On 15 January, the companies announced they would negotiate as a group with OPEC, not with individual countries, and none would do a deal with Libya without the consent of the others. Their logic was that negotiating country by country would lead to leapfrogging. If one country got better terms, another with poorer terms would insist on an improvement to their agreement, and the demands would keep spiralling upwards. The companies concluded it would be better to agree the same terms for everyone, and hold the line.

McCloy persuaded the State Department to send John Irwin, a former corporate lawyer now under secretary at the department, around the Middle East to show the government's support for the companies' position. No sooner had he set off than the fragile union of companies and the US government began to fray. The shah warned the American ambassador that if the companies insisted on negotiating with OPEC rather than with each country, any agreement would be defined by its most radical members, notably Libya. It would be better now for the companies to run two sets of negotiations, one with the more moderate Gulf countries, the other with the Mediterranean countries, including Libya.[8]

He was also indignant that the United States government had chosen this moment to get so directly involved, when for so long its role in oil negotiations had been intentionally ambiguous. It had grown used to treating the oil companies as a convenient buffer. As long as the producing countries negotiated with the companies, Washington could pretend that oil was simply a commercial issue. The moment the government intervened, it became a foreign policy matter, and more consequential as a result. In Tehran, the US government now blinked. Advised by John McCloy, the companies arrived thinking they had the full support of their government for unified talks. But they quickly discovered that they were alone. The shah's foot-stomping had worked. The State Department had fled. The talks began on 19 January, and quickly turned into a rout. 'We were seen to back off,' said Henry Schuler, who worked for Bunker Hunt. 'And we were seen to back off and off and off, and later developments showed that we constantly moved back.'

The companies agreed to split negotiations. Iran and the Gulf producers threatened an embargo if the companies did not meet their terms, and secured an increase of thirty-three cents per barrel in the posted price, and a guaranteed five cents a year more until 1975. Yamani told one of the companies' lead negotiators that they were fooling themselves if they thought the agreement would hold. Now they had tasted blood, the countries would soon be back for more.

The second round of talks, this time with Libya and the Mediterranean producers, began in Tripoli at the end of January. Without the presence of the Gulf producers, there was no moderating influence on Libya. Gaddafi was sick, in bed, and was represented by his 28-year-old deputy prime minister, Major Abdel Salam Jalloud. Before 1969, Jalloud had no experience of government, but he had become Gaddafi's most trusted executive, the man who made his revolutionary dreams real. He was earthier than Gaddafi, lean, handsome in his double-breasted suits, with the easy swagger of a Sicilian gangster, and a taste for drinking and nightclubs. His job was to bully the Western oil companies, and he did it with relish. He summoned their executives for talks, and kept them waiting for hours before sauntering in with no apology. He told them they were from backward countries, threw ashtrays at them, and hurled their written proposals at their feet.[9] [10]

Jalloud said that Libya had the right to increase prices whenever it wanted to. There would be no five-year agreement on prices. The US government had made an 'evil and unwarranted decision' to waive the usual antitrust rules and allow the oil companies to collude. Libya would now 'take all action necessary to achieve her rights' and 'if the oil companies do not agree they will suffer a continuing headache. Our battle will be long and tortuous and we want to prove to the governments of America and Europe that Libya is not a fertile land for exploration by profiteering companies.'[11] The companies agreed to a ninety-cent increase in the price per barrel of Libyan oil, retroactive to the previous March, and an increase in the tax rate. In just a few months before the Tripoli talks, the price of Libyan oil had risen by 53 per cent. Now it surged again. The Gulf countries looked timid for agreeing to much weaker terms in Tehran. The Libyan newspaper *Al Youm* reported that, 'The Government succeeded in recovering a large part of the people's right, their wealth, which the companies have been plundering for the past 10 years.'[12] Soon, it would go after the rest.

On 13 August 1971, Nixon summoned his economic team to the presidential retreat at Camp David. Unemployment and inflation were both rising, and he wanted to reset the economy before he began campaigning for re-election.

Nixon's rise to the presidency was as astonishing in its way as Gaddafi's. He had grown up in Whittier, a small farming community south-east of Los Angeles. He was one of five brothers, two of whom died by the time he was twenty, exhausting the family's finances. His father was a disappointed bully, his mother a devout Quaker who passed on her inner rage at life's injustices to her son. Through sheer hard work and a win-at-all-costs approach to politics, Nixon reached Washington and emerged from Congress to become Dwight Eisenhower's vice president in 1952. He was a scratchy, conservative everyman to balance Eisenhower's glistening record as a military hero and emblem of the liberal establishment. In 1960, he lost the presidential contest to John F. Kennedy, but triumphed in 1968, an unloved but strangely inevitable force in American life.

Nixon much preferred to spend his time and energy on foreign policy. He had spent the previous two years trying to bring a peaceful end to the Vietnam War, and pursuing a more engaged and less confrontational relationship with the Soviet Union and China. But as his re-election year approached, fixing the domestic economy became his priority. He craved his own version of FDR's New Deal, Kennedy's New Frontier, and Johnson's Big Society, a major domestic agenda demanding primetime coverage. Markets operated at their own speed, with no regard for the political calendar. Trusting them to solve economic problems, Nixon feared, rendered politicians irrelevant. He was at heart an interventionist.

The discussion at Camp David circled around some unusual themes. In normal times, the Federal Reserve could keep the economy within a narrow band of healthy growth by using interest rates. It could reduce them to stimulate borrowing, investment and economic activity, leading to more employment, and higher inflation. Or it could raise them, which does the opposite. Higher interest rates lead to less investment, fewer jobs, and lower inflation. But these were not normal times. The United States was experiencing both rising unemployment and rising inflation. Its economy had grown stagnant. The problems had grown beyond the Fed's reach. Inflation was too high for it to cut rates, and unemployment was too high for it to raise them. It was stuck in a pattern of 'stagflation'.

There was a third option which brought its own less knowable risks. Since the end of World War Two, the dollar had traded at a fixed price linked to gold. An ounce of gold was worth $35. Delegates from forty-four countries had met in the New Hampshire town of Bretton Woods, and agreed to fix this price to stabilise global trade and limit inflation. It meant that war-ravaged countries could trade with each other without worrying about fluctuating exchange rates, as their currencies were fixed to the dollar, which was fixed to gold. Governments would have no incentive to print money to finance their spending. The gold standard was credited with helping the global economy back to its feet.

But by 1971, the system was under severe strain. To meet foreign demand for dollars, the US Treasury had printed four times as many as could be exchanged for physical gold at the set price. If too many countries came and demanded gold for their dollars, the Treasury would quickly run out. The system was running on vapours. Supporting the rest of the world's economies with the gold standard had made America's exports cheap and its imports expensive. When its economy was booming, it could easily afford it. But in 1971, the US ran its first annual current account deficit since 1888. It had to borrow to fund its trade with the rest of the world. The time had come for it to end its post-war largesse, and take care of itself.

But decoupling the dollar from gold would instantly destabilise the global economy. The value of the dollar would plummet. The oil-producing countries which received much of their income in dollars would suddenly be getting much less per barrel than they had expected. The fixed dollar amounts specified in their contracts with the oil companies would buy far fewer imports. For the United States, devaluing the dollar would make its exports even cheaper for foreign buyers, and thereby increase employment. But that would only exacerbate inflation.

Nixon's answer to inflation was wage and price controls, and a 10 per cent tariff on foreign imports until the new international monetary system settled into place. It was interventionism on a grand scale: pushing on the gas by devaluing the dollar, while slamming the brakes with wage and price controls. The political pragmatists in his cabinet saw it as a way to wriggle out of recession long enough to win the election. The orthodox economists considered it a dangerous sugar rush, which would spike the economy briefly, only to send it into a deep and dangerous funk shortly afterwards. An economist hovering at the edges of the Nixon administration as an adviser, Alan Greenspan, wrote in *The Wall Street Journal*: 'In a free society, controls cannot supersede the law of supply and demand. In a society in which they can, justice cannot prevail.' Nixon had stolen the most basic functions of the economy, setting supply and demand, from consumers and businesses. They were now being manhandled by government.

Two beavering Nixon acolytes, Donald Rumsfeld and his assistant Dick Cheney, were put in charge of the Cost of Living Council. They had ninety days to draft a new system of wage and price controls. Three thousand IRS agents were drafted to enforce the new controls, but Rumsfeld's team were struggling to write the rules. They lacked the expertise and the staff. When they needed someone to work on oil prices, they picked Charles Owens, a young Texan whose job was arranging the council's public service announcements on the radio. Cheney assumed a Texan must understand oil.

With a day to go before their ninety days were up, Rumsfeld, Cheney and their team pulled an all-nighter. In a fog of cigarette smoke, Cheney sat at the typewriter, and they did the best they could. Their twelve-page document listed the foods and products subject to the price controls, and those exempted. Dressed broilers, flour and cigarettes were controlled. Live poultry, wheat and leaf tobacco were exempt. Dill pickles and packaged slaw were controlled, cucumbers and cabbage exempt. Custom wigs and taxidermy made to order were exempt, mass-produced leather goods were not. Over time the regulations grew to be thousands of pages. A few hours before their deadline, the council submitted their cobbled together draft to the Federal Register. 'It was a terrible idea in effect for a lot of reasons,' Cheney reflected later. 'It undermines the whole notion of a free economy.'[13]

Initially, Nixon's plan seemed to work. By the end of 1971 and into 1972, inflation fell and employment rose, giving him the economic bounce he needed to win re-election. But it could not last, and the predicted slump soon followed. Not for the last time, Nixon sacrificed common sense for a brief illusion of control.

In December, Libya nationalised BP's concession on a flimsy pretext: retaliation for Britain's support of Iran when it seized Greater and Lesser Tunb, two barely inhabited islands near the mouth of the Persian Gulf, claimed by two other sheikdoms. The Libyans could have simply broken off diplomatic relations with London. But there was no drama in that. OPEC was meeting that very moment in Abu Dhabi, and with this one flourish Libya reset its agenda.

Libya's representative at the United Nations justified the treatment of BP on the grounds that Britain had 'violated the treaties that it had itself imposed on the Sheikdoms of the Arabian Gulf,' when it withdrew from what became the United Arab Emirates earlier in 1971. Libya 'had replied in the only way understood by the imperialists – by nationalizing the evil interests of Great Britain in the Libyan Arab Republic and withdrawing our deposits from British banks.' He added, 'the United Nations lends a deaf ear to the loud cries of the small and weak, while it listens attentively and obediently to the words and whispers of the Big Powers.'[14]

Lawyers argued the finer points of Libya's actions in letters to *The Times*. Could a government arbitrarily break contracts with foreign companies? Who owned the oil in the ground during a concession, the company or the country? A year earlier, when BP went along with the other international oil majors and yielded to Libya's demands that it raise the price of its oil, it thought it had bought time and goodwill. Now it informed Libya that it had recruited a renowned international lawyer, Professor Sir Humphrey Waldock, to act as its arbitrator to settle the matter legally.

BP refused to market Libya's oil, and warned its customers it would sue them if they bought 'hot oil', oil from Sarir which they considered theirs. In late December, BP heard about a tanker leaving its terminal at Marsa al-Hariga loaded with oil from its concession. It decided to hunt it down. The *Capetan Elias* was sailing under a Panamanian flag, heading for a refinery in Priolo, a town on the Sicilian coast. When the tanker arrived in Sicily, BP agents boarded with a court order demanding samples of the oil for testing, to determine its origin. They asked the captain who were the sellers and buyers. The ship belonged to a Greek company registered in Panama, which said the oil was not theirs. It was on its way to a refinery owned by an Italian firm, SINCAT, which claimed they were just refining it and sending it on. The sellers turned out to be Linoco, the Libyan National Oil Company, which now owned BP's assets. When BP finally tracked down a representative of Linoco in Tripoli, Engineer Anis Ahmad Scoter, he said the oil did come from BP's former Concession 65 in Sarir, but that now it belonged to the Libyans. There was nothing Professor Sir Humphrey Waldock or anyone else could do about it.

6

I Will Use My Power

The Intercontinental Hotel in Geneva was an ungainly Lego block of a building, white and grey on the outside with all the charm of a municipal car park. But it was conveniently close to the United Nations and the city's diplomatic heart, and had fine views out towards Lake Geneva and Mont Blanc. Diplomats and politicians from around the world loved to convene and haggle behind its smoky glass doors and windows. None loved it more than Zaki Yamani.

When he came through, he took over two of the largest suites on the eighteenth floor, one for meetings, the other for his personal use. His staff piled the coffee tables with flowers, crystal jugs of pomegranate juice, pale green logs of pistachio paste and boxes of dates. He kept a portable trampoline in his private suite. Every few hours, he would jump up and down on it to keep his blood flowing during long negotiations.

On 21 January 1972, it had been drizzling and close to freezing all day when the OPEC delegation led by Yamani and executives from the oil majors gathered once again. The light was fading outside. The two delegations sat at long, narrow tables, thirteen men on each side. On one side were representatives from the main oil-producing countries. In the middle sat Yamani, their lead negotiator, dapper in a dark suit and leather boots. Next to him was his deputy, Faisal's son, Saud al-Faisal, whom the king had asked Yamani to mentor. Behind them crammed aides and representatives from other OPEC countries, men in cheap brown and grey suits, many wearing thick, black-rimmed spectacles, looking like the junior faculty of an engineering school. On the other side were the representatives of the Western oil majors, from the United States, Britain and France, sleek men fattened by corporate life, who had prepared for this encounter over lunch at the St Regis Hotel in New York. Their orders were simple: keep Yamani and his peers in their place, and don't let them change a thing. The issue was what the Arabs called 'participation' and the men across the room considered theft.

Like most of their OPEC peers, the Saudis did not want to nationalise their oil industry straightaway. They recognised that the oil companies had built Saudi Arabia, without laying claim to it. Ibn Saud had chosen the Americans as partners rather than the British for just this reason. The British, he knew, would feel compelled to colonise. It was in their nature to impose their vision of civilisation, and their break-ups tended to be lingering and torturous. Only the French were worse. The Saudis appreciated that the Americans were more clinical. They wanted the oil and a route out to the world's markets. They wanted money and national security. And for that they were willing to obey the law, to pay, and to teach the next generation of Saudis. They were also the world's ascendant power, not a collapsing empire. If Saudi Arabia were to have a great friend in a dangerous world, it made sense to have the richest and strongest one.

But four decades after Ibn Saud's original concession, as demand for oil had surged, production in the Middle East had ballooned, and the Saudis had learned the technicalities of the oil business, their fundamental relationship with the US oil companies remained the same. American employees lived and worked in their pockets of air-conditioned suburbia dropped into corners of the desert, while the Saudis and other nationalities lived separately, less comfortably. The Americans ran the oil operations, drilling, extracting and refining the oil, preparing it for export. They paid the Saudis a fixed price for what they took and kept roughly half the gross profits for themselves. Now the Saudis wanted more, to 'participate' in owning their oil, to have a greater role and stake which could grow over time as they became more expert in the industry.

Anyone who had been to Yamani's office and seen his chart showing the 'greening' of Aramco, the number of Saudis taking on managerial positions, would have understood how he saw the future of the company and his country. He wanted partnership and real profit sharing with the oil companies instead of tax payments. He wanted Saudi Arabia to be treated as an equal by the Americans and Europeans, rather than as an asset to be managed and milked. Saudi oil was generating enormous profits for Western companies and governments, which were also receiving major contracts in non-oil sectors like arms, construction and agriculture. But the process of industrialising Saudi Arabia for a future beyond oil was going slowly, and the talks on ownership of that oil came down to skin-deep prejudice and respect.

The initial question for this new round of negotiations was what exactly participation meant. Yamani spoke as if Aramco could be divided up like cheesecake. Saudi Arabia gets 20 per cent now and more later. After all, the cheesecake did belong to them. The company's American shareholders insisted it was not so simple. Twenty per cent of what? If it was equity, then the Saudis would be within their rights to argue for some degree of executive control. They would be entitled to know how Aramco operated, down to the last detail, and this was not a straightforward matter. Each shareholder had its own production rights, and rights to buy certain amounts of Aramco oil. There were rights to use Aramco's refineries and rights to sell oil in certain countries depending on demand and local taxes. And perhaps trickiest of all, there was the whole downstream business of selling oil products. Should the Saudis be let in on the great mystery of pricing gasoline for cars and trucks? And if that, should their 20 per cent include a nickel of every quarter made on every candy bar and soda sold in gas stations across America? Should 20 per cent give Saudi Arabia, a producing country and potential rival, access to the oil industry's most tightly held secrets?

That afternoon in Geneva, the moment Yamani said the subject for discussion was participation, the oilmen started to squirm. BP's representative said he could speak only for his company. The same went for everyone on his side. They could not speak for each other or the countries they came from. Yamani knew this was nonsense. For decades, it had been tacitly and explicitly assumed that the oil companies negotiated on behalf of their national governments as a bloc. They had brought their collective power to bear on the producing countries to keep down the prices they paid for oil. But now when the producers wanted a greater stake, the companies tried to scatter, and force Yamani to chase them into every corner of the room.

'This is quite simple,' said Yamani coolly. 'We want a share in the equity capital of our existing concessions. We would start with a minimum and build up to a maximum over a period of years.' The minimum would be 20 per cent and the maximum 51 per cent, representing control over the assets conceded to the companies when the producing countries were at much earlier stages of development.[1]

'Why are you unhappy with the existing arrangements?' asked Texaco's representative, Al DeCrane.

Yamani said that countries had a basic right to acquire the natural resources within their own borders. All they wanted was a greater share, while continuing to work with the oil companies. From a legal point of view, he added, circumstances had changed, justifying a change in the agreements. When the original concessions were granted, no Saudis had experience in the oil industry. Their country was still young and needed money. Its people had no idea how to find, extract and refine oil. Now there were thousands of Saudi graduates with specific expertise in these areas. All new agreements being signed contained provisions for participation.

And just look around, Yamani said. 'The trend now is to nationalize all resources.' The Algerians had assumed a majority stake in their oil and national gas industries; Libyans had begun the process of taking back their oil without the bother of talks; and it was rumoured the Iraqis were preparing to follow soon. Would the oil companies prefer that?

DeCrane kept at the legality issue. 'If a country has exercised its sovereignty by granting concession rights, why shouldn't the party who has relied on the agreements feel that he has a right to question nationalization? You cannot ignore legal rights given by contract.'

'You are exaggerating your rights,' said Yamani. 'An agreement with the Government does not give immunity from nationalization, and a state cannot bind its successor not to nationalize – even if they have promised not to do so.'

Yamani argued that gradual participation was the best way to ensure stability for the producers and the companies. The world had changed since the original concessions, and they needed a new deal to reflect that change.

'There is no legal right in our opinion to force us to agree,' said DeCrane.

'I don't care about your legal views provided you are prepared to discuss in a reasonable and practical matter,' said Yamani, now flashing his blade. 'If you say there is no right to ask for participation then that is the end of the matter. If you are prepared to discuss, then we will. We have the power to move in other directions.'

'It is important to distinguish between a right and a power.'

'Good, I am glad we understand each other. For example, I own this glass and I have the right to break it. Don't make me nervous or I will use my power.'

Yamani had thought deeply about the evolution of Saudi law in a time of accelerating prosperity and modernisation, and what it meant for oil. He believed that Shari'a law, the religious rules derived from the Quran, the Sunna, and the consensus of scholars, was organic and constantly evolving. It was not fixed by tradition or society. Shari'a survived because of its adaptability. Its provisions were constantly scrutinised and updated through a process of investigation and analogy, the comparison of situations over time. If it failed to account for the public interest and welfare of today, it would be as useless as the more extreme forms of capitalism and communism appearing in the West.[2]

He offered the example of a scholar of the Hanbali school, one of the four schools of Islamic justice, passing a group of Tatar men drinking wine. His followers urged him to stop the men drinking. But he refused. God banned Muslims from drinking wine as it would be a distraction from their faith. But the Tatars were not Muslims, and drinking kept them from activities more damaging to public welfare, such as murder and rape. It was better for everyone if they kept drinking than if they stopped. Shari'a was a moral code derived from religion to guide secular activity as it evolved, not to freeze it in time and place.

'The spirit and general principles of Shari'a are as valid today as they were yesterday, many centuries ago, and as they will be tomorrow many centuries to come,' Yamani wrote. 'They are like a green oasis in the desolate desert of our lives which is overcrowded with problems and conflicting ideologies.'

Shari'a, Yamani argued, was capable of great philosophical, legal and psychological subtlety. It was not subject to the rigid dogmas of left and right, which were causing the young in particular to feel spiritually bereft. While socialists and capitalists duked it out over the rights and duties of owners, Shari'a established that owners had distinct rights, but none greater than the obligation to serve the community. It illuminated the path to social justice, a concept endlessly discussed, but rarely realised, in the West.

The evolution of Shari'a applied as much to oil and its ownership as to any other aspect of Saudi life. In Islam, all property is owned by God, and therefore by the community. Private ownership is permitted on the condition that it benefits the community. Regarding the ownership of minerals, scholars disagreed. Some believed that all 30,000 gold sovereigns paid to Ibn Saud under the terms of the concession belonged to the state. If someone was authorised to search for or extract minerals, they could receive wages as labourers and contractors, but no right to ownership, which remained with the state. Others believed that owners could claim the right to minerals found beneath the surface of their land, but they had to pay a portion of any proceeds to the state as a royalty. Either way the state would benefit.

It came down to how you interpreted a saying attributed to the Prophet: 'People are partners in three things: water, grazing and fire.' Scholars took fire to include all sources of energy. Like water and grass in the desert, the fossil fuels lying beneath the desert were not the product of any human effort. They were simply there, and so must belong to everyone. Their extraction, refinement and transportation took work and merited compensation. The seemingly simple, yet infinitely complex question was, how much? Yamani had Faisal's full backing to torture the companies in Geneva.

When Yamani pressed the oilmen to agree in principle on participation, they blithered over the technicalities of its implementation.

'I have an agreement with my landlord for a considerable period of years on my flat in London,' said Total's representative. 'He cannot put up the rent or take away some rooms unilaterally.'

It was a breathtakingly stupid comparison, as if he had never seen the vast oilfields of Ghawar in Saudi Arabia or Ahvaz in Iran, the flares lighting up the desert night. As if he had no idea what it meant for a people to change in one generation from being nomads to controllers of the greatest store of natural wealth ever discovered; from being imperial whipping boys to having the world by its throat; or the sense of divine providence often attributed to this gift.

All that the man from Total could see was a rental contract.

'The oil concession agreement deals with the most important commodity in the world,' Yamani replied. 'We are as concerned with stability as you are. If we were not sincere about this, we would let it go a few years and then take the whole cake.'

'The oil industry comprises both the companies and the producing countries and unless we both live up to our agreements in good faith, both will suffer,' said the man from BP.

'We will suffer,' said Yamani, losing patience. 'You will lose your shirt.'

Yamani had run the numbers. He and Faisal had calculated that they could cut production for a while, and still be fine. Saudi

Arabia was struggling to find ways to spend and invest all the money that was pouring in. The change was as destabilising as it was invigorating. A pause might even be welcome. The time had come for the oil companies to accept new terms and for the Western consumers to pay a price for oil that reflected its true cost. 'The consumer can do without you but not without us,' he said. 'We have the oil in our ground and he must pay for his needs.'

OPEC and the Saudis had made up their mind, but the oil executives still thought there was room to haggle, to hold on to their exorbitant rights.

'You are asking us to sell something,' said DeCrane. 'We are still trying to explore areas of mutual interest.'

'Don't regard oil concessions as the Holy Bible,' said Yamani. 'If you are not prepared to move you will lose everything.'

'You will suffer more than us if there is a bust up,' Yamani told the executives across the table. This was why the Gulf states had asked him to lead the negotiations. He was fearless. 'The oil is ours and you need it. To me stability is important and it is therefore better to provide it by agreement than unilateral action. You will suffer far more than we. If you wait, it will cost you a lot more later.'

As Yamani elaborated the terms of his deal, the executives grew hysterical. Saudi Arabia and its negotiating partners wanted to acquire 51 per cent of the equity capital in their oil companies over time, and pay book value for it. Book value in this context meant the amount of capital invested in the assets minus liabilities. It was what the companies would have received if they sold off their assets and paid off all of their liabilities. It was a backward looking number, which took no account of the assets' capacity to make money in the future. It was far less than the assets' intrinsic value, the value of their future cash flows.

'This is just confiscation,' said Mobil's representative. 'You must know that. Book value is appropriate for bankruptcy and not for a going business.'

'You put no value on my title to the oil,' Yamani replied.

BP's man complained: 'You appear to confront us with a choice between part nationalization, creeping nationalization and prompt nationalization. No commercial concern could accept these terms.'

Yamani repeated that he was not negotiating. These were the terms. If the oil companies could not accept participation on the grounds of changed circumstances, for a price determined by the producers, there was nothing more to be said. The executives tried once more to lure him into a country-by-country, company-by-company negotiation. Again he refused, and asked if he should adjourn the meeting so the companies could consider his offer.

Calouste Gulbenkian, the great Armenian oilman of the early twentieth century, said: 'Oilmen are like cats. One never knows when listening to them whether they are fighting or making love.'[3] Faced with Yamani's intransigence, the executives began to shift. Esso's representative, C. J. Hedlund, had strongly rejected OPEC's offer. But when Yamani asked if he rejected any form of participation, he wavered. 'I can't be sure how to answer. It's not like dealing with sin or motherhood. I can't agree with what I have heard but also can't reply that I'm against it in every form.' Slowly the others swung in behind, Mobil, Gulf, Socal, BP, Total, Atlantic Richfield, all but DeCrane of Texaco. They were ready to hear more.

'Long live Esso,' said Yamani, and he adjourned the meeting.

The participation talks continued after Geneva, and as he grew more confident, Yamani delighted in goading the majors. Their executives arrived at meetings bristling with files and documents, primed to dispatch the upstart producers. For another round at the Intercontinental in Geneva, the companies' team arrived with a green file containing questions for Yamani, his possible answers, and reams of follow-ups. Everyone took their seats, the companies at a table, Yamani alone on a small stage in the hotel. A representative from the companies began reading out the first question. Yamani held up his hand and started to ramble on about everything but the question. The executives stared at their script, the output of several sleepless nights, blown up in seconds. Yamani was not so easily managed. When he finally asked some questions of his own, one of the executives stammered back, '[W]e're not authorized to even think about that.' Another pleaded, '[I]t's not in your best interest to go into that.' Yamani closed the meeting, saying, 'I want to deal with the principals.'

When the top executives came to see him, it was more of the same. They prepared, calculated, drafted and rehearsed, and Yamani sauntered in, seemingly fresh from sleep and breakfast.[4] They charged at him, bloodshot and snorting, and he swung his hips to elude them. Their over-prepared demands simply delayed the inevitable.[5] Yamani's skill, one executive said, was to drive 'you to the wall with sweet reasonableness.' Yamani put it differently. 'When discussions become heated, I become more patient. Patience is essential.'[6]

In Riyadh, Yamani often brought one of his Pomeranians or a cat into meetings, to add to the sense of genial and distracting chaos. The senior executives at Aramco's partners once became so frustrated by Yamani, they decided to go over his head and deliver their message directly to the king. They sent the president of Aramco, Liston Hills, who flew into Riyadh in a sandstorm, and drove to the palace with Frank Jungers, the company's chairman. Hills told his driver to leave and come back later, imagining the meeting would go on for some time. When they went in to see the king, Hills sat beside him, with Yamani opposite. Hills gave the king a letter explaining Aramco's position. Faisal put it on a side table without opening it. The two men had a friendly discussion, but Faisal did not mention participation. After a few minutes, he rose and said he had to leave. Hills did not understand that Faisal did not negotiate. He listened, and liked people who spoke quickly and straightforwardly. He gave his decisions later, in private. When the meeting was over, Yamani offered Hills and Jungers a ride to the airport. Yamani drove, with Jungers in the passenger seat, and Hills in the back. As he drove, Yamani reached into his robe and produced the envelope. 'Perhaps you could use this,' he said, grinning and handing it back to Jungers. He had opened it and read it while walking to the car. He had known the king would never open the letter himself. Faisal did not want to embarrass the Aramco men by being negative. Yamani was his negotiator and there was no getting past him.[7]

For the executives who had to shuttle between New York, Europe and the Middle East, wherever the next round of participation negotiations happened, it was thankless work. They left Manhattan with strict orders from men used to having their way, only for Yamani to brush them aside. He ran such rings around them that they suspected him of bugging their conversations, and flew from Riyadh to Athens, a four-hour flight, to guarantee a secure line to head office. When they returned to New York, the despondent executives were told they were pathetic to have been outsmarted by these 'savages'.[8]

7

Open Flow

West Texas had its own views on the evolving crisis. On Thursday, 16 March 1972, nearly two hundred members of the Texas Independent Producers and Royalty Owners Association (TIPRO), ranging from sleek senior executives of the global oil majors to sun-worn single well owners, jammed into the rooftop ballroom of the Holiday Inn in El Paso to give their forecasts for the coming months.

The Texas Railroad Commission had made an unusual trip from its base in Austin to the heart of the oil industry. The commission's name was deceptively modest. It was formed in 1891 to regulate the rates and schedules of Texas railroads. In 1917, it was given the additional responsibility of regulating the transportation of oil. But as the federal government took more responsibility for rail, the Railroad Commission's duties expanded to oil production and price setting as well as transportation. It became the primary oil and gas regulator in Texas, and the standard setter for the rest of the country. The decisions made by its three-person elected committee reverberated around the world. A few weeks later, Steve McQueen and the crew of *The Getaway* would drink and shoot pool in the Holiday Inn after staging car chases on El Paso's sun-bleached streets. Today it was hosting a wake for Texas oil.

One by one, for two and half hours, the oilmen stepped up to the microphone and said the same thing: demand for energy in America kept on rising, but domestic production was stuck. To plug the gap, the country was becoming increasingly dependent on oil from overseas, from countries which did not have America's best interests at heart. That winter, the country had experienced its worst energy shortages since World War Two. There were too few refineries to handle the oil there was, and consumers paid little attention to requests to change their habits. As the environmentalists ruefully joked, there was no point talking population control to couples making love.

Everyone agreed on the source of the problem. In 1968, prospectors had found huge oilfields in a remote part of Alaska, but environmentalists had blocked the building of a pipeline to bring the oil to a port, where it could be shipped. 'Militant environmentalists,' said M. A. Wright of Humble Oil, had caused millions of dollars of equipment to be left idle in the Yukon. Without more domestic oil, the United States risked having to import over half of its petroleum requirements by the end of the 1970s. 'One can imagine what would become of the United States if our major source of energy was controlled by foreign powers,' said B. E. Milner, the vice president of Atlantic Richfield.[1] 'It is imperative that we regain a balanced perspective between our ecology and our standard of living,' said R. F. Tucker, president of Mobil Oil's North American division. Oscar Wyatt Jr of Coastal States Gas Producing snarled that perhaps it was time Texas stopped sending oil to refineries on the East Coast, and kept Texas oil in Texas. Foul-mouthed, low-slung and powerful, Wyatt was an old-school wildcatter, an independent prospector. He had grown up poor, flown bombers during World War Two, and started in the oil business selling machinery parts from the trunk of his car. He particularly loathed opportunists like George H. W. Bush, the son of a rich senator from Connecticut, who came to Texas looking to make his fortune. To Wyatt's horror, Bush had arrived in West Texas on a plane owned by an oil services company, where his father sat on the board.[2]

The way these meetings usually worked was that the oilmen told the commission how much oil they expected to produce and sell in the coming months. The commission set an overall production target, based on what it thought the market required, then told each producer how many barrels it could pump. Around 45 per cent of the production target was assigned to the large constituency of small landowners, whose wells tended to produce a few barrels per day. The rest was divided among the bigger, more productive wells. The system was called 'prorationing', and its stated purpose was to limit waste by keeping unneeded oil in the ground. Critics said it was nothing but a means of price fixing. By the mid-1960s, the monthly calculations by the commission's 400 staff in ten offices around the state were monstrous, taking into account 6,000 producers, 8,500 fields, 210,000 wells, and about 3.25 million barrels of oil per day. Wars, changes in consumer habits, new technology and new discoveries were constantly forcing the Railroad Commission to adapt.

The commission's chairman, Byron Tunnell, was a lean, beaky politician, who had grown up in Tyler on the edge of the great East Texas oilfields. Over the century since oil was discovered, it had transformed the United States, and Texas. By 1929, Texas was the biggest oil-producing region in the world. In 1953, it still yielded more oil than the entire Middle East and twice that of the Soviet Union. But in Saudi Arabia, you could drive for miles south of Dhahran and have no idea that beneath you lay the world's largest oil reserves. The land and the oil beneath it was owned by the king, and conceded to Aramco for a limited time. There were no boundary disputes. The simple goal of Aramco's drilling, production and transportation system was maximum efficiency. The company operated over a vast area with just a few rigs and an almost invisible lattice of pipelines. Engineers picked a site, put up a rig and drilled down. It took a couple of months for men working twenty-four hours a day in shifts to establish if a well was wet or dry. If the well was productive, they capped it with a 'Christmas tree', a machine that controlled the pressure, and sent the oil away in pipes for refining and shipment. Then they would dismantle the rig, and 'skid' it to another site on a trailer with tyres soft enough not to sink in the sand. By the late 1950s, Aramco was producing more than a million barrels of oil a day with fewer than 200 wells. It was as Zen as oil production could be.

Texas was a land of speculators and jostling, no-good neighbours. In 1930, a wildcatter discovered the largest oilfield found up to that time, just south of Kilgore, 30 miles from where Byron Tunnell had grown up. Speculators poured in, buying tiny lots across the field, putting up rigs in their back gardens and even right in the middle of town. The craftier ones fitted their drills with 'whipstocks', metal sheaths which dug a well that curved into their neighbour's property and sucked out their oil. Above ground, the heist was invisible. At one point there were twenty-seven wells on a single acre of land around Kilgore. The price of land rose 2,000 fold, and within a year of the discovery, a new well was being completed in East Texas every hour. The wildcatters pumped their wells as hard and fast as they could, treating their land with unnatural ferocity.

The commission struggled with the speed of change. When it tried to control the chaos of the 1930s, many producers ignored it and kept on producing 'hot oil', oil that had been extracted in breach of laws and regulations. The small-time drillers hoped that soon enough they would have the money to pay off the inspectors and rule-makers. The question of how to manage Texas oil reserves over the long term became ideological rather than scientific. The big oil companies presented compelling technical evidence that Texas was dissipating its precious asset. Many of the wells in Texas did not produce much oil, as little as ten barrels a day. These last gasp 'stripper' wells were only economically viable if the price for oil was kept artificially high. But there were lots of them, and their owners were a formidable political force, capable of smothering the scientific and economic reality in rhetorical bilge. When an ex-mayor of Amarillo, E. O. Thompson, ran for a seat on the commission in 1935, he said: 'The issue is not one of big business versus the small man. It is greater than that. The real issue is shall Texas youth continue to have free opportunity amid their natural resources? Or shall our youth in the near future be forced through lack of opportunity to work for some big company in a chain filling station?' Ugly, low-yield wells were just more Texan. The Railroad Commission sat between the two sides: the smallholders who felt any regulations or production limits were an intrusion on their fundamental rights; and the large companies which wanted to sustain prices and supply over time by managing the oil reservoirs more carefully.

By the late 1960s, the fight was reaching its end. The old school Texas wildcatters and roughnecks were already fading into poetic legend. 'The oil industry is a truck and crew setting out from a motel about sunrise and striking out across a trackless wasteland for forty miles,' wrote a former roustabout in 1967. 'You live on black coffee and canned beans. And at night maybe a smile from a waitress. On weekends you make the drive-in malt shop and the movies and the dives in Roswell, or pick up a paperback at a newsstand before bedtime.'[3] The real action had moved to Alaska and the Middle East. Texan oil had evolved from the 'shotgun shack' towns of its pioneering days, to an age of modern oil cities along the Gulf of Mexico which managed production of a quarter of America's energy needs, and thrummed with money and power.

That day in El Paso, Tunnell had grim news. As soon as the presentations were over, he announced that, starting in April, Texas was to pump at 'open-flow', 100 per cent of its capacity. It was the first time since 1948, when America's post-war reserves needed replenishing, that Texas's wells would be pushed so hard. Across Texas, every barrel that could be pumped this month should be pumped, short of damaging the reservoirs.

'This is a damn historic occasion and a sad occasion,' said Tunnell. He said that instead of creating incentives for more exploratory drilling, Washington had been 'kicking the dog to death', trying to end the special tax treatment of oil companies, and arguing that Texas's pro-rationing system was a racket, paid for by the rest of the country. Perhaps if there was another war, Tunnell said, the commission might authorise the depletion of Texas's major reservoirs of oil, but 'I sure as hell won't do it just to protect the caribou on the North Slope' of Alaska.

The caribou had become Tunnell's shorthand for what he considered the insanity of America's oil industry. Deep below the frozen wastes of Alaska lay all the oil America needed, enough to restore its independence, and end its reliance on foreigners. And there it would stay, if the environmentalists had their way, for the sake of a few dopey animals.

If the federal government was serious about protecting America's oil and gas industry, said Tunnell, there were obvious ways to do it: restrict foreign imports; expand offshore drilling; raise the artificial limits on the prices of petroleum products;

and allow drilling in Alaska. More American oil would mean less room in the market for foreign alternatives.

The truth was more straightforward. Texas had mismanaged its oil. Instead of trying to become more efficient, Texan producers had spent years demanding their politicians protect them from the realities of the market with tax favours and by limiting the amount of foreign oil allowed into the country. But Texas could no longer meet rising demand with its overpriced oil. Open flow meant there was no more spare capacity it could play with to manipulate prices. Even with shipping costs, foreign crude was much cheaper, and more profitable for the oil majors. A barrel of Texas oil cost ten to fifteen times as much to produce as oil from Venezuela or the Middle East. Politicians from states which needed lots of fuel oil to get through the cold winters were tired of subsidising Texas.

If the import quotas protecting Texas oil were lifted, the price of oil in America would plummet, and domestic production would slow down. But the quotas in their current state, were costing Americans some $4 billion each year in tax breaks and subsidies for Texans. The hundreds of thousands of royalty cheques going to Texans with minuscule drilling operations were the price of America having its own sources of energy. The Texans argued that it was a national security matter, not an economic one. For the residents of Massachusetts and Maine it was simply a question of getting cheaper fuel to heat their homes, no matter its source. The talk of national security was nonsense.

Most Americans had a vision of the Texas oil industry far removed from hardscrabble suffering. They saw a wealthy, clubby industry, whose leaders feasted on steaks, sitting beneath mounted steer horns in the petroleum clubs of Houston and Dallas. They saw events like the independent producers' annual convention, where wives were invited to 'Coffee, Screwdrivers and Bloody Marys' at 9.30 a.m., and talks on 'The "How-to" of Handling Your Hairpieces' and 'The Business Man's Wife . . . Asset or Liability!' This was a conservative, complacent industry. Certainly not one that King Faisal in his majlis would deem worthy of protection.

The shah of Iran and King Faisal were both second-generation rulers, the sons of strong fighters and personalities who had dominated their countries. Aside from that, they could scarcely have been more different. Faisal maintained traditional dress and habits, and preferred to run his country from his favourite old palace in Jeddah. The shah adopted the airs and pretensions of a French king. In his office, he had gold-plated telephones, cigarettes and ashtrays, gold fixtures in his lavatory, and mirrored fragments pressed into the ceiling to make the room sparkle.[4]

Faisal was self-effacing, but quietly decisive. The shah was extravagantly vain, and dithering. After lunch, Faisal went home for a nap. The shah spent his afternoons with prostitutes selected by Madame Claude, Europe's top brothel keeper, and flown in from Paris. He called these sessions 'gardesh', outings. Faisal was effortlessly inscrutable. Every flicker of the shah's grim moods passed up through his ramrod body, and across his pinched and anxious face. Faisal kept his own counsel. The shah held secrets. Despite regular doses of Valium, he slept poorly.

To the West, the shah and King Faisal presented a choice. The shah was a more recognisable character, a man who yearned to be taken seriously by Europe and the United States, and wanted his country to rival their economic and industrial power. He was a Persian, not an Arab, well-disposed to Israel. But which of the two would be the better ally in the Middle East, the most reliable source of oil and the strongest defence against Soviet expansion? Was it the unprincipled, grandiose, temperamental shah? Or the glowering, anti-Zionist king, whose wealth outstripped his needs, and his power his desire to use it?

In May 1972, Nixon and Henry Kissinger flew from Moscow to Tehran. Kissinger was the undisputed star of Nixon's administration. He was Jewish, and his family had fled Germany for the United States in 1938 when he was fifteen. While a professor of government at Harvard, he had built ties in Washington, and advised the governor of New York, and perennial presidential candidate, Nelson Rockefeller, on foreign policy. Nixon appointed him his first national security adviser. They proved a relentless and formidable team, deeply intellectual, obsessed with history, strategy and politics. Kissinger's European bombast and charm balanced Nixon's chewy determination. Their shared ambition was to reinvent American foreign policy, to be realistic and engaged with the world, and clear the toxic air of Vietnam and the Cold War.

Before they arrived in Tehran, there had been a surge in terrorist activity in Iran. Several hundred, mostly middle-class young people, many educated abroad, had forged overlapping groupings attached to various communist ideologies. There were Marxists, Marxist-Leninists and Maoists, all yearning for revolution. They had established themselves in Iran's rural north, shifting beyond 'guerrilla theatre' into something more menacing.[5] In the four months leading up to Nixon's visit, they had set off eleven explosions directed at American targets. Sixteen guerrillas had been killed fighting the authorities, thirteen had been executed, and ten sentenced to life imprisonment. All were tried in military courts. The US embassy worried that the SAVAK was stoking resentment by being so heavy handed.[6]

While the shah feted the president at a state dinner, three

Japanese terrorists hired by a Palestinian splinter group arrived in Tel Aviv on an Air France flight from Rome. As they arrived at passport control, they tossed several grenades and opened fire with Kalashnikov assault rifles, which they had hidden in their bags. They killed twenty-four people and wounded seventy more. The customs hall was strewn with bodies and pools of blood.[7] The Marxist Popular Front for the Liberation of Palestine claimed the attack was revenge for the killing of two Palestinians who had hijacked a Sabena flight to Tel Aviv three weeks earlier, and died resisting Israeli troops.

After the state dinner in Tehran, the Iranian prime minister, Abbas Hoveyda, and Kissinger crashed a press party at a hotel. Kissinger was astute about using reporters to achieve his political ends. He understood the value of controlling their stories. But he also enjoyed their ribald company. Still in white tie and tails, he plumped down on a pillow on the floor, and began smoking a tall hookah pipe. To the roars of the assembled journalists, the belly dancer hired to amuse them undulated closer and closer to Kissinger until she fell into his lap.[8]

The next morning, Nixon and Kissinger spent two hours with the shah in the Saadabad Palace. Nixon had first met the shah in 1953, when he was vice president. He asked him about the stories of domestic discontent. The shah said, '[W]e just put subversives into jail.' Nixon assured him he did not have to worry about American liberals 'griping' about human rights.[9] The US embassy in Tehran knew little about the purpose of Nixon's visit except that he was going to brief the shah on his meetings in the Soviet Union. Its greater significance emerged six weeks later when Kissinger sent out a memo in the name of the president, instructing the government to give the shah whatever weaponry he wanted, from planes to smart bombs. Previously, the Pentagon had been cautious with the shah, selling him armaments that his military might reasonably use, and no more. Nixon's sudden open-handedness was baffling. In a stroke, he had made the shah America's unassailable ally in the Middle East.[10] One unconfirmed but widely circulated story was that the shah had earned Nixon's loyalty by funding his re-election campaign via secret accounts in Mexico.[11]

The night of Nixon's meeting with the shah, the staff of the Iraq Petroleum Company (IPC) in Baghdad received instructions not to go home. The office was closed, and around midnight a convoy drove up and Saddam Hussein, Iraq's vice president, stepped out.[12]

Since the nationalist Ba'athists seized control of Iraq in 1968, Saddam had solidified his place as a progressive and lethally effective leader. He had grown up in grinding poverty, with a violent mother and an abusive stepfather known in his village as Hasan the Liar, for his false boast to have performed his pilgrimage to Mecca. Hasan forced his stepson to work on a farm from the age of six. Saddam started school later than other boys, but quickly proved highly intelligent and gifted with a prodigious memory. As an adult, he rose through the Ba'ath party, acquiring a reputation for physical courage and political ambition. In 1959, he was part of a team who tried to assassinate the Iraqi prime minister, Abdul-Karim Qasim, on a street in Baghdad. A legend grew that Saddam escaped arrest by gouging a bullet from his leg with a penknife, and then fleeing to Syria on a donkey.[13] By the time the Ba'athists launched a bloodless coup in 1968, Saddam was the party's deputy secretary general. He said he wanted to turn Iraq into a Stalinist state.[14]

His first government assignment was to run the misleadingly named Office of General Relations, which included Iraq's notoriously vicious secret service. None of Saddam's peers wanted to touch it. Stealthily, Saddam took over more and more departments, education, propaganda, and *fellaheen*, which took care of the country's peasants. He moved into an office next to the president's and by the start of 1969 was vice president.

To distract the country from its serious economic problems, Saddam stoked fears of foreign plots. In December 1968, sixteen Jews were among thirty people arrested in Basra and charged with spying on behalf of Israel. Saddam turned their trial into a national spectacle. Fourteen of the accused, including nine of the Jews, were sentenced to death. They were hanged and left hanging in Liberation Square in the centre of Baghdad. When Saddam came to see the bodies, crowds cheered him. He had communists tortured in the prison known as the Palace of the End, and like Stalin encouraged his own party members to spy on each other for any lapse in their loyalty. By 1970, he had consolidated his power under the largely ceremonial president, Ahmed Hassan al-Bakr. Now he turned to curing Iraq's sick economy with oil. Economic independence would be essential to the country's political authority.

Nine years earlier, the previous government had expropriated 99.5 per cent of the concession areas belonging to the Iraq Petroleum Corporation, a consortium of Western companies led by BP, Shell, Esso, Mobil and the Compagnie Française des Pétroles. But it had left the companies to keep operating production. The Iraqis suspected the IPC's members were producing less oil than they could in Iraq, because they would rather pump oil in countries where they did not have to share the profits. BP owned most of the concessions in Kuwait and Iran, and would rather sell the oil from there that it owned outright. The Iraqis suspected the IPC had also given up exploring for new oilfields.

Saddam now took control of relations with the IPC. To the

companies' surprise he was remarkably well informed about the political issues and the state of the global oil market. He told the companies that he was happy to draw on their expertise, but that he alone would control the production volume and prices for Iraq's oil. In mid-May 1972, he gave them two weeks to accept his terms. He did not hear back.

The night he arrived at the IPC, he told its staff exactly how the nationalisation was to occur, which offices to take over and how to tell the foreign staff what was going on. He advised them to show the greatest courtesy as they seized the IPC's assets. He predicted the companies would try to sabotage the production facilities by removing parts of the machinery, so he had sourced replacement parts from friendly countries. Whatever happened, production would go on.

Saddam named 1 June 'Victory Day', because overnight 'our wealth has returned to us.' Radio Baghdad put it in even starker terms: 'Arab Oil for the Arabs'.

Posters appeared all over Baghdad showing greedy British oil executives, Uncle Sam being sprayed with oil by Iranian soldiers, and a grotesque caricature of Moshe Dayan, Israel's defence minister. In June, Saddam was lavishly received in Paris. He rewarded the French with privileged access to Iraqi oil on economic terms favourable to Iraq. But Ghanim Abdul Jalil, the chairman of Iraq's national oil company, said the deal was about more than money. It was also about Israel. He said, 'It is our right to be against governments that are against us . . . There is a strong relation between the Palestinian problem and oil.' France's position, which was 'not against the Arabs', made it a friend. 'We will protect the interests of our friends.'[15]

Bunker Hunt had become Gaddafi's quarry. While Yamani was negotiating participation in Geneva, the Libyan government kicked out Hunt Oil's employees and cut its share in production from Sarir by half. The Libyans hired oil specialists from the UK to run its production facilities and export terminals. In June, Hunt flew to Libya for the first time since 1967, when he had presented King Idris with the gold key, to try to strike a bargain. But he was too late.

Far away in Dallas, surrounded by his porcelain birds and prize cattle, Hunt had never played the game in Libya. He had not invested in schools, hospitals, or any of Gaddafi's vanity projects. He had no political credit. The Libyans demanded half the profits from the oil he had been selling from his unnationalised share in Sarir since BP was nationalised, and a 50 per cent ownership stake in his remaining operations. He offered to sell the ownership stake in return for two years' worth of production. The Libyans refused, saying that oil in the ground was not Hunt's to sell. It already belonged to them.

The anti-Western mood in Libya darkened. In August, a crowd stormed the British embassy in Tripoli, trashed the offices and burned a Union Flag. The alleged provocation was the British government's decision to refuse asylum to two Moroccan air force officers involved in an abortive coup d'état in Rabat, who had fled to Gibraltar. The Libyans were looking for any reason to rile the West. By the end of 1972, Libyan oil was surfacing in Bulgaria, Yugoslavia, the Soviet Union, Cuba and Spain. What the Libyans did not receive in cash, they got in goods and services: an airport runway from the Bulgarians; oil engineers from the Russians. No sooner did BP stop one ship trying to dock on the East Coast of the United States, than another popped up veering around the Mediterranean to avoid detection. Tankers were leaving Tobruk and being rerouted out at sea to avoid detection.

In December, the Iraq National Oil Company complained

that brokers were offering Iraqi crude they did not have in order to feel out prices. Once they knew what they might get, they went to the Iraqis and tried to buy supplies. One European refiner received more offers for Iraqi oil than Iraq could even produce. The Iraqis called these offers for non-existent oil 'Arabian nights dreams of brokers'.[16] Anyone with oil contracts fixed before the dollar was devalued demanded that prices go up as compensation. Buyers refused and the brokers profited by piecing together the broken promises.

It was not only in the Arab countries that the old order was collapsing. Since 1956, when Egypt took control of the Suez Canal, and Moscow and the international oil companies broke off their connections to Israel, Iran had been supplying Israel with oil through a pipe, forty centimetres in diameter, which snaked through the Negev desert from Eilat, on the Red Sea, to Ashkelon, on the Mediterranean. To avoid discovery by the other Middle Eastern producers, Iran had registered its legal partnership with Israel in Liechtenstein. But a decade later, Israel's need for oil was growing, so it negotiated with the shah a new 50-50 partnership, and began seeking financing to expand the pipeline to nearly triple its width. A new company was registered in Switzerland, and funding came from an improbable source: Deutsche Bank, and its chairman, Hermann Abs. Abs had been the most powerful commercial banker under the Nazis, and was imprisoned after the war for his service to the Third Reich. But he had since prospered and become a central figure in Germany's post-war resurgence. He agreed to provide Israel with a low interest loan to pay for construction.

For years, the Israelis and Iranians went back and forth on the terms of supply, investment, profit sharing and secrecy. The shah wanted the money, but he was also desperate that the trade remain secret. For Yaakov Nimrodi, a Mossad spy who served as Israel's liaison with Iran's military and secret services, the shah's capricious behaviour exemplified the 'Persian philosophy of life: flexibility in everything, moving in such a way that the sheep remain alive, while the wolf is also satisfied.'[17] Or as the shah put it himself, '[I]f the choice is between a shape without contents and contents without shape, then the second choice is preferable.'

Once the expanded pipeline was completed in 1969, a specially commissioned fleet of tankers began pulling up to Kharg Island, the main loading terminal in the Persian Gulf, and filled up with Iranian oil. Their paperwork listed an innocuous destination, often Gibraltar. The ships set off and returned three weeks later, higher in the water, their holds empty, with no record of having docked anywhere. They had been to the deep-water port at Eilat, disgorged their oil, and come back. Once the oil reached Ashkelon, the Israelis took what they needed and sold the rest. Independent brokers shuffled the paperwork to hide the origin of the oil and its intermediate stop in Israel, and leased tankers to ship it west across the Mediterranean or north into the Black Sea.

Out at sea, the flags and markings of the tankers were changed as an extra precaution. The oil was often cheap and heavy, needing extra refining at its destination. But the buyers, notably General Franco's poor, isolated, fascist Spain, were grateful for it, and the shah, whom the Israelis called 'the landlord', liked the backdoor money. In its first, and busiest, year of operation, the pipeline carried 10 million tons of oil, shipped by 162 tankers coming and going through the Red Sea right under Saudi Arabia's nose.[18]

While the oil majors made decisions in boardrooms high above New York, Dallas and Houston, a separate, scruffier world of oil trading was evolving. The long era in which oil prices were administered by the majors was coming to an end. With more sellers, more buyers and booming global demand, the market was descending into very lucrative chaos.

A judge in Sicily then ruled against BP's attempt to stop ships carrying their Libyan oil, noting the absurdity of his court 'being asked to ascertain whether BP is or is not the owner of the petroleum held by SINCAT, in the possession . . . of Linoco, which acquired it from Arabian Gulf Exploration Company, which extracted it from the Sarir deposit, which was the subject of Concession No. 65, of which BP acquired half from Nelson Bunker Hunt, with the consent of the Libyan Government.' This was a wild goose chase and BP should give up.

The situation was completely out of hand, and there was no way of controlling it.

The teams that had opposed each other in Geneva in January met several more times over the next months, Yamani insisting and cajoling, the companies procrastinating. Saddam's actions had focused minds. 'Yamani whispered never threatened,' said one executive. 'His deadliest tactic is to probe for holes in your argument by calmly repeating question after question until finally you're so weary you'd hand over your grandmother.'[19] Faisal broadcast a rare warning: 'The implementation of effective participation is imperative and we expect the companies to cooperate with us with a view to reaching a satisfactory agreement. They should not oblige us to take measures in order to put into effect the implementation of participation.'[20]

But the companies kept searching for wiggle room. They wanted to give up a lower share of ownership, and be paid for the loss of profits they would have made if their concession had run its full term. They asked to buy back a greater share of the government's oil to guarantee supply without going into the more volatile spot markets. Yamani was resolute, and warned them to stop 'delay and procrastination.'[21]

After Geneva, they met in Saudi Arabia, London, San Francisco and Beirut. Oil executives far preferred meeting in cities where they could eat and drink in decent restaurants, and find whatever nightlife they wanted. London was the key listening post for the oil industry. Executives could conspire and share information here, far from the scrutiny of the US Justice Department, with its pesky obsession with antitrust laws. Beirut was a compelling mix of French and Arab culture, with restaurants and decadent nightclubs lining the Mediterranean seafront. Cairo and Tehran also had their glitzy charms compared to the grim austerity of Riyadh.

In Beirut, the oil companies' team met Yamani at the Bustan Hotel in Beit Mery, which looked out over the city. They gathered each morning, stayed for lunch, and talked into the afternoon. Yamani was friendly but resolute. His terms were the terms, and he asked the companies to produce a complete and final offer.

Throughout the talks, Saudi Arabia's oil production kept rising, and the world kept consuming. Britain clung to the deluded hope that it would be saved by recently discovered oil in the North Sea. 'Unfounded optimism,' Yamani called it. At the end of September, he gave his first concrete, long-term estimate of Saudi oil production. It would increase 20 per cent a year to 20 million barrels per day by 1980 – more than the current demand of the United States, the world's largest oil consumer. If anyone still questioned Saudi Arabia's influence and wealth, Yamani put their doubts to rest.

On Thursday 5 October, at a meeting in New York, the five OPEC countries led by Yamani reached an agreement with the oil majors. Yamani asked everyone to keep the terms secret until they were approved. But by the following Monday, the news was out, leaked by a French executive who had attended the talks. Everyone had predicted that the majors would accept 20 per cent participation. They agreed to 25 per cent, rising in increments to 51 per cent and majority control by 1983. The Saudis were the most conservative of the Middle East's oil producers. They had not forced nationalisation on its partners. But through steady negotiation they had opened the path to controlling their own oil.

Yamani now travelled from New York to Washington with a proposal. He had been observing the dispute over import quotas. The Northeastern states were concerned about fuel shortages in the coming winter, and wanted the government to let in more oil from overseas. The Texans were resisting, fearing that cheaper imported oil would drive down the price of their own crude. Yamani offered to sidestep the problem by selling oil directly to the United States at a fixed price outside the quota system, provided it was exempted from all restrictions and duties imposed on other foreign oil, and Saudi Arabia was allowed to invest in its downstream refining and marketing. The Americans would be guaranteed a steady supply of oil, while the Saudis would be able to invest their increasing oil revenues. Yamani said the deal would create an 'economic bridge' between the producers and consumers.

Kissinger rejected the idea. He suspected the Saudis were angling for preferential political treatment. A deal would infuriate America's own producers and bypass the majors. It might provoke a rash of bilateral arrangements between the developed countries in Europe and Japan, and individual producer countries, which would drive up prices.[22] Kissinger saw no risk in rejecting the Saudis, because he saw no way they could fight back.

At the conclusion of the participation deal, Yamani had warned his fellow exporters not to exploit their newfound power. 'The world needs our oil, and we, in our turn, need the world. In other words, we are like the human body: when one part of it is hurt, all the other parts are affected.'[23]

A year later, the body would be torn to shreds.

PART II

8
The Rapids

In 1953, Pierre Wack, a young French economist, was working on a government study about reviving France's economy. He visited Japan to study its post-war recovery and extended his trip to spend several weeks with a revered garden designer, Kokobe-San. One day, Kokobe-San took him to a corner of a garden covered in unremarkable brush. 'Look at this,' he said to Wack. 'Look at it really. This is real. It is. And it is much more important than to be beautiful. Never forget, what is, is.' Unblinking observation, and a refusal to be distracted by convention or noise, would define Wack's later work as a corporate planner.

He was also deeply influenced by the Russian mystic George Gurdjieff, and his philosophy of acceptance and understanding beyond our five senses. He believed in intuition and the flashes of insight that came from Zen meditation. Later, when he was the head of planning at Shell's London headquarters, Wack burned joss sticks in his office and meditated cross-legged on the floor. He practised a form of evolved simplicity. Every day he had the same lunch of smoked salmon, brown bread and butter, coleslaw, an orange and, ever the Frenchman, a glass of white wine. Before he made a presentation, he would shiver for five minutes to put his mind and body into a near trance. He travelled for weeks at a time, observing the world and 'breathing in' ideas that might shape Shell's future. He called his presentations 'breathing out'.[1]

Wack despised traditional corporate forecasts. Reams of data were distilled into monolithic and unimaginative predictions, lines on graphs extending from past to future with minimal variation. His alternative was scenario planning, an integration of different macro and micro inputs producing a variety of possible outcomes. Ideally, the scenario planners came up with two or three visions of the future, and a set of options that executives could consider and act upon. Scenarios offered interpretations and choices, rather than sterile projections.

At Shell, Wack was given the latitude to abandon the traditional processes and pursue his ideas. As he pitched his new methods and findings, he realised it was not enough to come up with well-thought-out scenarios if the decision makers were not willing to consider them. Often these decision makers were locked into mental models about the world and their businesses which had congealed over time. Executives who had been promoted for exercising good judgement in the past, struggled to imagine a different world of sudden and calamitous change. Trying to jolt them from their linear forecasts was like pouring 'water on a stone'. The scenario planners had to reach beyond logic to consider the psychological work of changing minds.

Shell's planners had reached a similar conclusion to the Texan oilmen about the coming years. The supply of US oil had been falling since 1970 as usage kept rising. In the short term, the gap could only be filled by Middle Eastern oil. That left the United States vulnerable to any price increases or production cuts the Middle Eastern countries decided to impose.

As they worked on their scenarios for 1973, Wack took the seven members of his team to an old monastery in the South of

France, owned by Shell Française. He wanted to get them 'in the green', out into nature, free of distractions, and thinking clearly. Over five days, he began with a series of intense discussions, which continued well past midnight, and resulted in physical fights between his planners. Wack considered these fights the point of mental and intellectual breakthrough. For the rest of the retreat, his team worked harder and more imaginatively to revise their scenarios.

The first step in designing scenarios was to understand the 'predetermined elements' of any situation. Wack explained that if there was a storm high up in the Himalayas, the Ganges would flood as it passed through the foothills towards the towns and cities downstream. The predetermined elements included the storm, the mountains, the river and what lay along its route. The chain of events was inevitable. But not all scenarios were so simple. In the Middle East, the price of oil was not simply a function of supply and demand. The causal chain was much funkier than flooding along the Ganges. To understand oil prices, you had to understand geology, drilling and transportation, not to mention the Arabs' historical, religious and political motivations, their attitudes towards the West, and their feelings about Israel.

As each country decided how much oil to produce, Wack's team identified another important factor: absorptive capacity. Countries with ample reserves and small populations, like Saudi Arabia, could only spend so much on their development. If they produced too much, they would not be able to absorb all the revenue. It was better for them to limit production, keep prices steady over the long term, and avoid being swamped by foreign currency. Their oil was often worth more if it was kept underground and sold for higher prices in the future. By contrast, countries with large populations compared to their reserves wanted to earn as much as they could as soon as they could to fund their immediate needs. Their decisions about how much oil to produce were driven as much by their domestic requirements as by global prices and consumer demand. Traditional oil company forecasts took none of this into account. Scenario planners had to separate the predetermined elements from the uncertainties, what was inevitable and what was possible under ever-changing circumstances.[2] The oil markets challenged all of their best efforts.

In early 1973, Wack presented his scenarios to Shell's senior managers. He assumed that over the next decade, demand for oil would push up against the limits of world supply. He said that Shell was 'like the canoeist who hears the white water around the next bend, and now needs to prepare for "THE RAPIDS" he will soon have to negotiate.' By paring their case down to this one vivid image, the planners hoped the executives would pay attention.

Wack explained that from late 1972 to 1973, the global economy had been booming. The oil industry was living in a traditional world of steadily expanding supply and demand. Companies built new tankers, and expanded their refineries and production. But soon they would hit The Rapids, where oil prices rose, production was restrained, the producing countries struggled to absorb their oil revenues, and consumers ran up deficits paying for more expensive oil, sending inflation higher. Beyond the rapids lay a new world to which governments would respond in one of two ways: either they would intervene with all kinds of top-down solutions, from price caps to energy-saving rules, and investments in alternatives; or they would let market forces work, and adjust to the new situation.

What Wack's team could not predict was when exactly these changes would occur, how much prices would increase, and the various participants' immediate reactions. But they estimated that supply and demand would start to converge in 1973, as the producing countries kept renegotiating prices and participation with the companies.[3] At that point, prices would soar. They convinced the executives that whether or not they were right about The Rapids, the company would be better off preparing for them.

Despite his academic credentials, Henry Kissinger thought himself too grand for economics. It seemed a lesser field than diplomacy. It was for bean counters not strategists. He boasted: 'When people tell me we are consuming six million barrels a day, they might as well say fifty thousand Coke bottles worth of oil. I don't know what that means.'[4] His fans adored him for his intellectual swagger, which had invigorated American foreign policy. But it left him ill-equipped to understand the looming energy crisis.

Two groups of people might have educated him. Unfortunately, he loathed both of them. He thought that the executives at the major oil companies saw Washington as just another resource to be tapped and exploited. They wanted a free hand to negotiate with the producing countries, but also expected the government to lard their profits with special tax treatment and subsidies. When things were going well, they wanted the government to stay away. When things went awry, they came begging for help.

Then there were the Arabists, a special priesthood within the State Department. They tended to come from White Anglo-Saxon Protestant (WASP) families with missionary or commercial links to the Middle East. They attended north-eastern private schools, like Exeter and Deerfield, and studied political science or languages at Harvard and Princeton. During their postings they learned Arabic poetry and collected lithographs of the desert and the souks. They bought intricate rugs to cover the floors of their homes in Washington, and retired with academic sinecures. They were appalled by what they saw as America's betrayal of the Arabs when it backed the creation of Israel. In his memoirs, Harry Truman wrote that some of these Arabists were 'inclined to be anti-Semitic'.[5] As support for Israel grew in Congress, the major political parties and the press, the Arabists came to see themselves as the last line of defence for Arab interests.[6] In Kissinger's view they were anachronistic snobs. He was determined to break their hold on US foreign policy in the Middle East.

Jim Akins was no traditional Arabist. He was born to a poor Quaker family in Akron, Ohio, and earned a degree in physics from Akron University. When he graduated he worked for the American Friends Service Committee in eastern Europe, and went on a walking tour through Greece and Turkey, which led to his fascination with the Levant. He travelled to Beirut, and taught physics and chemistry while trying to get a job with the Foreign Service. He was admitted in 1956. Over the next decade he learned fluent Arabic and served in Kuwait and Iraq before returning to Washington as director of the State Department's Fuels and Energy Office. He was not another simpering WASP besotted with Arabia. He had a much clearer view of the region, its characters, its interests and what lay in store.

In 1970, Nixon set up a Task Force on Oil Imports which concluded that US demand for oil would reach 18.5 million barrels per day by 1980, of which 5 million would need to be imported, mostly from Canada and Venezuela, America's western hemisphere allies. The task force believed that there was no way the United States would be forced into dependency on unreliable sources in the Middle East. Akins was not so sure. By 1973, imports had already reached 6 million barrels per day, with the eastern hemisphere contributing more than half. The United States had no spare production capacity and all of its projected growth in demand now had to come from overseas. If production ceased in any one of seven countries, Saudi Arabia, Iran, Iraq, the Federation of Arab Emirates, Kuwait, Libya or Venezuela, the world would face a temporary oil shortage. If two stopped producing, there would be a crisis. To convince anyone, though, Akins needed a political patron with a very thick skin.

Bill Simon grew up in affluence in New Jersey, but after his mother died when he was young, he watched his warm, ineffectual father slide through the rest of his life in a state of ebbing gentility. By the time Simon left Lafayette College in Pennsylvania, he had completed his military service, got married, had his first son and run up $5,000 in debt. He sustained himself on menial jobs, from washing windows to making beds, and his wife Carol's irregular earnings as a model.[7] One day, he bumped into a friend working at a securities firm on Wall Street. The friend invited him to come to his office at 9 a.m. on Monday for an interview. For three days, Simon sat in the lobby of his friend's employer. His friend would occasionally pop out and apologise that everyone was busy. Finally, on Thursday, the personnel manager appeared and grudgingly invited him in to see the head of the municipal bond department. During his brief interview, Simon swapped jokes about college fraternity life, and was offered a low-paid traineeship. 'I didn't know a thing about municipal bonds, but when I joined the trading desk I immediately felt right at home. I went from the fraternity of Delta Kappa Epsilon to the fraternity of Wall Street – and found similar camaraderie.'

World War Two had removed a generation from Wall Street. Simon was surrounded by a new, younger generation of men 'full of life and energy, ambition, and mischief'. Municipal bonds, a once dozy area of the financial markets, would power the post-war growth of America's towns, suburbs and cities. Simon loved the small-town and regional politics around financing roads, sewers and schools, as much as he did the fast-twitch trading floors of lower Manhattan. He travelled and networked, while Carol juggled a fast-growing family.

He thrived in the locker-room culture of traders. In Hollywood, Florida, for a bankers' convention, a colleague arranged for dozens of live chickens to be delivered to his hotel room. Simon swatted them out into the hallway with a pillow, where it took four bellhops to corral them into the lifts and out of the hotel. Another year, another colleague left a dead barracuda wearing a bowler hat and bow tie in Simon's toilet.

Simon eventually landed at Salomon Brothers, a smaller rival to the white-shoe firms which dominated the bond markets, like Morgan Stanley and Smith Barney. Its traders were notoriously aggressive and risk-taking. Simon had found the perfect environment for his talents. As head of the municipal bond division, Simon ruled over a trading room, where a board covered half the length of the longest wall, which the youngest trainees would run around updating with the latest bond prices. He would stand at the corner of his desk drinking ice water, glass after glass, to stay cool. He preferred it to coffee, which made traders physically and mentally agitated, and led to frequent, time-wasting visits to the bathroom. He smoked, spoke on the phone, and issued orders to as many as three hundred traders and salesmen at a time in an atmosphere of 'barely controlled mayhem'. Yelling was the preferred mode of communication. He was so effective, that Salomon also put him in charge of the even larger government bond department, which handled US Treasury bills, notes and bonds, which fund the federal government.

Simon's guiding theory as a bond trader was to always hold bonds. If you are sitting on the sides waiting, no one cares about you. But if you own assets, you are at the centre of the flow of information. Being in the loop, understanding buyers and sellers, is the key to making money. A small loss one week might inform you about the thinking of buyers and sellers, which will help you generate a profit next week. And if you're big enough and people pay attention to what you do, you can eventually make the market buckle to your will.

One day in 1969, Simon told one of his bankers to 'buy', meaning borrow, $50 million at a 5.25 per cent interest rate to buy some bonds. The banker couldn't do it. Every time he tried to close the deal, the market saw him coming and the interest rate went up. He came bleating to Simon who told him to try selling instead; to lend money he didn't have at the same 5.25 per cent interest rate. Sure enough, the market reacted by assuming money was now cheap, and the rate on the loan fell to 4.5 per cent. By acting swiftly and surreptitiously, Simon's banker was able to 'buy' his $50 million for 4.5 per cent, and earn a profit on the money he 'sold' at the higher rate. Simon had taught him a lesson in 'making' the market instead of falling victim to it. Four years later, Simon would be setting the direction for the most valuable commodity market in the world: the market for oil.

As head of one of the most active government bond trading firms, Simon made frequent trips to Washington DC, to the Treasury and to Congress. He gave money to Richard Nixon's successful 1968 and 1972 presidential campaigns, and soon after Nixon's second victory, he was contacted about joining the administration. Nixon was initially hostile to Simon, considering him yet another member of the East Coast establishment he so loathed, a 'Cadillac Liberal'. But his staff insisted he meet him.

Simon flew down to Camp David where Nixon lectured him about history, politics, the past and future, the balance between means and ends, before concluding, 'I am so thrilled you are going to join my administration.' Simon had barely said a word, but accepted the role of deputy secretary of the Treasury, under George Shultz. It was an ideal position for a man of Simon's experience, who described himself as a 'market man', all steak and creamed spinach, 'who recognized the fact that economics is, at its essential level, a study of people's behavior in the marketplace.'[8] In 1972, Simon made over $2 million at Salomon Brothers. Starting in February 1973, his government salary was $42,500.

Shultz was an academic economist, who often hosted fellow conservative economists like Milton Friedman and George Stigler for dinner in Washington. Friedman and Stigler believed ardently that markets functioned most efficiently under the lightest possible touch. They took a sniggering glee in the coarse humanity exposed when governments and regulators got out of the way. After Stigler died, Friedman reminisced about a trip they made to Europe in 1947. Britain was 'in a sad way two years after the war. Food was rationed and poor. Price, wage, and exchange controls were extensive and rigid, and appeared to be widely accepted and respected. Black markets doubtless existed, but they were small and well hidden.'

In Paris, by contrast, life was vastly more invigorated. The food was better and people seemed to be getting on with things in the absence of much oversight. Stigler asked the clerk at the hotel where they were staying, 'Could you direct me to the closest outlet for the black market in currency?' The clerk reached into his jacket and pulled out his wallet. 'Go no further, gentlemen.' Stigler's conclusion was that 'the British obey all laws, the French obey no laws, the Americans obey only the

Ibn Saud in Kuwait, 1910. The photographer, Captain William Shakespear, wrote he was 'of genial and very courteous manner'.

Ibn Saud's army on the march near Habl, January 1911.

A lavish royal banquet held for an overwhelmed American diplomat, 1947. Ibn Saud tucks into the hump of a young camel.

A new oil well sprouts in the desert. Two locals gaze on beside a Beechcraft plane owned by Aramco, 1948.

A ship scarcely fit for a king: President Franklin Roosevelt decks out the USS *Quincy* with ornate rugs to host Ibn Saud, 1945.

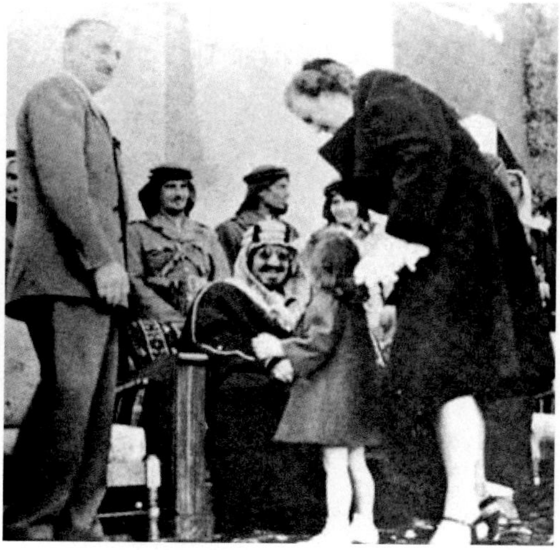

Visiting the Aramco compound at Dhahran in 1947, a delighted Ibn Saud greets the American mothers and children living in the company town.

Ibn Saud and his son Faisal drive through the Eastern Province in 1947. A faint reflection shows one of the oilfields that would make them the richest men in the world.

(*Above*) As part of their extensive training, Aramco employees take a test at the company's stabiliser plant in Dhahran, 1955.

(*Left*) Aramco workers at the Ras Tanura refinery on the Persian Gulf, mid-1970s.

The Al-Aqsa mosque, one of the holiest sites in Jerusalem, burns as firemen try to tame the flames, August 1969.

Denis Michael Rohan stands on trial for setting fire to the Al-Aqsa mosque, claiming he was sent to prepare for the Second Coming, October 1969.

Just two years before the fire, Israeli soldiers stood outside the Dome of the Rock celebrating victory in the Six Day War, June 1967.

Rising powers: Yasser Arafat (centre) sitting to the right of Colonel Muammar Gaddafi of Libya at the funeral of Egypt's President Nasser, October 1970.

Vice president Saddam Hussein of Iraq meeting his close friends and commercial partners, the French, in Paris, June 1972.

Gaddafi (right) with Abdessalam Jalloud, Libya's prime minister and the thorn in the side of the oil industry, July 1973.

Pictured in the mid-1970s, Zaki Yamani's negotiating style was to drive the oil companies 'to the wall with his sweet reasonableness'.

King Faisal joining thousands of Muslim men on their pilgrimage to the holy city of Mecca, 1967.

William Simon, the all-action energy czar and later treasury secretary, playing in a pro-celebrity tennis tournament in New York, 1974.

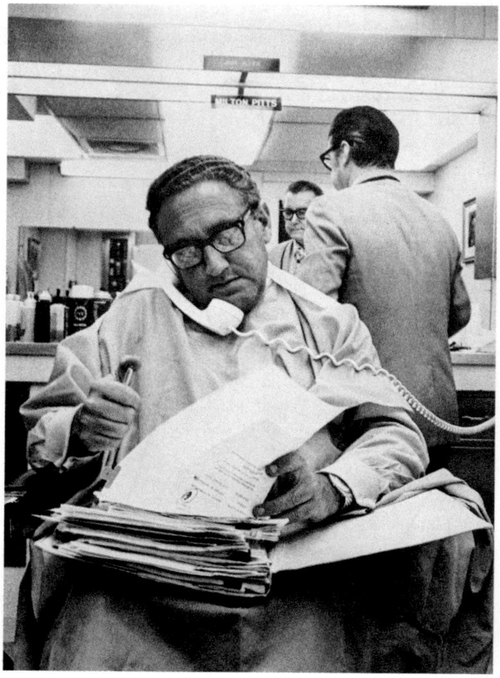

Henry Kissinger running the world from the White House barber shop, 1972.

Donald Rumsfeld, a beavering acolyte of Nixon, announcing price and wage controls in an ill-fated attempt to control surging inflation, 1971.

Nixon and Brezhnev practising détente at Nixon's home in San Clemente, California, June 1973.

War is coming: flanked by President Georges Pompidou and his wife Claude, a ponderous King Faisal is feted by the French at Versailles, May 1973.

The embattled Prime Minister Golda Meir and Moshe Dayan visit Israeli troops on the Golan Heights two weeks after the outbreak of war, October 1973.

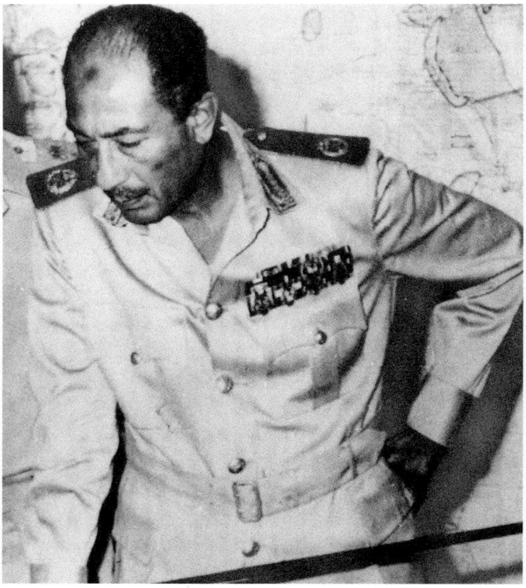

Egypt's unassuming yet determined President Sadat strategises the invasion of Israel during the Yom Kippur war, late 1973.

Israeli troops captured by Syrian soldiers in the Golan Heights during the early days of the war, October 1973.

Egyptian soldiers captured by the Israelis near the Suez Canal in a makeshift prison of barbed wire, November 1973.

good laws'. The British situation was depressing, the French glorious, if chaotic, the American perhaps ideal.[9]

In 1971, Stigler published an article describing the ways in which certain industries, companies and occupations used their political influence to introduce regulations to their own advantage. 'The machinery and power of the state,' he wrote, 'is a potential resource or threat to every industry in the society. With its power to compel, to take or give money, the state can and does selectively help or hurt a vast number of industries. That political juggernaut, the petroleum industry, is an immense consumer of political benefits.'

There was no more egregious benefit than the oil import quota system. In 1959, President Eisenhower was persuaded to impose quotas on the import of foreign oil as a matter of national security. If there was ever to be another global conflict, or regional conflicts in the distant corners of the world where foreign oil came from, American homes would go unheated, cars would stand still in driveways, and industry would grind to a halt – as long as the economy depended excessively on foreign oil. Controlling the import of foreign oil would stop this happening. The actual effect of quotas was to protect inefficient American producers from competition. Tired wells in Texas, Oklahoma and California, which squeezed out a few barrels a day, were allowed to survive in a world where Saudi wells were gushing thousands of barrels a day. American consumers were paying billions of dollars more than they needed to. The argument for national defence, Stigler observed, was 'calculated to elicit uproarious laughter at the Petroleum Club'. The import quota system was a regulatory racket designed to stifle change and protect industry profits at the expense of consumers.

Friedman expressed the same view more vividly than the civil Stigler. 'Few industries sing the praises of free enterprise more loudly than the oil industry,' he wrote shortly after the Six Day War. 'Yet few rely so heavily on special favors.' Friedman believed that if all the regulatory props for the oil industry were removed, there might be a temporary disruption to US production, but over time, a much healthier and more competitive domestic industry would emerge, naturally protected from foreign oil by the cost of transportation. The supposed threat of international disturbances like Middle Eastern conflicts was a smokescreen. It was the oil companies who kept prices artificially high, for no reason but their enrichment.[10]

These dinners at Shultz's house helped Simon to organise the instincts he had developed on Wall Street into a coherent intellectual framework. They provided a graduate seminar in economics that could be as intimidating as it was inspiring, though as Shultz recalled, Simon gave as good as he got. Simon had no doubts about his pragmatism and decisiveness, honed on the trading floors, but as he read the economic classics and argued with future Nobel laureates, he began to grasp 'the crucial philosophical underpinnings' of policy, and to appreciate 'that ideas have consequences.'

'A Jesuit priest would argue that the Lord is the only creative force of life,' he said later during his time in Washington. But 'money, well manipulated, is a fantastic form of creativity. And I am a creative man.'[11]

As demand for oil in the industrialised world kept rising faster than supply, the price had to go up. Nixon's commerce secretary, Pete Peterson, said in a speech to oil executives in Chicago, that countries would be 'forced to engage in a wild and cannibalistic scramble not only for energy but for external earnings to pay their bills.' There would follow a destructive competition to offer the lowest cost exports, which would harm every country which took part. These changes, he said, would have 'crucial economic and political implications . . . The era of low-cost energy is almost dead. Popeye is running out of cheap spinach.'[12]

One of Simon's first duties at the Treasury was to run the president's advisory Oil Policy Committee, and examine the dreaded import quota programme. One meeting of the committee was all it took for Simon to disband it. 'It was abundantly clear that its goal was not to solve problems – that would entail taking responsibility, which was to be avoided at all costs – but to ruminate, incessantly.' He assembled his own team of six experts, five from government, including Jim Akins, and one former Exxon executive to teach him about energy. They met at nights and weekends, bringing Simon up to speed on every aspect of the energy business, from oil and gas extraction to petrochemicals, trucking and hydroelectricity. At 10 p.m., a delivery of pizzas and burgers arrived to keep them going into the early hours. Within weeks, Simon was convinced that Stigler, Friedman and Shultz were right: government was the problem. If you ended the quota programme and let supply naturally meet demand, consumers would be happy and prices would take care of themselves.

That spring, *Foreign Affairs* published an article by Jim Akins titled 'The Oil Crisis: This Time the Wolf Is Here'.[13] Akins laid it all out in forthright, pungent language: the coming oil shortages; the geopolitical implications; and the threats from Arab countries to use oil as a weapon against the United States. 'The common response among Americans has been: "They need us as much as we need them"; or "They can't drink the oil"; or "Boycotts never work."' None of those answers made sense, Akins wrote. 'The threat to use oil as a political weapon must be taken seriously.'

The problems began with the forecasters, who 'had only marginally better success than those who foretell the advent of earthquakes or the second coming of the Messiah.' Before, during and after World War Two they said the world was about to run out of oil. Then they predicted that by 1970, the last fossil fuel electricity plant would have been built and that the cost of sending meter readers to people's homes would be higher than the electricity itself. In the 1960s, they said oil would soon prove so abundant that its price would fall to $1 a barrel and stay there. They relied on the exaggerated productivity estimates provided by American oil companies and well owners and missed the dwindling production of domestic gas, and the need for oil to make up the gap.

Akins estimated that by 1980, the US would be consuming 24 million barrels of oil per day, of which around one third would have to come from the eastern hemisphere. The gap between supply and demand was narrowing to the point where prices had to rise sharply. The age of cheap oil was ending more quickly than the West dared fear. The task force and Akins differed widely on the consequences for America's relations with the Arab world.

Akins did not believe there were easy alternatives to Middle Eastern oil. If demand kept rising, it was widely assumed, then the oil companies would switch effortlessly to reserves in friendly neighbourhoods like Alaska, the North Sea, Indonesia or Canada. Alaska still needed approval for a pipeline to carry its oil across hundreds of miles of frozen wastes to a shipping terminal. If its oil came on stream by 1980 it might cover the projected decline in existing US production, but none of the growth in demand. Indonesia could provide at most 2 or 3 million barrels per day, and the North Sea a fraction of Europe's growing needs. Saudi Arabia, by comparison, was reckoned to be sitting on more than 150 billion barrels of reserves, perhaps even double that amount. It was bound to become more important to the industrialised world.

Akins agreed that it might be possible to develop alternative energy sources, such as geothermal, solar, and nuclear fission, and to limit consumption through efficiency and conservation measures. But these would take years, while the crisis was imminent. 'To lock simply at the world's oil reserves and conclude that they are sufficient to meet the world's needs can no longer be acceptable,' Akins wrote. 'We could allow ourselves such fatuities as long as we had large spare oil production capacity, and while our overseas imports were small. We can do so no longer. Our security and balance-of-payments problems are large and growing. Whether we focus on today, or 1980, or 1985, it is abundantly clear that we must move on a variety of fronts if we are to avoid a situation which could lead to or even force us into highly dangerous action.' There was no good denying it. The United States, western Europe and Japan absolutely needed Middle Eastern oil.

Pierre Wack compared the world to a cherry tree. It was easy to be impressed by the trunk and the boughs, billowing pink in the spring. But if you really wanted to understand what was going on, you had to study the fruit growing on the smaller branches, and how each cherry developed on the same tree. In 1973, the same crisis was brewing for all of the consuming countries – but each one faced a different situation.

Italy and France depended on oil for three-quarters of their energy needs. The British only needed oil for half of theirs, but a coal miners' strike meant they suddenly needed more.

France and the UK maintained good relations with the Arab countries, and a robust trade in industrial and military goods. Germany and the Netherlands did not, largely because of their support for Israel. France and West Germany, the two largest countries in the EEC, had very different national energy markets. France's was largely state-controlled, and focused on stable prices. West Germany's was more free-wheeling, allowing lots of participants, and prioritising supply. While Britain and Italy faced fiscal ruin if oil prices kept rising, West Germany believed it was economically strong enough to cope. Japan relied on oil imports for over three-quarters of its energy needs, and three-quarters of these imports came from the Gulf. It could not fathom letting enmities driving events 6,000 miles from Tokyo derail its post-war industrial miracle, but the likelihood was getting stronger.

The countries also differed in their relations with the United States. West Germany, bordering the Soviet bloc, depended on America for its security, and hosted large US military bases. France wanted a European foreign policy more distinct from America, and felt entitled to its own policies towards the Middle East. Three days before the Six Day War in 1967, Faisal visited Pompidou's predecessor, General de Gaulle, in Paris. De Gaulle was seventy-six, a grand relic, isolated from his own government and people. Talking in private, Faisal unspooled his familiar themes. He challenged Israel's right to exist, and the Jewish people's claim that Palestine was their ancient homeland: 'Most Israelis are not originally from Palestine. They are Khazars from the Caucasus who planted themselves in eastern Europe.' This was an old and baseless antisemitic trope: Jews came to Europe from the central Caucasus in the late tenth century, when the Khazar empire fell; they had never lived in Palestine, and so had no claim to the land. Even if the Jews had ever lived in Palestine, Faisal went on, that was no reason to let them back now. 'By this logic, the Arabs would be able to return to Spain, because they were once there. And if the Arabs had to leave Palestine because the Jews used to be there, then the Americans ought to return to the European countries they came from and leave America to the Indians.'[14]

De Gaulle had been sidling away from Israel for several years, calling his position 'pro-Arab neutrality'. But France had continued to sell arms to Israel, notably a powerful fleet of sixty-five Mirage fighter jets. Yet the day after Faisal's visit, De Gaulle announced a partial arms embargo on Israel, which became a full embargo eighteen months later.[15] France's Arab friends were delighted. France was importing half of its oil from the Middle East. Unlike the US and UK, France's oil majors controlled just a sliver of production in the region. Pandering to Faisal, the French told themselves, was necessary for economic survival. In May 1973, Faisal returned to Paris on a five-day state visit. He hosted an elaborate dinner for President Pompidou in the Hall of Mirrors at Versailles. The French rolled out the best of their exports, jet fighters, SECAM colour television sets and Concorde.[16]

The problem with the consumers lacking a coordinated approach to Middle Eastern oil, Akins noted, was that the Arabs could pick them off one by one. They could say, we will only keep supplying you if you submit to our position on Israel, and they seemed willing to sacrifice huge amounts of income to make their point. Akins could see it. The Texans could see it. The Aramco executives in Saudi Arabia could see it. The diplomats posted around the Middle East could see it. Pierre Wack could see it. The Arab leaders and their emissaries to the West made the same points again and again. Yet the Washington establishment could not imagine being humbled by desert kingdoms, which had so recently been docile, grateful recipients of whatever crumbs the oil companies allowed them. Kissinger could not see past Akins's provenance. Here was yet another State Department Arabist crying wolf on behalf of the Arabs. But this was no false alarm.

9

Trips of the Fox

Between 1967 and 1973, there were no formal declarations of war between Arabs and Israelis. Informally, the fighting never stopped. The Arabs went freelance, with terrorist splinter groups, funded by oil-rich countries, assuming the work of armies. The Israelis assigned their fight to intelligence and specialised commando groups. The cycle of violence and vengeance spun faster, with no regard for the niceties of conventional warfare. Civilians were not spared.

Along the western side of the Suez Canal, Egypt built up its forces with Soviet support and exchanged heavy shelling, commando raids and aerial dogfights with the Israelis stationed opposite. Between 1969 and 1970, this War of Attrition killed thousands on each side. To Israel's east, Saudi and Israeli troops skirmished in the Arava Wadi, running 115 miles from the Red Sea to the Dead Sea, skimming the border with Jordan. Palestine Liberation Organization fighters skulked in the foothills of Moab and Edom just inside Jordan. At night they stole across to raid Israeli settlements and industrial plants. The Saudi Arabian and Jordanian troops assigned to guard the border made no effort to stop them. Israel responded by sending night patrols of paratroopers into Jordan to ambush the fighters where they hid. In March 1970, the PLO fired mortars over the border to destroy an Israeli chemical works, while the Saudi brigade camped nearby. Israeli units fought the Saudi and PLO forces away from the border and established a forward post inside Jordan. It was the first time Israeli and Saudi troops had engaged directly with one another.

Israel fortified the border with mines and barbed-wire fences, but there was still the problem of tracking the enemy raiding parties across such a wide and forbidding area. Helicopters and vehicles went only so far. The best trackers were the Negev Bedouin and their camels. In order to move the camels as quickly as possible whenever they found freshly marked tracks, the Israelis built special platforms on the back of large jeeps. The Bedouin would sit up front with the camels strapped to the back. The 'camels on alert' strategy was an old-fashioned counterpart to Israel's high-tech war against Egypt. But it was no less effective.[1]

The third major front for Israel was in Gaza, where Yasser Arafat's PLO and George Habash's Popular Front for the Liberation of Palestine (PFLP) were active. Israeli units under Ariel Sharon, the swaggering hero of the Six Day War, moved in and pursued their targets house by house and block by block. They flushed them out of bunkers built under citrus groves and dense cactus hedges. Undercover units of Israeli Jews and Arabs had been posing as locals, pretending to be market vendors, sitting in cafes, riding donkeys, even playing the parts of PLO and PFLP members in their own hideouts. Sharon bulldozed houses to widen the streets and make it harder to hide. He eventually pushed for Jewish settlements to extend into Gaza like fingers prizing open the area. His tactics were controversial but effective in finding and killing the enemy.

While Israel shored up its borders, the Arab terrorists went international.[2] They targeted Jews and their allies wherever they could find them. Collectively, they were the 'fedayeen', the men willing to sacrifice themselves for a greater cause. The PLO oversaw the groups within this loose federation, with various degrees of control. Its own paramilitary wing, the Palestine Liberation Army, had a commando unit, the Popular Liberation Forces, which operated inside Israel. The PFLP specialised in airline hijackings and attacks on airports. Other groups in the network included Fatah, supported originally by Egypt; Al-Saiqa, funded by Syria; and the Arab Liberation Front, backed by Iraq. There was also the PFLP-General Command, which broke away from the PFLP to stage its own operations. The Black September Organization (BSO), took its name from the month in 1970 when King Hussein of Jordan attacked the fedayeen and drove them out of his country.[3]

After Nasser died in the autumn of 1970, no one expected much of his unassuming vice president and successor, Anwar Sadat. He had joined the army in order to help drive out the British, then befriended Nasser, and after the revolution in Egypt in 1952 taken a series of largely ceremonial jobs. He became vice president in 1969 and, after Nasser's death, emerged from a brief power struggle as president. He was a devout Muslim, who dressed with a nonchalant elegance in pressed military uniforms and beautiful suits, his overcoat sometimes slung over his shoulder. He disliked the formal offices of Cairo, and preferred to run his government from his own villa on the Nile, and government houses around the country. He said that 'the key to everything – politically, economically, and militarily – was to redress the situation following from the 1967 defeat, so as to regain our self-confidence and the world's confidence in us.' It would be 'one thousand times more honorable' for him and the entire army to die crossing the Canal than to continue suffering the 'disgrace and humiliation' which followed the Six Day War.

Sadat began his presidency by purging his government of the

Nasser loyalists who had been around in 1967. He reduced the power of the secret police and, in July 1972, expelled the 15,000 Soviet military specialists and advisers in Egypt. Their presence had put Egypt in the middle of the Cold War, and precluded any lasting peace with Israel, given its support from America. Sadat hoped that the expulsion would draw the United States into talks, at least, about Israel pulling back to its 1967 borders. In 1970, he began threatening to invade the Sinai and reopen the Suez Canal, which had been closed since the Six Day War due to Israel's presence on its east bank. But as time passed and nothing happened, few believed Sadat had the nerve or military capability to start a war.

He was not the only Arab leader agitating for open conflict with Israel. At a banquet in Mecca early in 1971, Faisal said: 'Who are the leaders of Communism, who sponsored its doctrines and assumed its responsibilities in the world? They are all Zionists who endeavor to destroy humanity in order to realize their aspirations for the domination of the world.' He added: 'I urge my colleagues, the leaders in every Arab country, not to accept any settlement that does not guarantee the restitution of usurped rights, the restoration of assaulted dignity and the safeguarding of the rights of their displaced brothers.'[4] But he was keeping the oil weapon in its scabbard.

By the early 1970s, Saudi Arabia was contributing hundreds of millions of dollars to the US balance of payments in oil company revenues, and defence and civilian contracts. Washington recognised the growing contribution of Saudi Arabia to the US economy, but there was a growing sense of embarrassment at being so closely associated with such a conservative, stagnant, anti-Israeli society.[5] An interdepartmental memo summarising the state of US-Saudi relations for Kissinger concluded that Faisal was in an 'increasingly bitter mood', and 'delay in political and social reform not only feeds domestic unrest but tends to discredit the U.S. within Saudi Arabia and elsewhere by seeming to associate us with an unenlightened, archaic social and political system.[6] The Saudis valued their relationship with the United States, but kept quiet about it so as not to alienate the conservatives in their own country, and among their neighbours. These tensions made the Saudis cautious and unpopular with their regional allies.

In 1972 Faisal told a Cairo weekly magazine that deploying the oil weapon would hurt the Arab countries without having the slightest effect on America which could find oil elsewhere. 'This proposal should be ruled out, and I see no benefit in reviving its discussion at this time.' A few months later, Prince Saud al-Faisal, the king's son and Yamani's deputy at the oil ministry, said that Saudi Arabia needed to sell oil just as much as the consumers needed to buy it. 'For us, a cut-off in oil supplies would be economic suicide. Oil won't be used as a political weapon as far as Saudi Arabia is concerned.'[7]

The Arabs had other means, however, for pursuing their war on Israel. Black September's attack on Israeli athletes at the Olympic Games in Munich in 1972 unfolded live on television. In a disastrous rescue attempt, five of the eight terrorists and all nine hostages were killed, some by West German police. But there were many other less-well-known attacks. In 1972 alone, in addition to the horrors of Munich, Arab terrorists hijacked a Lufthansa flight and forced it to land in Yemen. Members of the BSO took over a Sabena Belgian World Airlines flight on its way to Tel Aviv and demanded the release of 317 Palestinians held in Israel. Israeli paratroopers dressed as mechanics attacked the plane and ended the siege. Three Japanese men hired by the PLFP killed twenty-five people and wounded seventy-six more when they opened fire with semi-automatic rifles and grenades at Lod airport in Tel Aviv. BSO terrorists hijacked another Lufthansa flight from Beirut to Ankara, demanding West Germany release the three surviving BSO terrorists from the Munich attack. The Germans complied. The BSO sent letter bombs to Israeli officials and embassies all over the world. One killed an Israeli diplomat in London. Many more operations were staged or foiled by police and intelligence services. German police estimated that there were nine underground Arab organisations in their country, with 110 subsidiary groups operating within a local community of 36,000 Arabs.

Israel's intelligence services and specialised army units were just as busy. They spent years tracking and killing the perpetrators of Munich, and targeting Palestinian fighters before they could attack. In February 1973, Israeli commandos took off in helicopters from frigates off the coast of Lebanon, and landed close to two Palestinian refugee camps where Palestinian fighters were being trained. They blew up buildings suspected of belonging to Fatah, and fought off the Palestinians who fought back. They killed at least fifteen Palestinians and wounded many more.[8] Two days later, Israeli fighter jets fired at a Libyan passenger plane which had flown into restricted Israeli airspace over military sites. The pilot of the plane had not responded to requests to land. The stricken Libyan plane crashed into the Sinai desert, killing 108 people. The Israeli government said that a few weeks earlier it had received a report that Palestinian terrorists planned to hijack and fly a jet into Tel Aviv. The downing of the Libyan plane was a regrettable but necessary act of self-defence. Israel's enemies suspected more malicious intent.[9]

Even the Saudis, who funded the fedayeen publicly and privately, were not immune to the violence. On the evening of 3 March 1973, a Black September group drove into the Saudi

Embassy in Khartoum, Sudan, where a diplomatic reception was taking place. They rammed their Land Rover into the US ambassador's car just as he was trying to leave. They took the guests hostage, and made a series of outlandish demands, including the release of Robert Kennedy's assassin, Sirhan Sirhan. Eventually, they released all the hostages except the incoming US ambassador, the American deputy chief of mission, and the Belgian chargé d'affaires, whom they took to the basement of the embassy, and machine-gunned to death. The order to kill came from Arafat. The Saudis asked the Americans to forget this 'unfortunate incident' and appoint a replacement ambassador, which they did a year later.[10]

Arafat had been at the University of Cairo at the same time as Zaki Yamani. They had witnessed the surge of Arab nationalism under Nasser. Their paths crossed repeatedly later in life and they considered each other friends. Yamani thought Arafat an effective and moderate leader, capable of delivering a state for the Palestinians. He was instrumental in securing Saudi Arabia's financial support for Fatah, Arafat's political organisation. The PLO had been founded in 1964 with the support of the Arab League to bring together the disparate Palestinian resistance. Its goal was to create an independent Palestinian state in the territory which was now Israel. After Israel's victory in the Six Day War, the PLO's more militant factions, notably Fatah, gained influence. In 1968, Yamani introduced Arafat to Faisal, and later arranged for Fatah to receive 100,000 Saudi riyals, around $30,000 at the time. It was the first of many transfers from the Saudis to Fatah and the PLO.[11] In 1969, Arafat became the PLO's chairman. Yamani excused his friend's violent ambition to erase Israel from the map as the necessary language of the oppressed. 'Sometimes, people have to talk in a certain way.'[12] Faisal considered the PLO the 'good fedayeen'.

Even by the paranoid standards of his militant peers, Arafat was unusual. He did not tell interviewers his age and described himself as the spokesman of the Central Committee of the Palestinian Resistance. He lived on the run, and made secret trips into Israel, which he called 'trips of the fox'. He encouraged his fellow fedayeen to do the same, to get to know the land which he assured them they would one day recapture. He claimed that the Israelis deliberately undercounted the soldiers they lost fighting the Palestinians, and misattributed their deaths to car accidents to conceal the real, much higher number. In his opinion, the Israelis were not great warriors. They only won in battle thanks to overwhelming American technology.[13] To restore Palestine, he believed he had to destroy Israel. Peace processes be damned, he was ready to fight for generations.

When Nixon met Sadat's national security adviser, Hafiz Ismail, at the White House in February 1973, he said that with Israel and Egypt so firm in their positions, it was a case of an irresistible force meeting an immovable object.[14] When Ismail and Kissinger met again in Washington soon afterwards, Ismail repeated that Egypt wanted to recover the Sinai and reopen the Suez Canal, and Kissinger repeated that he was only ready to discuss a general theory for how the sides should proceed, and not specifics. Anything but a step-by-step process would trigger Israeli pressure on the United States, and limit the effectiveness of its involvement. If Egypt wanted the US to participate, then it would have to accept its terms. Ismail looked despondent, knowing that Sadat was ready to take any provocation as a justification for war.[15]

Kissinger and Ismail met again secretly near Paris in May during American talks with the North Vietnamese. Kissinger insisted that neither the French government, the press, nor even the US Embassy knew about the meeting. He and a small group from the National Security Council and the state department left the US embassy in an unmarked car without a police escort. An American general had overseen the preparations, along with the CIA. They drove to the Moulin St Fargeau, a quaint old farmhouse with pretty gardens, which had been restored by a rich American.[16] Kissinger told Ismail bluntly that there was nothing the United States could do for Egypt since it was the defeated enemy and Israel the mightier force.[17] Israel had no need to negotiate peace so long as it held the upper hand.

Meanwhile, Israel's own resolve was hardening. The issue was not whether the 1949 or the 1967 borders were correct. What mattered now were the borders that gave Israel the security it believed it needed. A new philosophy of defensive borders was articulated by Yigal Allon, a former general and interim prime minister, who would serve as Golda Meir's deputy prime minister during the Yom Kippur war. If Arab countries lost a war, he argued, they lost prestige. Israel's wars were existential. Defeat could mean the extinction of the country, the stated ambition of many Arab leaders. 'Israel cannot afford to lose a single war,' Allon wrote. 'To lose a single war is to lose everything, and this is a most real and stark fact.'[18] Allon accepted the need for negotiation with Arabs, but premised on Israel's security needs.

Sadat believed that Egypt could not negotiate from the position of humiliation, and loss of territory, inflicted by the 1967 war. His speech became more violent. He told Egypt's parliament to expect an 'era of total confrontation' with Israel. Unless there was 'peace-based justice' there would follow the 'nightmare to end all nightmares', a situation 'much worse than Vietnam' for the United States, as in the Middle East its vital interests were at stake.[19] Abba Eban, Israel's foreign minister, had told Kissinger that Israel's well-drilled forces had nothing to fear from the Egyptians. 'The army across the Canal is unshaven, playing cards; there is no vigilance.'[20]

The Americans and Soviets were keeping a close eye on the situation. They had specific information on the military preparations by the Arabs and the Israelis. The Egyptians were moving missiles, Mirage fighters and bombers up to Cairo, and had recalled their reservists. The Moroccans had sent a squadron of planes to Syria. Israel was recalling its reservists, and had deployed advance hospitals for 1,000 wounded. At a meeting at his country retreat north of Moscow, Brezhnev told Kissinger that across the Middle East, military committees were meeting 'not just to have a few drinks.'[21]

10

War Is Coming

Nixon disliked Brezhnev the communist. But as a Russian, he liked him very much.[1] Where Nixon was rigid and formal, Brezhnev was all hugs, sobbing and naked displays of emotion. In June 1973, Brezhnev travelled to the United States, visiting Washington DC, the presidential retreat at Camp David, and Nixon's Californian home, Casa Pacifica in San Clemente, on the coast between Los Angeles and San Diego. At their first meeting in the Oval Office, Brezhnev said that when he left Moscow it was raining – a good omen, according to Russian folk tradition. He then showed Nixon his cigarette case. Brezhnev's health was poor, exacerbated by his smoking and drinking. He explained that his case had a timing mechanism, which meant that once he closed it, it would not open for another hour, stopping him from chain-smoking. 'That's a way to discipline yourself,' laughed Nixon.

While they were at Camp David, Nixon walked over to Dogwood, the guest cottage where Brezhnev was staying, to bring him to dinner. When he arrived, he said a 'very handsome, full-bosomed Russian girl came out' and shook his hand. Brezhnev's aide told the president it was his masseuse. As they walked away, Nixon put his hand up to his nose and noted that the woman had been wearing Arpège, one of his wife's favourite perfumes. French. Expensive. Some masseuse.[2] Brezhnev's constant travel companion at the time was Nina Korovyakova, a statuesque nurse, and rumoured KGB agent. She towered over Brezhnev, provided him with massages and physiotherapy, and even brushed his teeth. Brezhnev had suffered from insomnia for many years, and Korovyakova managed the combination of sedatives and tranquillisers that helped him sleep. He took them in the afternoon with a shot of Zubrówka vodka, flavoured with bison grass, which left him groggy the rest of the day. Korovyakova was rumoured to offer more than medical services to the priapic Brezhnev.[3]

The main topics at Nixon and Brezhnev's meetings were nuclear disarmament and economic cooperation. But on the last night of Brezhnev's visit, after dinner and a session of heavy toasting in Casa Pacifica, the general secretary requested an unscheduled meeting with Nixon. It was a breach of protocol and Brezhnev would not specify the subject. Nixon had begun taking Dilantin, an anti-seizure drug effective at calming nerves, during his 1968 campaign. Combined with limited amounts of alcohol, it can cause people to slur their speech. He also regularly took Seconal, a sleeping pill,[4] and Valium, but still struggled to sleep.[5] By the time the two leaders met at 10.30, there was a good chance both were heavily sedated.

Brezhnev's hope, Kissinger suspected, was to catch Nixon off guard and alone, without his advisers.[6] When the two leaders met in Nixon's study, along with Kissinger, and the Soviet foreign minister and ambassador to Washington, Brezhnev said he wanted to raise the stakes in the Middle East. He insisted that the Americans agree to four principles: the withdrawal of Israeli troops from the areas captured in 1967; the recognition of the pre-1967 borders; the free passage of ships through the Red Sea; and guarantees that these principles would be respected. It was more than Nixon could agree to. He wanted more latitude to start negotiations. If the two superpowers insisted on these terms before negotiations even began, the Israelis were unlikely to show up. Without them, Brezhnev insisted, the Arabs would not consider direct talks with Israel, and 'we will have difficulty keeping the military situation from flaring up.' Nixon held firm, promising he would work towards a settlement, but arguing that 'we can't abstractly beat the issue to death . . . we can't take [an] intransigent position.' Brezhnev again brought up the risk of a military confrontation, with the Soviets backing the Arabs and the Americans compelled to support Israel. 'I am categorically opposed to a resumption of the war. But without agreed principles that will help [the] situation in [the] area, we cannot do this.' Brezhnev then began dialling back his demands. Perhaps they could just agree on the withdrawal of troops, and not even write it down, make it public, or even tell the Arabs. A gentleman's agreement would suffice to enable the Soviets and Americans to keep talking behind the scenes. Nixon called the meeting to a close, promising to think about all Brezhnev had said.[7] Brezhnev, however, still had energy to spare. Pat Nixon complained she heard the secretary general and his masseuse romping through the night in her daughter Tricia's bedroom.[8]

If the Arabs needed any reminding of the superiority of Israel's intelligence capabilities and military daring, it came on the evening of 9 April 1973. An agent in Lebanon had informed Mossad that three of the PLO's top officials were living in apartment buildings on the same street in the heart of Beirut. The only way to reach them was to send in targeted assassination teams to kill them at close quarters. They would have to sneak in, complete their mission, and escape before they were caught. If any member of the team were captured, the Lebanese would torture and kill them.

Operation Spring of Youth was assigned to Sayeret Matkal, an elite unit of the Israel Defense Forces, trained for secret combat operations in hostile countries. Twelve commandos divided into six couples, half dressed as men, the other as half women, stole into Beirut from the sea. They strolled through the city like any other couples taking the night air. Around 11 p.m. they split up, each pair with instructions to take out one target. A doctor waited for them in the street in case they were injured. They blew the doors off their targets' apartments, killed them and ran out into the street. As the Lebanese police arrived, the commandos in drag, blonde wigs and lipstick, fired wildly with their machine guns to provide cover for their escape. Elsewhere in the city, Israeli paratroopers blew up a building killing thirty-five PFLP members. With the mission complete, the soldiers raced back to their dinghies, and out to missile boats waiting 12 miles offshore. By dawn, they were back in their beds in Israel. They had killed fifty PLO men, in addition to the three top targets, and seized valuable documents. The sheer bravado of the operation led to the resignation of the Lebanese government. Israel, it seemed, could do whatever it wanted. No ramshackle Arab army stood a chance.

Anwar Sadat, however, remained unfazed. By the spring of 1973, word had reached the CIA of his contacts with Faisal. They had become close friends during the Islamic Congress in 1955, when Faisal was crown prince, and Sadat a minister of state. Now the king had agreed to back Sadat's use of force to provoke negotiations with Israel. Faisal needed progress towards an Arab-Israeli settlement to justify his relationship with the United States.[9] He also wanted a return of Jerusalem to Arab control. But the reports sent to Washington from its embassy in Jeddah advised the State Department not to take the Saudis seriously. They were 'fundamentally timorous', desperate for a relationship with the United States yet worried that it made them easy targets for Arab radicals. They were 'almost pathetically eager' for US support for even the slightest aspect of the Arab cause to justify their friendship, but Faisal had been 'deeply disturbed' by the attack on the Khartoum embassy. He was too frightened to condemn or cut off Fatah and continued to provide the organisation with support as an insurance premium against domestic terrorism.[10] This was a man too conflicted to hold the world hostage.

When Senator Henry Jackson, an ardent supporter of Israel, visited Saudi Arabia in March, he insisted on bringing a rabbi friend. Faisal refused, so Jackson visited when the king was out of the country. Frank Jungers of Aramco told the senator, '[I]f there is a war, as we suspect there may be, Saudi Arabia is not going to stand on the sidelines. There's going to be an embargo.' Jackson dismissed the idea.[11] Even when the Saudis told Kissinger to his face that they were ready to use oil as a weapon, he refused to believe them. Yamani visited the White House in April 1973, accompanied by his deputy, Prince Saud. Kissinger was on typically bumptious form. Yamani said that while Saudi Arabia had the reserves to end America's oil shortage, it was under heavy pressure from the rest of the Arab world not to do so until the United States pushed Israel to withdraw to its 1967 borders. Kissinger dodged, talking about the difficulty of negotiations, the need for discretion, and blaming the Arabs for their impatience. He said that in the US there were always elections round the corner, which kept shortening the time frame to do anything. Prince Saud said the US should at least try to show interest in a settlement. Kissinger promised he would.

When the conversation turned to oil, and the growing threat of shortages and rising prices, Kissinger was dismissive. 'There are always "unemployed intellectuals" who find it fashionable to write dramatically about whatever subject is fashionable at the moment. This year the subject is oil.' Yamani asked if Kissinger meant that the problems would not develop. 'Oh, we'll have problems,' Kissinger replied. 'It is necessary to see the problem, however, in a wider perspective . . . and it has to be handled in a statesmanlike manner.'[12]

Soon after he returned home, Yamani was working with Faisal in the king's office listening to the radio station Voice of America. A State Department spokesman was reported to have said that Yamani was speaking for himself when he said the US should put pressure on Israel. It was not formal Saudi policy. The implication, clearly leaked by Kissinger, was that Yamani had been freelancing. Hal Saunders, one of Kissinger's most trusted advisers on the National Security Council, said the issue was not whether it was a good idea to engage more meaningfully with the Saudis, but rather, '[H]ow can we have a rational dialogue without getting bogged down in Faisal's anti-Zionist emotionalism?' Short of Kissinger going to Riyadh armed with the full authority of the president, there was no point sending some lesser official to be peppered with Faisal's invective. Talking to Yamani in Washington, Saunders added, was unhelpful as he was a 'technocrat with a limited political role.'[13]

The Saudis tried another channel for communicating their message: the oil companies. On his way back from a tour of Britain and an extended medical visit to France, Faisal stopped in Geneva where Aramco's leaders were holding one of their regular meetings with Yamani. The guests at the Intercontinental were used to seeing foreign delegations sweep through, but nothing like the king in his flowing white robes, striding through the corridors flanked by his Nubian bodyguards. Faisal was friendly, but frighteningly clear. 'War is coming. And I wish to protect Aramco from the inevitable Arab wrath when it does.' America's unconditional support for Israel, he said, had to change. 'Action must be taken urgently; otherwise everything will be lost.'

The executives took Faisal's message back to Washington, and to meetings with the heads of the biggest companies in America. Frank Jungers met thirty-eight chief executives over the course of a few days in New York, Detroit, Milwaukee, San Francisco, Los Angeles, Dallas and Houston. But he said that Washington seemed to think that Faisal was 'calling wolf when no such wolf exists except in his imagination.' Mobil ran newspaper advertisements emphasising America's dependence on Arab oil. Chevron wrote a letter to its shareholders, prompting supporters of Israel to invade and deface its headquarters.[14]

Faisal spent the hottest months of the summer at his palace in Taif, in the Hijaz mountains. On 4 July, he greeted the correspondents from *The Christian Science Monitor* and *The Washington Post* in his reception hall, and spoke in Arabic with a translator, his voice rising higher as he became more exercised. 'The United States stands behind Israel, but gains nothing from its support of Israel . . . The real interest of the United States in this region is to cooperate with the Arabs.' The American diplomats in Jeddah reported that Faisal was making an 'entreaty rather than a threat.'

When the American ambassador attended a reception in Riyadh for the Emir of Bahrain later the same month, he was surprised to see Arafat standing next to Faisal in the official receiving line. The US did not recognise Arafat as the official voice of the Palestinian opposition to Israel, but the ambassador had no choice but to shake his hand.[15] Faisal had spent the past year trying to convince the West that he was serious about an oil embargo. Arafat had long been urging the Arab oil producers to freeze or cut production as a weapon against Israel's supporters in the West. His presence that day was yet another signal from Faisal that the time for subtlety was over.

The president's daily briefing of 4 August noted that Faisal was delaying any decision on increasing Saudi oil production until he received more clarity about America's commitment to resisting communist influence in the Middle East, and its willingness to apply pressure on Israel to end the Arab-Israeli status quo. Despite all that Faisal and Yamani had said, the briefing noted, 'it is not yet clear how the Saudis will try to use oil to advance their political objectives.'[16]

While Faisal was open about his support for Arafat, his broader relationship with the Palestinians remained fraught. In September, a group of Palestinian attackers calling themselves the 'Punishment Squad' stormed the Saudi embassy in Paris. They took five Saudis hostage, bound them hand and foot, and boarded a Syrian plane for Kuwait. As they flew over Riyadh, they threatened to throw the hostages from the plane unless the Saudis helped secure the release of a Fatah leader being held in Jordan. The Saudis refused. The terrorists eventually surrendered to the Kuwaitis. When the Saudi hostages landed back in Jeddah, they were treated as returning heroes, and rewarded with medals and cars. But Saudi Arabia's pride was hurt. Faisal had funded the PLO and thought he had a special relationship with Arafat. But now this.[17] Faisal was in Algiers for the Arab summit when the attack happened, and it was left to his younger brother and minister of the interior, Prince Fahd, to fine tune the Saudi position: Paris was the work of a lunatic fringe, whose actions only served Zionism and Saudi Arabia's enemies. Saudi support for the mainstream fedayeen would continue.[18]

*

The Gulf's other oil powers wanted to modernise as quickly as they could, to transform their societies with their sudden fortunes. The Saudis were less interested in hurtling forwards into a new world than about losing the old. Faisal had brought an austere order to his realm. In fifty years, the country had progressed from the Middle Ages to the twenty-first century. Whether or not they liked the change, people were exhausted and unsettled.[19] A newspaper editor in Jeddah explained: 'We like to move like the camel who walks slowly but goes a long way. It is better than to hurry like the gazelle, who runs too quickly and breaks a leg in the sand.'[20] By the summer of 1973, the tension between old and new, caution and haste, was becoming unbearable.

Faisal had seen kings murdered and monarchies overthrown across the Arab world. In 1951, Jordan's King Abdullah was killed at the Al-Aqsa mosque in Jerusalem by a Palestinian tailor's apprentice who resented his accommodation of Israel. Abdullah's son, King Hussein, survived an assassination attempt when the bullet intended to kill him bounced off a medal on his chest. The frequency and cunning of the efforts to kill Hussein were almost comic. A bottle of nose drops that he took for a sinus problem was replaced with sulphuric acid. A servant tried to stab him while he slept. A cook poisoned his food, but was foiled when the palace cats, which tested the king's meals, dropped dead. There were numerous failed bombings and shootings. The phlegmatic Hussein gave up on bodyguards, and moved around Jordan alone, with a Colt .38 tucked in his belt. Risk, he had come to believe, was his natural element. Like water to a fish.[21] Others had been less fortunate. King Farouk of Egypt was ousted by a group of revolutionary army officers in 1952. The last king of Iraq, Faisal II, was killed by one of his own army officers in 1958, as he tried to flee the royal palace in

Baghdad. In 1962, republicans in Yemen toppled their last king, Muhammad al-Badr, who flew to Saudi Arabia and launched a resistance movement which survived until 1970.

In every case, Faisal saw echoes of his own problems: conflicting views of how to stand up for Palestine, violently or through diplomacy; a sudden rush of oil money destabilising society, corrupting the elite and alienating the middle and lower classes; nationalist feelings channelled through charismatic young army officers. Faisal understood that his survival, and the survival of the Al Sauds, depended on managing these forces. In early September 1973, he told NBC television: 'We do not wish to place any restrictions on our oil exports to the United States in any way but . . . America's complete support for Zionism and against the Arabs makes it extremely difficult.' Other Arab countries had accused the Saudis of 'being in collusion with Zionism and American imperialism against the Arabs.'[22] Nixon tried to keep oil separate from politics, telling a press conference that the United States was not more-Arab than pro-Israeli 'just because the Arabs have oil and Israel had not,' and urged both sides to negotiate.[23]

But time had run out on the Americans' hedging. On 23 August, Sadat went to meet Faisal in Riyadh. He told him that the war would soon be starting. By the end of the month, he and President Hafez Assad of Syria had set a date for their attack. They had named it Operation Badr, after one of the Prophet's decisive battles. This would be a holy war as much as a nationalist and political one.

Anarchy was now spreading through the oil markets. Around twenty-five buyers had travelled to Riyadh in May hoping to buy a share of Saudi Arabia's participation oil. They were mostly independent refiners from the United States, Europe and Japan, plus Petrobras from Brazil. The rules were simple and non-negotiable, a display of Saudi strength. They set the selling price and there would be no haggling. Buyers had to take it or leave it by the end of the day. The government would decide if you got any oil at all, and then how much, and in what proportion, of the different types of crude, light, Arab-heavy, Arab-medium and 38-gravity Berri crude. They would not pit the buyers against each other. This would be a clean, four-day process to sell 70 billion barrels of oil, delivered over the next three years. The price of crude had already risen from $1.84 to $2.30 per barrel over the previous year. The Saudi sale price lifted it a further twenty-five cents. Every time the producers prodded the market, it lurched upwards.

Gaddafi then delivered his coup de grâce by seizing Bunker Hunt's assets in Sarir. The official decree called the nationalisation 'a warning to the United States to end its recklessness and hostility to the Arab nation.' Gaddafi said it dealt America 'a strong slap on its cool, arrogant face', and presaged 'catastrophe' for its interests in the Arab world. The State Department's initial reaction was meek and technical. It acknowledged that the 'Libyan Government has a right to nationalize industries,' but said that it should pay prompt and adequate compensation. It took a month for them to call Libya's action 'invalid and not entitled to recognition by other states.' Hunt called them a 'big joke', and accused the other oil companies of making him a 'sacrificial lamb'.[24]

The unravelling of the old pricing system spread fear. Panicked companies and countries began buying oil to stockpile it as prices kept rising. The value of a cargo of crude loaded before the Saudi auction and dispatched to northern Europe rose fifty cents during its journey. Even the lowest-quality heavy, high-sulphur oils were fetching high prices. By

August, the markets were frantic. Desperate American refiners were hurtling around the Middle East offering to buy oil at any price. They had no experience buying oil anywhere but the United States at market prices from the majors. They did not understand the behaviour and psychology of Middle Eastern sellers. An internal memo sent to staffers at *Petroleum Intelligence Weekly* said of one of these rube companies, 'You can imagine what a screwing it may be in for *if* it winds up with a contract.'[25]

Libya's Jalloud laid the blame for the escalating global energy crisis on the United States. For years, he said, American companies had kept the price of their oil artificially low as part of a wide-ranging 'imperialist scheme' to control the world's natural resources and ensure the 'rich become richer and the poor poorer.' The US military, he noted, was the largest single institutional consumer of petroleum, much of it coming from the Middle East. 'We do not want to see America, Europe or Japan without heating in the winter or with their cars at a standstill. But at the same time we do not want oil to become a weapon for them to turn into a means of destruction and destroy us with it. We want oil and energy to reach innocent people so they can travel and be warm not so that it can be transformed into murderous weapons aimed at ourselves.' The United States had no business telling Libya how much oil to produce and at what price. 'We refuse that Libya should be a milk cow which depletes its oil in ten or fifteen years.'[26]

By now even most crude buyers had given up trying to understand what was going on. Tanker shortages meant buyers and sellers fought to get scarce tankers to the right place at the right time, or risk a sharp change in their price per barrel. The slightest touch on the scale by a producer sent prices skidding upwards. For unscrupulous traders, such volatile markets were paradise.[27] For the countries which depended on Middle Eastern oil, a more dramatic series of events threatened catastrophe.

In April 1956, Moshe Dayan, the chief of the Israeli general staff, stood beside the grave of Roi Rotberg, a 21-year-old officer who had been living at a kibbutz a mile from the Gaza border. Palestinian gunmen had grabbed Rotberg while he was working in the fields. They killed him, mutilated his body and dragged it across into Gaza, where they left it. Dayan wrote his eulogy in half an hour, and read it from a piece of creased paper. He was tragically clear-eyed about Israel's fate and its duty. It was no good blaming the murderers. 'Eight years have they sat in the refugee camps of Gaza, and seen, with their own eyes, how we have made a homeland of the soil and the villages where they and their forebears once dwelt.' The price in blood would have to be paid by the Israelis, who had to be 'morning and evening, armed and ready.' There was a 'surging sea of hatred and vengeance' at Israel's borders, hundreds of thousands of Arabs 'waiting for the moment when their hands may claim our blood'. Israelis had a duty to the millions who had died without a homeland. They could never rest, or lay down their arms, because if they allowed the slightest crack in their defences, they would suffer Roi Rotberg's fate. He warned of the day that 'tranquility blunts our alertness'.

In November 1972, the commander in chief of the Egyptian armed forces, Marshal Ahmed Ismail Ali, led his officers stationed along the Suez Canal to the top of their 65-foot fortifications. He asked them to look out towards the Sinai, past the Israelis massed on the other side, and tell him what he should do once they had invaded their former territory.

During their preparations for war, the Egyptians communicated in an ancient Nubian language incomprehensible to the

Israelis listening in. At 2 p.m. on 6 October 1973, Zero Hour, the order went out: Oshriya. Strike.[28] Some 222 Egyptian fighter jets took off and crossed the Canal. Egyptian soldiers scrambled out from behind their fortifications and launched boats into the Canal shouting 'Allahu Akbar'. They pointed their specially made German water pumps at the Israeli earthworks, cutting channels for their tanks to drive through. The falcons were flying south across the Arabian Peninsula, and war had begun.

The next day, Dayan sat on a boulder in Galilee, looked towards the Golan Heights where Syrian tanks were surging through Israel's northern defences, and wept.[29]

11

Volcano

Simcha Dinitz and Anatoly Dobrynin, the Israeli and Soviet ambassadors to Washington, were the only foreign ambassadors permitted to drive into the underground parking lot at the State Department and take the private elevator up to Kissinger's offices on the seventh floor.[1] When he visited Kissinger on the final day of September, all Dinitz wanted to talk about was Schönau.

Two years earlier, in 1971, the Soviet Union had lifted its ban on Jewish emigration to Israel. Thousands of Russian Jews boarded trains that crossed Czechoslovakia and Hungary, and stopped in Austria, the first non-communist country on their route. The Jewish Agency, the largest Jewish organisation in the world, took a lease on Schönau Castle, a former Habsburg estate 20 miles south of Vienna, to process these waves of immigrants before sending them south. Golda Meir hated the fact that Jews had to set foot in a country with a strong Nazi history. The Austrians were uneasy about seeming to abandon their neutrality on the Middle East. Israeli politicians visiting Austria made a point to visit Schönau, which came to be seen as a pocket of Israel.

On 28 September, two Arab men boarded a train heading from Moscow to Vienna when it stopped in Bratislava, in Czechoslovakia. Of the train's seventy passengers, thirty-nine were Jews heading for Schönau. When the train stopped at the border town of Marchegg, the Arabs pulled machine guns and grenades from their suitcase, and took three Russian Jews and an Austrian train guard hostage. When they reached Vienna, they took a Volkswagen bus belonging to the Austrian railroad, and forced the train guard to drive them to Schwechat airport.[2] Four armed policemen approached them when they stopped on the runway. One of them shouted to the driver, 'Come on out, you shitty dog. I'll spit the whole magazine into your stomach.' The driver asked a photographer standing nearby what the policeman had said. 'He's annoyed because he's on duty now because of you.'[3]

The attackers had been sent by a Syrian-backed Palestinian organisation, al-Sa'iqa, to distract Israel from the Arabs' preparation for war. In Washington, Tel Aviv and Jerusalem, no one was looking to Israel's northern and southern borders and the threat of war. The politicians and media were focused on Vienna. While Egypt and Syria moved forces into position to attack, an Israeli minister said, '[Y]ou would have thought Israel's front line was not Suez but the Danube.'

The terrorists demanded a plane to fly them and their Jewish hostages somewhere in the Arab world. At first the Austrians refused. But by the afternoon, the foreign ministry summoned the Lebanese, Israeli and Egyptian ambassadors and instructed them to talk with the terrorists. They returned with the demand to close Schönau. The decision fell to Austria's chancellor, Bruno Kreisky. 'My guiding principle in politics was to protect human life at all costs, and I acted upon this principle from the moment that I became embroiled in the hostage affair.'

Kreisky was born shortly before World War One to a non-observant Jewish family in Vienna. He considered himself an 'acculturated' Jew, one who was fully part of Austrian society, but who retained elements of his Jewishness. This was different from the assimilated Jews, who had erased all trace of their Jewishness to become fully Austrian. The distinction mattered socially in the late Habsburg era. It did not matter to the Nazis as they pursued anyone with the slightest Jewish lineage.[4] Kreisky escaped to Sweden in 1938 but more than twenty members of his family died in the Holocaust.

He was elected chancellor in 1970, the first socialist in fifty years to hold the job. He considered his Jewishness irrelevant to his politics, and said that to divide people into Jews and non-Jews was to perpetuate Hitler's murderous prejudice, proving that 'the yellow patch is still with us even today.' He thought the idea of a global Jewish community was 'imaginary', since there was little in common between a Jew from Eastern Europe and a Jew from Tunisia besides their religion.

In 1972, he had watched West Germany's disastrous mishandling of the Arab terrorist attack on Israeli athletes at the Munich Olympic Games. The Germans had negotiated, refused the help of Israel's special forces, and tried to rescue the hostages as the terrorists prepared to fly them out of the country. The three terrorists arrested were released just a month later in a hostage swap for the passengers on a hijacked German plane. The episode was a catastrophe for Germany's relationship with Israel.

Kreisky dreaded a repeat, and immediately promised that Schönau would be closed in return for the release of the hostages. The terrorists released them and flew out of Vienna to Libya on a small Cessna. Most Austrians supported Kreisky, but three days later, a furious Golda Meir swept into Europe. She told the Council of Europe in Strasbourg that '[A]ny government which strikes a deal with these killers does so at its own peril,' and that Kreisky had delivered a 'great victory' to the terrorists and the Arab states. She then flew on to confront Kreisky.

Meir had been born in Kiev, under the threat of Russian pogroms against Jews. In 1906, her family emigrated to the United States. As a teenager she became fascinated by Zionism and in 1921 left for Palestine, and life on a kibbutz. She became deeply involved in negotiations for the creation of Israel, and was one of twenty-five signers of its declaration of independence in 1948. She was a stoutly built, chain-smoking defender of her country, unblinking at its challenges. After Israel's victory in the Six Day War, she said: 'There is nothing Israel wants so much as peace. With all the bleakness of the desert, the desert of hate around us is even more bleak.' She trailed all of her country's righteous fury and defiant resolve.

The chancellor ordered his staff to take good care of Meir, to offer her coffee and cakes, a shower in the small bedroom behind his office, and to find out if she kept kosher. But when she arrived, she said all she wanted was 'Negotiations! Negotiations!' Kreisky stayed behind his desk, and leaned awkwardly across to shake Meir's hand. She set her large, black handbag on the floor, and sat down. Closing Schönau, Kreisky told her, did not mean an end to Jewish emigration through Austria. The Red Cross would soon open a camp in a different location, and operations would resume as before. Nothing had really changed, and lives had been saved. 'It might be that my way is not the way to fight terrorism,' he said. 'However, yours is not either.' Meir was implacable, banging the desk with her fists. She said Kreisky had betrayed the Jewish people and become a hero to the Arabs. The day after the attack, Egypt's President Sadat sent a minister to Vienna to congratulate Kreisky. 'You and I belong to two different worlds,' said the chancellor, also now banging the desk.'[5] 'Indeed we do, Herr Kreisky,' said Meir. 'You and I indeed belong to two very, very different worlds.'

When Meir landed at Ben Gurion Airport, she told

journalists: 'I think the best way of summing up in a nutshell the nature of my meeting with Chancellor Kreisky is to say this: He didn't even offer me a glass of water.' Israel's labour minister, Yosef Almogi, called Kreisky a 'Jewish Kapo', comparing him to the Jews in concentration camps who were recruited as supervisors by the Gestapo. President Nixon called Kreisky and accused him of giving in to 'international blackmail'.

For Kreisky, the defining argument for his decision was that four weeks after he closed Schönau, the number of emigrants each month passing through Austria from Russia was its highest ever. But Israelis saw a Jewish man who had betrayed them. Kreisky's ambivalence towards Israel was not unique in Europe. The continent's need for oil would expose its true feelings towards the young Jewish state.

The failed war in Vietnam and the strains of the Cold War had convinced Nixon and Kissinger to reset America's foreign policy. The purpose of the Nixon Doctrine was to reduce America's responsibility to its allies. It would honour its treaties, provide nuclear cover for its friends, and offer military and economic support to allies who needed it. But it was not going to patrol the world with its own forces the way it had been. The policy required much more advanced diplomacy, as America was now going to engage far more with its supposed enemies, to talk, negotiate, trade, and relax the most fraught relationships, while solidifying the good ones.

Nixon's first secretary of state was an old friend, a successful Wall Street lawyer, William Rogers. Rogers had served as attorney general under Eisenhower while Nixon was vice president, but he had no experience of foreign affairs. By appointing him to state, Nixon hoped to minimise the department's influence, while he ran foreign policy from the White House with

Kissinger, his national security adviser. The first term had proved a great success. Nixon reopened relations with China, and visited Beijing to meet Chairman Mao. He travelled to Moscow to sign the Strategic Arms Limitation Treaty agreements (SALT I), the first time that the United States and the Soviet Union agreed to limit their swollen nuclear arsenals. Nixon and Kissinger restored America's confidence overseas, as the miseries of Vietnam began to recede.

Rogers mostly accepted his diminished role, and in August 1973 resigned to make way for Kissinger, who became secretary of state, while retaining his White House position. Kissinger had always idolised European statesmen like Metternich and Bismarck, who used strength and guile to achieve their nations' interests, without too many of the squeamish constraints of morality. Even they might have envied his extraordinary power over American foreign policy, which now grew as Nixon became distracted.

Early in the morning of 17 June 1972, five men were arrested trying to bug the offices of the Democratic National Committee in the Watergate building in Washington DC. Nixon was re-elected in a landslide in November, but investigations by reporters and the FBI were accumulating evidence that the burglary was part of a much larger conspiracy run from the White House on behalf of Nixon. Over the course of 1973, several of Nixon's closest aides were either convicted of involvement in the burglary, or decided to resign. The Senate began televised hearings on Watergate. John Dean, the former White House counsel, revealed he had spoken to Nixon on many occasions about covering up the scandal. The president's former appointments secretary then revealed that since 1971, all of Nixon's conversations and telephone calls had been recorded. The Justice Department and the Senate demanded the tapes, but

Nixon refused, knowing what they contained. The tussle over the tapes corroded Nixon's credibility, confidence and mood, and left a vacuum in foreign affairs which Kissinger was happy to fill.

On the evening of 4 October, the new secretary of state took over the Metropolitan Museum of Art for a dinner for the diplomats of the United Nations, the Nixon Doctrine in action. He welcomed his guests in the Great Hall, before they walked south to the museum's Fountain Restaurant. The dinner took place around a reflecting pool containing fey bronze statues of the muses prancing. It began at a very *mondaine* 9.30 p.m. Kissinger was sleek and bustling as he greeted representatives from almost all of the 135 member countries of the United Nations. Only a few, notably Iraq and Libya, had boycotted the event. The Chinese wore Mao jackets, the Africans exuberant dresses, the Europeans sombre tuxedos. The State Department had exceeded its budget to serve a feast of smoked trout, roast veal, lemon mousse and Californian wines.

In his toast, Kissinger called the UN 'the treasury of man's noblest aspirations'. The great practitioner of realpolitik and the transactional pursuit of national self-interest said that the United States was now 'ready to begin the journey toward a world community,' and that 'peace will come when all – the small as well as the large – have a share in its shaping, and that will endure when all – the weak as well as the strong – have a stake in its lasting.'

Kissinger's policy of détente, relaxing the tensions of the Cold War through diplomacy, did not convince everyone, notably the French, who thought it naïve at best, duplicitous at worst. What was good for America was not necessarily good for its more vulnerable allies. Michel Jobert, France's spiky foreign minister, told the UN General Assembly: 'A famous actress used to dress in nothing but perfume. I fear that dressed so scantily in détente, we might also end up shivering.' The day after Kissinger's dinner, four transport planes arrived in Cairo from Russia to take the Soviets in Egypt home. Moscow had been watching Sadat's preparations, and had little faith his attack on Israel would succeed. If this was going to become a proxy war between the United States and the Soviet Union, the Soviets wanted to minimise the damage to themselves.

Early in the morning of 6 October, Meir summoned the US ambassador to Israel, Kenneth Keating, and told him there was likely to be an attack on Israel that afternoon. The Egyptian forces had been put on alert, and the Syrians were positioning their forces in the Golan Heights close to the 1967 ceasefire lines. Kissinger was roused from his bed at the Waldorf Astoria hotel in New York. He promptly sent a message to Faisal asking him to intervene with Sadat and Assad. He said he had urged the Israelis not to act pre-emptively, spoken to the Soviets, and tried getting hold of the Syrians, but their foreign minister would not answer his phone.[6]

Faisal cabled back that this war was simply the 'link in the chain' of Israel's aggression towards its neighbours. 'If the United States does not act to deter Israel, the volcano which has so far been quiet in the Middle East will be active again and its holocaust will not be confined to this region alone, but will develop into an all-out Third World War.' It was up to the United States now to persuade Israel to withdraw and grant the Palestinians 'their rights in their territory and homeland.'[7] He could not have chosen a more provocative word than 'holocaust' to express his fury at what was now happening.

That afternoon, Kissinger called a meeting of the White House Situations Action Group, WSAG, composed of members of the National Security Council staff, the CIA, and the departments of State and Defense. Oil was a prominent concern.

Kenneth Rush, Kissinger's deputy at state, said, 'If there is an embargo, we're all in a helluva fix. We only have 30 days' supply and the Europeans have about sixty days. And that is to catastrophe. Within fifteen days there would be panic.' Europe was highly vulnerable to any cut-off by Libya, while Japan, observed another attendee, had 'about a 10-minute supply'. Faisal was the key to avoiding an embargo, but he would not press for peace talks so early in the conflict.[8]

Rush's numbers were off. A White House paper the following day calculated that if there was an Arab embargo, the United States had 210–250 days' supply. But there would be serious regional shortages almost immediately, and the president would quickly have to introduce either mandatory allocations or even rationing. The next day, a crowd broke all the windows at the Egyptian embassy in New York.

When the WSAG met the following evening, Kissinger laid out his strategy. He wanted to end the war with the Israelis on top, but not having won a crushing defeat. If possible, the Arabs, and their Soviet backers, had to emerge with their dignity intact, and a willingness to engage in peace talks led by the Americans. Israel had to feel in control, but still vulnerable enough to be open to negotiations. Kissinger was confident that once the Israelis recovered from the initial shock of the attacks, their military superiority would prevail, especially with strong American support. The goal was for all sides to retreat to the 1967 ceasefire lines, where they had begun on 6 October. Kissinger predicted that the Arabs would resist any quick stop to the fighting, screaming that 'they are being deprived of their birthright'. But he reckoned by Thursday, four days later, the Israeli counterattack would have succeeded to the point where the Arabs would be 'on their knees begging us for a ceasefire.' While this played out, Kissinger said, the Americans 'should try and be enigmatic.'

He then returned to the question of oil. William Clements, the deputy secretary of defence, said, '[N]o one is telling it like it is on the fuel shortage.' Kissinger could not understand how the country could be so vulnerable and unprepared. He asked Bill Simon, representing the Treasury, what Nixon should say on the day of a cut-off. 'He institutes rationing,' Simon said. It would be a bureaucratic hell. 'They talk about it's affecting the middle of the barrel, but I say you can't do that without affecting the whole barrel.' Kissinger pointed at Simon and Clements. 'Does anyone here understand what these two are talking about?'

The middle of a barrel of crude, around 25 per cent of its volume, consists of fuels like diesel and heating oil. During refining they separate at temperatures in between the lighter fuels like gasoline, and heavier residues like asphalt. Around 50 per cent of a barrel of crude yields gasoline. Simon's point was that if the only fuels that had to be rationed were diesel and heating oil, the 'middle of the barrel', that would be challenging enough. But if you had to ration the rest of the barrel, including the gasoline that millions of Americans used to fill up their cars, the government would have a much bigger problem.[9]

As OPEC's delegates arrived in Vienna for new talks on oil prices, the newspapers were full of reports from Egypt, Israel, Syria and Washington. During the first twenty-four hours of the war, the Arabs terrorised the Israelis. Syrian tank divisions surged southwards towards the Sea of Galilee, and Egyptian infantry burst through Israel's frail resistance in the Sinai. Israel could not afford to fight a long war, and already it was facing devastating losses of men and materiel. Egypt had invested heavily in Soviet anti-aircraft missiles, which shredded Israel's vaunted air force as it tried to support its ground troops, stumbling backwards in retreat. Moshe Dayan suggested setting off a nuclear bomb simply to freeze the conflict. Golda Meir told him to forget it.[10] In one day, the Arab armies appeared to have reversed the humiliation of the Six Day War.

The coincidence of war with a fresh round of oil price negotiations made it clear that it was no use pretending any longer that the economics of oil could be separated from the politics of the Middle East. Yamani had warned that the pricing formulas agreed in Tehran in 1971 would not last, and they had duly collapsed under the strain of rising inflation, devalued currencies and higher prices for other commodities. The producers felt insulted to be still negotiating with companies rather than directly with the consumer countries' governments who might actually influence the issues at hand. This was not how serious global powers were treated.

OPEC's lead negotiators were Yamani and Jamshid Amouzegar, Iran's dapper finance minister. Amouzegar was an American-educated engineer and lawyer, who had served in successive Iranian governments. Like Yamani, he was considered a moderate and technocrat. His wife was German, and he related easily to his Western counterparts. He and Yamani had negotiated alongside each other in Tehran two years before. The oil companies were represented by George Piercy of Exxon, who had negotiated with the producers in Tehran, and André Bénard of Shell, a hard-headed French engineer who had fought with the Resistance during World War Two. Bénard had only been assigned Shell's Middle East portfolio a few days before. To his astonishment, the governments of the consumer countries did not send a single foreign affairs expert to advise him and Piercy, nor an economist to gauge the effect of price rises on consumers. They had no context for what they were discussing. The war meant that on OPEC's side, the moods and demands changed by the day, depending on whether the Arabs or Israelis looked to be winning. But when Piercy and Bénard called their corporate headquarters for guidance they heard nothing back. As they negotiated terms with the gravest economic and political consequences, the politicians in the consumer countries vanished, not wanting their fingerprints on any deal which emerged. The price of the world's most important commodity was being settled by two influential ministers on the producer side, with direct lines to the rulers of their countries, and two under-informed, under-powered executives on the other, whose calls home went unanswered.

The oil companies' best hope was that the negotiations in Vienna would yield an agreement on gradual, predictable increases in the prices and costs of oil. The Americans thought they could get away with chiselling away at the producers with a succession of small increases, ten hard-fought cents at a time. The Europeans thought it would be simpler to offer one big increase, of three to five dollars a barrel, and stop the poisonous drip of endless talks. But these differences over tactics were irrelevant, since the consumers had no leverage: no political power; no alternative sources of energy; and no flexibility in demand. They had no choice but to buy OPEC's oil. They could give in immediately to OPEC's price demands, with no guarantee that the producers would not soon come back for more. They could walk away, hoping the producers would cave, which was unlikely. Or they could play for time, saying they had to consult the consumer governments before agreeing to any new terms. They chose the third.

On the night of 11 October, after three days of halting talks, Piercy and Bénard asked to see Yamani in private. He invited them to his hotel suite, and offered them drinks and dates from Dhahran; the best in the world, he told them. Yamani had proposed a doubling of the posted prices. The companies had met in New York and could not agree on what to do and nor could they get the US government to say anything to appease Faisal on Israel.[11] Piercy told Yamani that OPEC's pricing strategy was endangering the world economy. The increase he was asking for was too big for the companies to agree to, without the consent of the consumer governments.

He and Bénard asked if they could suspend the talks for fifteen days and return home for consultations.

Yamani fell silent while he thought. He called Amouzegar, and spoke to the Kuwaiti delegate who had bustled over in his pyjamas. He asked if the companies would accept a retroactive date of 1 October for any deal, in return for the two-week recess. Piercy said he did not have the authority to agree.[12] Yamani said he was going back to Saudi Arabia. Bénard asked when they would next see him. He said he did not know. They should listen to the radio, like everyone else. The companies were no longer party to this decision. Yamani returned to Riyadh on a plane lent to him by Shell. Bénard returned home to Holland, gave up his company car and took up cycling.[13]

12

What Do We Do if the Oil Is Cut Off?

Within hours of Yamani's departure from Vienna, John McCloy sent a letter from the chief executives of the four Aramco companies to Nixon, explaining the consequences of the collapsed OPEC negotiations. The free world was already operating 'wide open', with no spare production capacity. If OPEC increased prices to the extent they were threatening, many countries would struggle to pay for oil. Market forces justified some increase, but the sudden doubling proposed by OPEC would be disastrous.

King Faisal was angry that the US had asked him to urge the Egyptians and Syrians to pull back to the ceasefire lines. He did not wish to be America's instrument in the conflict. It was now all but inevitable that Saudi Arabia and Kuwait would cut production as retaliation for the United States' flagrant support for Israel. There was a high probability that if one producer took action against the US, there would be a 'snowballing effect that would produce a major petroleum supply crisis.' McCloy warned that the United States risked being driven from the Middle East, and replaced by European, Japanese and even Soviet interests.

At last, the message was getting through. On Sunday

morning, 14 October, the WSAG met for nearly two hours in the White House Situation Room. Kissinger asked: 'What do we do if the oil is cut off?'

'Suppose the Egyptians are badly defeated,' he mused. 'I don't think they will be, but it is not beyond the realm of the possible. We might lose all outlets and get cut off.' Of the Saudis, he asked, 'What if they limit production over the long term and we can't handle it with diplomacy and other pressures?' Despite all of the warnings, the invasion, and Faisal's recent references to an 'all-out Third World War', Kissinger still did not believe the Saudis would cut off oil supplies to the United States. 'All I have received are hysterical calls from oil companies,' he said.

John Love, the former governor of Colorado, had joined the Nixon administration three months earlier as its first director of the Energy Policy Office. A genial lawyer from Denver, he had been a popular governor for ten years. Silver-haired, handsome, often compared to the actor William Holden, he was a terrific retail politician. Under his leadership, Colorado had attracted new jobs and businesses, and its skiing and tourism industries had boomed. Unlike many more conservative Republicans, however, Love favoured government intervention to protect the environment. He signed water- and air-pollution acts and spoke out against reckless growth and use of the land. On paper, he seemed an ideal choice to achieve Nixon's goals, a Western governor with executive experience, a pro-business reputation, and credit with environmentalists.

But he was ill-prepared for the back alleys and flick knives of Washington. He was given one assistant and three secretaries, and relegated to a small office in the Old Executive Building,[1] the administration's Siberia. He struggled to find time with the president. Now he faced Kissinger's full glare.

Love spoke to the WSAG in vague technicalities. The US was

consuming just short of 20 million barrels of oil a day. A cut-off by the states around the Persian Gulf, not including Iran, plus Libya and Algeria, could lead to the United States being short by 500,000 barrels a day. The US could surge its own production in the south-west and California and find 100,000–200,000. A boost in coal production might replace another 200,000 barrels, but that would require changes to the law. Restrictions on demand, such as factory closures, a lower speed limit and a gasoline tax might save a couple hundred thousand more. Then there was the weather. A cold winter would mean higher demand for heating oil. If Europe were embargoed too, there would be a stampede for the few remaining sources of oil, such as Iran and Venezuela. Within a month, Love predicted, there would be shortages of everything.

Kissinger was reluctant to let it be known that the government was contemplating the worst. 'Let's not talk about consequences,' he said. 'We don't want to make it happen. We should be low key . . . but if there is a fait accompli, we want to know what to do.' Love replied: 'We will have to move on an allocation program.'

Nixon supported Israel in public, but in private often spoke contemptuously of Jews. Arthur Burns, the Jewish chairman of the Federal Reserve, listened to Nixon rant about Jewish organisations he believed were corrupting the country, and destroying his plans to transform America's place in the world through trade, arms reduction and dogged diplomacy. Burns did not believe Nixon was antisemitic, but that he would lurch that way for political advantage.[2]

Kissinger, who was Jewish, said that when it came to Israel and Jews, the president 'shared many of the prejudices of the uprooted, California lower-middle class from which he had come.'[3] In the spring of 1973, Golda Meir met Nixon in the Oval Office, to ask him to pressure the Soviet Union to allow Jews to emigrate in greater numbers to Israel. Afterwards, Kissinger was recorded saying: 'The emigration of Jews from the Soviet Union is not an objective of American foreign policy. And if they put Jews into gas chambers in the Soviet Union, it is not an American concern. Maybe a humanitarian concern.' He and Nixon did not believe it justified straining the US-Soviet relationship.

Like Faisal, Nixon considered communism a Jewish conspiracy against the United States. If one of his critics or opponents were Jewish, Nixon often pointed out the fact when he attacked them in private. He believed that a 'terrible Jewish clique' was undermining his executive powers and that the Justice Department was 'untrustworthy' as it was 'full of Jews.'[4] He wanted to unleash the Internal Revenue Service on the Democratic Party, particularly 'the Jewish . . . the big Jewish contributors of the Democrats.' He instructed his aide H. R. Haldeman to 'investigate some of the cocksuckers.'[5]

When the Bureau of Labor Statistics reported on inflationary pressures in the economy in 1971, Nixon raged against a 'Jewish cabal' trying to undermine him.[6] He seemed to particularly enjoy making racist and antisemitic remarks in front of Kissinger, who saw no point in challenging him, and even ensured that at National Security Council meetings with the president, he kept the number of Jewish staffers to a minimum.[7] Kissinger believed that Nixon thought that 'Jews formed a powerful, cohesive . . . and predominantly liberal' group in the United States, and that they 'put the interests of Israel above everything else.'[8] William Safire, Nixon's speechwriter, said that Nixon's real hatred was for liberals, and that 'Jews in Hollywood and New York, were part of the target.' Safire believed Nixon's was the 'towel snapping, locker room kind of antisemitism, and not something he thought of or something he carried out on.'[9]

Nixon's private views did not undermine his support for Israel. When Golda Meir asked the United States for supplies three days into the war, Kissinger and Jim Schlesinger, the secretary of defence, worried about how much to send, and by what means so as not to antagonise the Arabs. Ronald Reagan, then in his second term as governor of California, had an elegant solution to the problem. Since the Arabs were reportedly exaggerating their success against the Israelis, he told Kissinger, 'Why don't you say that you will replace all the aircraft the Arabs claim they have shot down?'[10] Israel was not prepared to fight a long war. 'When Israel fights, men drive their trucks to their posts, because the truck the military will use,' said Admiral Thomas Moorer, the chairman of the joint chiefs of staff. Its economy contracted as men went to fight. To win quickly, Israel needed America's financial and military support immediately.[11] Nixon had the final say. The Arabs would be offended if the US sent any supplies at all. 'If we are going to take heat for this, well, let's go,' he said. He told Kissinger there was no point sending a few planes. 'By golly,' he said, 'just go gung-ho.'[12] By the night of 13 October, American transport planes were flying towards Israel carrying supplies. Operation Nickel Grass had begun.

The European countries with American air bases on the continent refused to allow the planes to land for fear of antagonising the Arabs. The Portuguese allowed them to use Lajes in the Azores, an airfield bedevilled by fifty-knot cross-winds and thick mists. Once refuelled, the planes flew east across the Mediterranean, keeping within a narrow corridor, making sure not to enter the airspace of Arab countries to the south, and European countries to the north. As they passed over the Strait of Gibraltar, they held their line right in the middle to avoid provoking the British or the Moroccans.[13] The ships of the Sixth Fleet strung out below them, tracking the planes and ready to defend them if necessary. Each ship handed their responsibility on to the next as the planes passed overhead. The smaller A4 fighter jets, the Phantoms and Skyhawks, needed to refuel three more times on three aircraft carriers, the *Kennedy*, positioned 100 miles west of Gibraltar, the *Roosevelt*, south-east of Sicily, and the *Independence*, near Crete. The transport planes could make it from Lajes to Tel Aviv without stopping. As they neared Israel, they were picked up by Israeli F-4 phantoms and escorted into Lod airport in Tel Aviv, where the pilots and crews were greeted by glamorous El Al flight attendants serving meals.[14]

At a meeting of the WSAG on 16 October, William Colby, Director of the CIA, said that Faisal was upset by the supplies being poured into Israel. 'He is inclined to blow off emotionally about things, but he usually calms down.' Kissinger said that even if Israel did not exist, Faisal would have used oil as a weapon. 'You put a man in a monopoly position and he will squeeze you.' As Kissinger pressed for more weapons to be sent more quickly to Israel, the news came over the ticker that he and Le Duc Tho had been awarded the Nobel Peace Prize.[15]

After the failed embargo of 1967, the Arab oil producers had set up their own organisation, the Organization of Arab Petroleum Exporting Countries (OAPEC), adjacent to OPEC, to focus more on their own interests; matters which did not concern OPEC members like Venezuela and Nigeria. The founders were Saudi Arabia, Libya and Kuwait, and by 1973 they had added Algeria, Bahrain, Egypt, Iraq, Qatar, Syria and the United Arab Emirates. Throughout the crisis and beyond, people spoke of OPEC and OAPEC as if they were interchangeable. Their members and their interests overlapped. Oil prices and production levels mattered as much to Indonesians as they did to the Kuwaitis. But OAPEC was the Arabs' precision instrument, and with the prospect of unsheathing the oil weapon, it now came into its own. On 16 October its member countries' oil ministers met in the Sheraton Hotel in Kuwait to discuss the breakdown of the OPEC talks in Vienna with the oil majors. If the companies could not agree to pay a higher price for oil, then the Arab oil-producing countries would raise the price unilaterally and the companies would have no choice. The companies had failed to respect the countries' rights to their own resources. Now, as Yamani had threatened, they would use their power. They raised the price of oil by 70 per cent, to match the prices on the spot market, which had surged since the outbreak of war. 'The moment has come,' Yamani told his fellow ministers. 'We are masters of our own commodity.'

George Piercy and André Bénard opened their newspapers the next morning to find the answer they had been waiting for that night in Vienna. 'The 16th of October was the demarcation,' Yamani said. 'It was the day that OPEC seized power. The real power.' Piercy called it an 'unmitigated disaster'.[16]

Like Yamani, the Saudi foreign minister, Omar Saqqaf, was one of Faisal's clever Hijazis. He came from Medina, from a family that claimed to be directly descended from the Prophet, and had worked his way up through the government to his position close to the king. Jim Akins once attended a meeting with Saqqaf and Prince Mohammed, Faisal's half brother, a powerful and plain-speaking influence in the court, nicknamed the 'father of two evils' for his temper and his drinking. The prince kept referring to Saqqaf as a Hadhrami, a man from the Hadhramaut, a province in Yemen. When they were alone, Akins said to Saqqaf, 'I thought you were from Medina.'

'I am from Medina,' he said.

'Does your family have some connection to the Hadhramaut?'

'We left there for Medina 700 years ago.'

Saqqaf had nonetheless won Faisal's confidence. He was tall, imposing, and spoke fluent English and French. He drank Scotch and often used his visits to Washington as the pretext for a week or two in Las Vegas. By the time he went in to see Kissinger and Nixon on 17 October, he had been kept waiting for two days while Operation Nickel Grass gained momentum. The Saudis clocked the insult. The president and Kissinger told Saqqaf they would seek a mediated peace between Israel, Syria and Egypt. At a press conference afterwards, an American journalist sneered at the minister:

'We do not need your oil. You can drink it.'

'All right,' said Saqqaf. 'We will.'[17]

Kissinger's initial anxiety about the war had eased into cockiness. 'We don't expect an oil cut-off now in the light of the discussions with the Arab foreign ministers this morning,' he said at the WSAG meeting that afternoon. 'Did you see the Saudi foreign minister come out like a good little boy and say they had had very fruitful talks with us?' The Saudis had been in an 'extremely conciliatory frame of mind'. In the meantime, the United States should keep pouring in military supplies to Israel 'until someone quits'. This meant sending more armaments to Israel than the Soviets could to the Arabs. Engagement to any degree meant the Arabs would 'scream bloody murder'. So now that they had started, the Americans should give the Israelis whatever they needed.

An hour later, the Saudis, and the rest of OAPEC, screamed bloody murder. They were cutting oil production by 5 per cent and would keep cutting it by 5 per cent more each month until Israel withdrew from all occupied Arab territories. In addition to the price rises from the day before, the production cuts sent the oil market spinning.

On 19 October, reports reached the Israelis that thirty Saudi tanks were moving towards Aqaba, the Jordanian port on the Red Sea. This was part of the Saudis' desultory military contribution to the war. The Israelis told the Saudis that if they attacked Aqaba, they would bomb Riyadh. The Saudi tanks retreated into the Jordanian desert, lost their way, and were rescued by Jordan's Royal Desert Forces, better known as the Camel Corps.[18]

Yamani called Akins to his office to explain what had happened in Kuwait. The Saudis had resisted the more radical demands to cut diplomatic ties with the United States, switch reserves out of dollars, and cut oil production by up to 50 per cent all at once. But there was enormous resentment among the Arab countries at the supply of sophisticated weaponry to Israel. If one Israeli child was hurt, Yamani complained, his picture appeared on the front of *The New York Times*. If thousands of Arabs were murdered, no one in America cared.[19]

That evening, Faisal was in his office when he learned Nixon had asked Congress to approve sending $2.2 billion worth of weapons to Israel, whose troops were now successfully fighting back. He was furious that Nixon had crossed him, promising his foreign minister an honourable peace then going straight to Congress to make such a large request to help Israel. That evening, the king called Yamani, and told him to come to the palace immediately.

'Write this down,' said the king. 'In view of the increase of American military aid to Israel, the Kingdom of Saudi Arabia has decided to halt all oil exports to the United States of America.' All the other oil-producing Arab states except Iraq and Libya joined him. The embargo which Kissinger never thought would happen was now in effect.

Frank Jungers, now chief executive as well as chairman of Aramco, asked Faisal how he planned to meet the logistical challenges of an embargo. 'I am not going to do it,' Faisal said. 'You are.'[20] On 22 October, Yamani summoned Jungers, two other Aramco executives, and the oil ministry's team from Dammam, to Riyadh. The embargo and the production cuts meant that Aramco would have to cut its total production by 23 per cent from September. Far more complicated was the allocation to countries. Yamani told the Aramco team that there would be three categories of countries, depending on their attitude to Israel. The Most-Favoured Nations would be those who broke relations with Israel. They were allowed either the same amount of oil they had received in September, or the average for the first nine months, whichever was higher. Neutral countries would share the remaining oil, based on what they had received during the first three-quarters of the year. The embargoed countries, the United States, and from 1 November, the Netherlands, Israel's most loyal ally in Europe, would get nothing.

Under its existing system, the four partners in Aramco sent in their tanker schedules twenty days before the beginning of each month. After some fine tuning, the schedules were sent to Dhahran. Here, unanticipated events, from mechanical failures to sick crews, were built into the month's planning. Aramco then arranged for the right amounts and grades of crude to be lifted from its various fields and brought to Ras Tanura at precisely the right time for loading and dispatching to sixty-eight countries. Now Aramco had to figure out a new system, calibrated under the intense gaze of the Saudi government. The Saudis needed these measures to bite. If they failed, the oil weapon would be as blunt as it was in 1967. They wanted to know how every barrel moved through the complex network of tankers, refineries and shippers to make sure none of their oil was going to boycotted countries. When Faisal ordered a 10 per cent cutback, Aramco cut 20 per cent to make sure it stayed well within bounds. In the early days of the boycott, its oil was on tankers heading to destinations around the world. Aramco did not know where much of it was. It was hyper cautious, worried that if it breached the Saudis' rules, it would be nationalised immediately.[21]

Every day, sometimes several times a day, the Saudis told Aramco what to do. The men on each side had worked together for years, and knew each other by their first names.[22] Tankers backed up all along the Persian Gulf, waiting for Aramco to figure out the new loads and destinations. When the Netherlands was embargoed, the Aramco partners were instructed to track down tankers which had already left for the great refineries of Rotterdam, and redirect them elsewhere. As countries moved from list to list, or begged for special treatment, Aramco juggled frenziedly to keep up.[23] One tanker had to go to Ceylon, which was running short of oil, another to Tanzania, an African friend. Aramco was no longer just an oil producer. It had become the trusted enforcer and front line of Saudi Arabia's war on Israel, an American company wielding the Arabs' weapon for them.

To mark its accession to the European Economic Community in 1973, Britain organised eleven days of cultural events. The Fanfare for Europe featured art exhibitions, essay competitions for children, classical music concerts, a beauty contest for Miss TV Europe, a vintage car rally, and a football match at Wembley Stadium, pitting a team with players from the EEC's newest members, the UK, Ireland and Denmark against a team from the six existing members. Only a third of the stadium was filled for the game. An exhibition of European candy, titled Sweets, at a gallery in East London was attacked by a group of visiting school children, who smashed through the Perspex protecting the exhibits and devoured some 50 pounds of sweets. The police warned the children to go to their doctors as the sweets may have been contaminated by rat poison spread on the gallery floor.[24]

The bleak Fanfare was of a piece with Britain's dishevelment after quarter of a century of post-war decline. The government was printing money to pay its bills, inflation was rising, and Prime Minister Edward Heath tried to protect consumers by fixing prices, as Nixon had. When he fixed the price of oil, Shell's fierce managing director, Frank McFadzean, accused him of putting Britain in the same category as Italy, which was 'in a state of near economic anarchy'. It was, he said, a 'humiliating position for any country to adopt.'[25]

When war broke out in October, Heath, in his desperation for Arab oil, refused the US access to British bases for planes carrying supplies to Israel, and stopped the sale of spare parts for Israeli weapons, including shells for the British Centurion tanks it had sold them. Heath's opponents accused him of the darkest cynicism. He believed his position was a necessary compromise. The day after the announcement from Kuwait, Heath's advisers told him the Arabs had him cornered. Britain's economy was already precarious. Now it was going to have to spend even more on oil. Its balance of payments would deteriorate rapidly, and the pound would collapse. Short of using military force, all Britain could do was comply, distancing itself from Israel in order to become one of the Arabs' Most-Favoured Nations.[26]

Kissinger was unimpressed. He called the British 'jackals' at a meeting with senior defence and intelligence staff. They had no principles, and were circling in the shadows to see what happened next. They were impotent and, like the Europeans in general, 'shits'.

The day after Faisal implemented the embargo, Heath invited McFadzean and his opposite number at BP, Sir Eric Drake, for dinner at Chequers, the prime minister's country residence. The executives briefed Heath on the situation. The war had cut supplies from the eastern Mediterranean by two-thirds. Once the fighting stopped, those supplies might be restored, but the Arab countries were likely to use oil as a bargaining chip in their negotiations. Heath had two obvious courses of action. He could go to the other industrialised countries and propose a rationing system for Middle Eastern crude, whereby the reduced oil supplies were allocated to each member in proportion to what they had been importing when the crisis began. And he could reduce demand by restricting supplies and introducing a rationing system, ensuring the most vital customers got what they needed, while everyone else cut their energy use.

Heath then proposed a third possibility. The oil companies could redirect oil from other markets to Britain. Surely this was their duty in a time of national crisis. If Japan went short, so what? Britain had to think of itself first.

The executives explained that the Arabs would be watching closely where their oil was going. Even though they couldn't track every barrel once it had left their terminals, they would be able to tell if supplies to individual countries were rising or falling, and who was trying to game the system. If Britain were seen to be cheating, the Arabs would be pitiless. If Europe tried forcing its oil companies to supply them at fixed prices, the Arabs would cut them off and sell their oil at higher prices to Japan.

For at least the next decade, the executives explained, the industrialised world had no alternative to Middle Eastern oil. Venezuela, Indonesia and Iran were close to producing all they could. Domestic coal production and imports could not fill the gap. Production of North Sea oil had yet to start, let alone reach significant volume. Industrial disputes had pushed the start of production to the spring of 1975. The only way to start sooner would be to bring in 200 welders from the United States, but then all the British workers would strike. If the companies offered bonuses to the British workers to work faster, that would breach the government's pay policies. In order to secure its supply of Arab oil, Britain had to throw Israel overboard. The country that drafted the Balfour Declaration, which paved the way for a Jewish state in Palestine, had to abandon the country it had helped create.

France relied on Arab states for just over half of its oil. Around a third came from the more militant countries, Algeria, its former colony, Libya and Iraq. When France left its North African colonies between 1955 and 1962, many Arabs had emigrated to France, and many French had stayed behind. Its leaders felt stronger economic, diplomatic and cultural ties to the Arabs than to Israel. They believed France was better served by having its own bilateral relationships in the Arab world, than falling in behind America. Spain under General Franco was so economically destitute and politically isolated it bought low-grade oil from whoever would sell it to them. Watching the Europeans react to the crisis, Kissinger saw only abject weakness. Despite the Americans' open support for Israel, their 'position with the Arabs is better than that of the Europeans who are kissing ass.'[27]

Jim Schlesinger, like Kissinger, was a former academic who joined the Nixon administration as an economist. He briefly ran the CIA before becoming secretary of defence in July 1973. Like Kissinger, he could be caustic, arrogant and alienating, even when he was right. He said that the French at least were 'self-assured', but the West Germans were 'pitiful'. In 1965, they had established formal diplomatic relations with Israel, at the cost of ties to several Middle Eastern countries. It had taken several years to win the Arabs back. Now the West Germans had discovered that Israeli ships had entered their waters as part of the American resupply effort after the outbreak of war. America had implicated them in their support for Israel without their consent. When the morose West German ambassador skulked over to the State Department to complain, Kissinger waved him off. The Germans were missing the bigger story: the Soviet radicalisation of the Middle East. Time and again, the Americans had tried and failed to stake out common positions with the Europeans. Now the countries of the West were 'bleeding ourselves slowly and unspectacularly'. The usually unsentimental Kissinger said he was 'struck by a profound sadness' at the collapse of a once treasured alliance.[28]

On the evening of 8 October, Vice President Spiro Agnew went to the Oval Office to resign. He had taken kickbacks for construction projects while he was governor of Maryland and would be accepting a plea deal of three years' probation, and a $10,000 fine for tax evasion. The administration was not ready to deal with simultaneous foreign and domestic crisis. When the British prime minister, Edward Heath, called and asked to speak to Nixon on the night of 11 October, Kissinger refused to connect him, because the president was 'loaded'.

Watergate was consuming Nixon. He was trying to resist demands for the White House tape recordings which he knew contained the evidence to destroy his presidency, the proof that he had approved a cover-up of the burglary. The previous July, six days after the break-in, he had spoken to his then chief of staff, H. R. Haldeman, about asking the CIA to stop the FBI's investigation as a national security matter. It was a flagrant, criminal attempt to obstruct justice. There was plenty of other material on the tapes to smear Nixon, his profanity, vindictiveness, willingness to pay hush money and engage in the dirtiest tricks against his opponents. But for a president to obstruct justice in this way was a resigning matter. Nixon's lawyers fought their way up to the US Court of Appeals for the District of Columbia Circuit. On 12 October, the court ruled that Nixon must hand over the tapes to Archibald Cox, the special prosecutor appointed by the Justice Department to investigate Watergate. The same day, Nixon appointed Gerald Ford, the house minority leader, as his new vice president. Months of political drama were now being condensed into days.

Despite the court's ruling, the White House kept squirming over the tapes. It offered to provide written summaries of the recordings. When Cox rejected the offer, Nixon demanded that the attorney general, Elliot Richardson, fire him. Richardson refused, and resigned. Richardson's deputy, William Ruckelshaus, refused and resigned as well. It was left to the number three at the Justice Department, Robert Bork, to fulfil Nixon's desperate request. The press called that night of 20 October the 'Saturday Night Massacre'.

Kissinger, meanwhile, was pursuing a ceasefire in the Middle East. The fighting had reached the point he had been waiting for. The Israelis, with American help, had battled back successfully, but the Arabs were not yet defeated. If the war stopped now, the Arabs would have been checked but not humiliated, and the Israelis would still feel insecure enough to negotiate a long-term peace. On 21 October, he flew to Moscow to discuss the details with the Soviets and then on to Tel Aviv. The next day, the UN announced a ceasefire between the Egyptians and Israelis. Gaddafi warned the Europeans that if they voted for the ceasefire, he would cut off their oil, as he had done to the United

States three days before. 'We are quite ready to do without oil revenues,' he said. 'Three quarters of my people live in tents and their needs are extremely modest.' The vote passed with European support and Gaddafi did nothing, his once strident voice drowned out by larger events.

The ceasefire was supposed to start at 16.52 GMT on 22 October, but the fighting continued. The Israelis were determined to keep strengthening their position. In order to get a better idea of what was happening, the United States sent an SR-71 Blackbird, its most advanced spy plane, on a 12,000-mile, eleven-hour, round-trip mission. The Blackbird was a third the length of a football field, built of composite material that absorbed radar, and could fly at supersonic speeds. Its cameras surveyed 100,000 square miles in an hour. When it reached Egypt, it flew down the Suez Canal past Cairo, veered over the battle lines in the Sinai, turned north towards the Golan Heights, then did a U-turn to retrace its route. Back in Rochester, New York, a special wing of a Kodak plant was equipped to process its film.

Kissinger arrived back in Washington on the morning of 24 October to hear of the renewed fighting, and to find the administration in further disarray. The news was dominated by the aftershocks of the Saturday Night Massacre, and the House of Representatives was preparing to discuss impeaching a president for the first time in over a century. The detailed images from the Blackbird showed him how much land the Israelis had taken since 22 October. They had surrounded Egypt's Third Army, cutting it off from supplies, and trapping it on the wrong side of the Suez Canal. There was no longer any doubt about which side controlled the war.

That night, word reached the White House that the Soviet Union had mobilised airborne troops to support the Syrians. It was seven hours ahead in Israel, and if the Soviets were going to attack, they would do so at first light. The US faced the prospect of going to war.

Nixon was drinking heavily to cope with his depression. He told Kissinger that the stress of Watergate had become so much he thought he might die.[29] Now, as the president lay drunk and medicated in his private quarters, Kissinger and the national security team made the decision to raise the military preparedness of US forces worldwide to DEFCON 3, one step short of imminent nuclear war. American ships of the Sixth Fleet sailed from across the Atlantic and Mediterranean towards Crete where they assembled. Six thousand combat-ready marines braced for amphibious landings in the war zone; helicopters, fighters and attack aircraft waited on carriers for the order to attack; destroyers with long range sonar and torpedoes scanned for underwater threats; store ships raced back and forth delivering food and supplies.[30] The scale of the armada dwarfed the Soviet naval presence in the eastern Mediterranean and gave Washington a range of choices, from simply showing the flag to a full-blown intervention.

By morning in Washington, both sides had backed down. Nixon's incapacity had been exposed. America's NATO allies were angry not to have been consulted, but as Admiral Thomas Moorer, the chairman of the joint chiefs of staff, put it: 'Those bastards never get up before about ten o'clock, and they wanted us to go around knocking on each door in all the NATO countries. Well, hell, by that time it was ridiculous.'[31]

13

The Shuttle

High up in the Hijaz mountains overlooking the plains of Mecca and Medina, shepherds in rough cloaks carrying wooden staves still strode through the streets of Taif. The town petered out into fields and orchards. Yamani could speak frankly here far from the formality of the royal households of Jeddah and Riyadh. Jim Akins had just arrived from Washington, promoted from director of fuels and energy at the State Department, to be the ambassador to Saudi Arabia. He had been appointed a month before the embargo. Akins was physically imposing, tall, with thick dark hair swept back over his collar. He could seem brusque and severe to some, reassuringly confident and correct to others. He spoke fluent Arabic, and there was no diplomat better informed about the intersection of politics and oil. The Saudis trusted him.

At the end of October, Yamani invited Akins to spend Eid-al-Fitr, the end of Ramadan, a day of celebration and fasting, at his home in Taif, close to Faisal's summer palace. He told the ambassador of his deep distress that the United States had ignored the king's warnings of an embargo, and was now sending its weapons to 'break the bones of the Arabs'.[1] The Americans seemed to assume that the economic benefits of dealing with them rendered their Middle East policy irrelevant. The fact was, the Saudis were so angry that the American companies lining up for Saudi contracts and investments were wasting their time. Yamani scarcely mentioned the rights of the Palestinians. What mattered to the Saudis and Faisal was to see an Arab flag back flying over Jerusalem, and the Americans had given no sign they were going to help make that happen.

On 27 October, Egypt and Israel had agreed a new ceasefire. This time the fighting actually stopped, and Kissinger wrote to Faisal requesting a meeting. 'The moment now seems right for a discussion between us on the implementation of Security Council Resolution 242 and a just and durable peace in the Middle East. As the president has told your foreign minister, he is prepared to engage in an effort in this direction but would not want to proceed without the benefit of your views.'

Resolution 242 was the United Nations Security Council's response to the expansion of Israel's borders during the Six Day War. It required the 'establishment of a just and lasting peace in the Middle East' and the application of two principles. The first was the 'withdrawal of Israel armed forces from territories occupied in the recent conflict'. The second was the 'termination of all claims or states of belligerency and respect for and acknowledgement of the sovereignty, territorial integrity and political independence of every State in the area and their right to live in peace within secure and recognized boundaries free from threats or acts of force.'

For Faisal, and many other Arabs, there were two major flaws in the text. In the first principle, 'territories' is not preceded by a definite article. If it were 'the territories' that would suggest all the land taken by Israel in 1967. Just 'territories' left the matter vague. It gave Israel room to haggle over the extent and terms of its withdrawal. The second flaw was the absence of any mention of the Palestinians. They did not constitute a 'State in the area', and the closest the resolution comes to mentioning them is further down, when it affirms the necessity of a 'just settlement of the refugee problem.' For all of its flaws, Resolution 242 remained the reference point for negotiations about Israel's borders and the creation of a Palestinian state. Competing interpretations of it would torture negotiators for decades to come, leaving oil and Israel on a permanent collision course.

Faisal did not respond immediately to Kissinger's letter. Akins had only just arrived, but now he set to work persuading the king that a meeting might be useful. Kissinger, he told Faisal, was Jewish but not a Zionist. He had taught history at Harvard, and saw his role in historical terms. He wanted to go down as an advocate for American not Israeli interests. After three days, Faisal wrote back to Kissinger, inviting him to Riyadh, while invoking his familiar themes. 'We, in agreeing to your wish, hope the results of this visit will prove beneficial for the future of this region and bring to it security and stability – it having been prey to chaos and instability since the founding of Israel, and fertile ground for communist principles which the region had not previously known.'

Kissinger's visit was scheduled for 8 November. The day before, Akins went to the palace in Riyadh to present his ambassadorial credentials formally. The chief of royal protocol called him in. He was evidently embarrassed, and it took several cups of coffee and a rambling political discussion before he got to the point. During the last major visit of a senior US official, when Vice President Spiro Agnew came, the Saudis had hosted a large group of aides and diplomats in government guest houses. 'We know they didn't mean to do anything wrong and we know Americans like to collect souvenirs,' the chief told Akins, 'but the Vice President's staff and the journalists stripped the government guest houses of all their silver. All the crystal vases and drinking glasses. Even the dinner place settings. It's not that we can't afford to replace them, but everything is crested and made especially for us. It takes about six months to replace missing items. Do you think you might be able to explain the problem to our American guests?'

Akins sent a cable back to the State Department, warning against a repeat performance. 'Saudi Arabia is still a very traditional Muslim country, and the impact of such petty thefts is greater than it would be elsewhere. (A thief who is a two- or three-time loser in Saudi Arabia has his limbs lopped off, starting with the right hand, for each successive arrest.) We hope therefore that any souvenir hunters in Secretary's party might confine their activities to shopping trips through the *suq*.'

He also called Nixon's chief of security who warned the travelling party: 'There will be an inventory after you have left your quarters. If anything is missing there will be a search of your baggage at the airport. If anything belonging to the guest house is found you will be removed from the official party and turned over to the Saudis for appropriate punishment.

Over the past year, the Saudis had listened to American officials, from the president down, saying they were committed to an early, permanent settlement to the Israel–Palestine situation. They had believed them until October, when the US had thrown its political and military might so visibly behind Israel. Now they were waiting for the Americans to show they were serious again. Words would no longer be enough. Faisal needed to see action towards restoring Jerusalem to the Arabs, or at least Old Jerusalem to an Arab state; the creation of a Palestinian entity in Gaza and the West Bank; and the return of other occupied lands by Israel. Without obvious and immediate progress towards 'justice', in Faisal's words, Saudi Arabia would continue to use its oil to apply economic pressure on the West, and the rest of the Arab world would be happy to resume fighting.

'We have quoted – without success – your earlier statements on being able to work no miracles,' Akins wrote to Kissinger. 'Saudis are attaching immense importance to your visit and if they cannot have miracles, they are prepared to settle for instantaneous results.' The schedule drawn up by the palace included a light dinner, followed by private talks with the king.

After Akins had presented his credentials and received his brief, he went to a welcoming party at Yamani's apartment. There were women present, and alcohol for the guests.

On 7 November, Nixon addressed the nation about the looming energy shortages. He warned that the supply of petroleum to the United States would soon fall 10 per cent short of its demands, and possibly more. Americans needed to use less energy, 'that means less heat, less electricity, less gasoline,' until new sources of energy could be found to reduce the dependence on foreign oil. He asked Americans to lower the thermostats in their homes at least six degrees, to achieve a national daytime average of 68°F (about 20°C). 'Incidentally,' he noted, 'my doctor tells me that in a temperature of 66 to 68 degrees, you are really more healthy than when it is 75 to 78, if that is any comfort.' He had ordered federal government buildings, including the White House, to go even further, turning down the heat to 66 to 68 degrees. He had asked state governors to reduce highway speed limits to 50 miles per hour. He called on his audience to show the 'spirit and determination that have always graced the American character' to reduce energy use. Earlier in the year, George Shultz had said of the need for energy conservation, '[W]e have met the enemy and it is us'.[2]

Nixon also said he would be taking measures to increase the domestic supply of energy, everything from loosening environmental regulations and pushing for the construction of the

Alaska pipeline to accelerating the licensing of nuclear plants. Nixon called his plan 'Project Independence'. He compared it to the Manhattan Project, which led to America's first atomic bomb, and the Apollo project which put Neil Armstrong on the moon. Nixon's ambition was for America to meet its energy needs from its own resources by 1980. It was a slop bucket of measures, from the mundane to the hyperbolic, but it was all the government had for now.

As Kissinger departed Washington, he received his final instructions: persuade Faisal to ease the embargo, then invite him to Washington right away for a big announcement with Nixon. He cabled back that inviting Faisal to Washington would hand the Saudis an unnecessary PR coup. While they were at it, he wrote sarcastically to Nixon's chief of staff, why not arrange an 'ecumenical joint communique at presidential tete-a-tete with Faisal and Golda in a New York synagogue just at Christmas Hanukkah season'[3]

Kissinger now began an epic run of 'shuttle diplomacy', the practice of flying back and forth between parties in a negotiation to nudge them forward. Each day, he woke up at 7 a.m. and read his updated briefing books, and any telegrams and intelligence reports that had come in overnight. His plane landed in some foreign capital in the morning, and he spent the day in meetings, followed by a formal dinner. Afterwards, his staff drafted a report of the day's discussions to send to Washington, and updated the action checklist for the following day. The repeated overnight refreshing of Kissinger's plans and actions, the constant accumulation of ideas, relationships and resources, kept the shuttle in motion. The staff called it 'thinking while flying'. At each stage in the negotiations, Kissinger wrote a report to his interlocutors. He said essentially the same thing in every report, but made sure each one had its own first and last paragraph to give the recipient the sense that he was talking only to them.[4] A large and rowdy press pack travelled with him, to report home and burgeon his reputation.

As he flew to Saudi Arabia on 8 November, his flight plan was carefully routed so that he took off from another Arab country, Jordan. His deputy, Joseph Sisco, was coming straight from talks in Tel Aviv with Golda Meir. The Saudis advised that no plane taking off from Israel would be allowed to land in Riyadh. The first act of diplomacy on this mission was to beg the palace for an exemption.[5]

Sadat warned Kissinger that Faisal would talk about communists and Jews.[6] The king was convinced that they had conspired to destabilise the Middle East. Two years before, British and French newspapers reported that his bigotry had taken a dark turn, becoming more hateful and paranoid as he grew older. He told an audience of journalists at a meeting of Islamic foreign ministers in Jeddah that Jewish conspirators pursued their goals through the spread of communism, and organisations like the Freemasons and the Rotary Club.[7] To an Egyptian interviewer, he repeated the medieval claim that Jews used the blood of Christian children to bake Passover bread, and said that he had personally heard of a case in Paris a couple of years earlier of five infants being killed and drained of their blood for this purpose.[8] On a visit to Nigeria, he said that the enemies of Islam were 'the Jews and the infidels who are the authors of all evil in the world.'[9] He considered Judaism a 'vast wilderness' which took 'heresy as guidance and indiscreet behaviour as forthright conduct. High morals in their opinion are to be immersed in the mire of corruptions.'[10] He had also taken to keeping copies of *The Protocols of the Elders of Zion* on a shelf outside his office to thrust on visitors. *The Protocols*, which were first published in 1903, purported to be the minutes of a meeting of Jewish elders who were plotting to take over the world. In fact they were a collection of the vilest antisemitic conspiracy theories cobbled together by a Russian journalist. In 1968, Faisal was reported to have funded the printing of 300,000 copies in various languages to stimulate unity among Muslim countries.[11]

As Kissinger approached the Kingdom, he went back to the press section and cracked jokes to ease his jitters. This was his first time in the Middle East. He was the first Jewish secretary of state to visit this bastion of reactionary Islam. 'Only WASPS can disembark here,' he told the reporters. 'I'd like to enjoy a little night life with you fellows in Riyadh, but I understand it starts at four in the afternoon and ends an hour later.'[12]

Omar Saqqaf greeted Kissinger at the airport, and held his hand as he introduced him to the rest of the welcoming party. The physical attentions of Arab leaders, the long embraces, kisses and hand-holding, became a running joke for Kissinger. At an event in Washington that winter, he said that he had to refrain from kissing the chairman of the organisation hosting the event, because 'after traveling two months through the Middle East I kiss every man in sight.'[13] When he embraced Golda Meir, she joked that she was surprised as she had only ever seen him hugging men.

The two foreign ministers spoke to the press in a room at the airport, and drank small cups of jolting, bitter coffee. The secretary had barely slept since leaving Washington three days earlier. When he arrived at the Red Palace in Riyadh, where Faisal worked, he was struck by its size. It was modelled after a nineteenth-century British official's residence in India, and built for Ibn Saud by his favourite contractor, Muhammad bin Laden. It was tall, sprawling, and bulging in the middle with verandas. Its gardens were a welcome patch of greenery in the drab capital. Faisal's welcome did nothing to allay Kissinger's anxiety. Two tall guards carrying swords walked ahead of him into a vast hall, where dozens of men in black robes, white headdresses and sunglasses sat along the walls. This was the friendliest group they could put together, the palace had assured Akins, including the younger, Western-educated members of the family. Faisal sat in an armchair on a dais at the far end, with a white telephone beside him. As he rose, all the princes did the same. As Kissinger approached, Faisal took a slight step forward, a minimal gesture of courtesy.

At dinner, when Faisal spoke the table fell silent. When Kissinger spoke, everyone resumed their conversations. Faisal told Kissinger that Jews and communists were conspiring to destroy the world. That Israel was the Bolsheviks' way of forcing America and the Arabs apart. Kissinger did not try to argue, but noted that the king's views, whatever else he thought of them, served Saudi Arabia's immediate tactical interests. Loathing the communists pleased America. Loathing Israel pleased the radical Arab militants, who threatened the Saudi monarchy.[14] As Kissinger left the dinner, he whispered to Akins, who had been sitting a few seats away, 'That was your idea of light dinner conversation?'

Later that evening, Kissinger and Faisal met with just their closest aides. Kissinger had been briefed on the dos and don'ts for a meeting with the king by the embassy's public affairs officer and translator, Isa Sabbagh. Faisal had a tendency to lecture his visitors, and Kissinger would have to accept the position of a student listening to a professor. If the secretary had any doubt about what to say next, he could fill the silence with 'Your Majesty . . .' There would be no jokes, or even much levity, but in case there was, the correct response was appreciation rather than guffaws. There would certainly be no kissing on the cheeks, as there was with Sadat. Finally, if Kissinger did at any point need to cross his legs, which was generally considered rude, Sabbagh advised him not to do it 'violently showing your voluminous thighs.'[15]

As the secretary's party waited for the king, Sisco told Akins not to join them. Akins said he had done all the work to set up this meeting and threatened to resign if he was not let in. Kissinger soon scuttled over. 'Where did you get the idea that you would not attend the meeting? Of course you will attend.' The relationship between the two men was already starting to founder. Kissinger's team resented Akins's closeness to the Saudis, and what they perceived to be his arrogance in explaining their motives.

For all of his intimidating theatricals, Faisal had a deep and very modern affection for America. He knew more English than he let on, was fascinated by America's economy and its technology, and had sent most of his children to American schools and colleges. During the 1950s and 1960s, his boys attended the Hun School and Lawrenceville in New Jersey, and went on to Princeton, Georgetown and Swarthmore, as well as Oxford and Cambridge.[16] They had rowed crew and played soccer. One of his daughters went to Wellesley. When his son Saud told him he wanted to drop out of Princeton, Faisal took time out of a trip to Washington to visit him at college and persuade him to stay, for his own self-esteem, and the family's honour.[17] The generation of Saudi princes who spoke fluent English and moved effortlessly among the American and European ruling classes were Faisal's legacy.

But the version of Faisal who met Kissinger that night was not the concerned college Dad. The man peering through clouds of incense was the implacable king, with his frozen sneer, who listened more than he spoke, picked lint off his burnoose when he was bored, and knew precisely the range and limits of his power. Kissinger opened by saying that he understood the king's frustration. Successive presidents had promised to resolve the dispute between Israel and the Palestinians. John F. Kennedy had written to Faisal in 1963 about the need for a just settlement. Lyndon Johnson told the world that no changes in the Middle East would be tolerated if they were brought about by force. Kissinger's predecessor, William Rogers, had said repeatedly that the United States considered a peaceful settlement a return to the borders before 1967. But nothing had happened. Israel's expansion had been tolerated. After the Yom Kippur attacks, it had received decisive military support from Washington. Kissinger understood how dispiriting it must have been for Faisal to threaten repeatedly to use oil as a political weapon, only to be ignored.

But that was the past. Now America needed Saudi Arabia's help. Nixon wanted Faisal to support a peace conference to resolve the October war, and to stem the rise of anti-Arab feeling in the West by lifting the embargo.

Faisal, in his reedy, mournful voice, launched into his usual rant about the communist-Zionist conspiracy, before concluding that more than anything he wanted the Israelis out of Jerusalem, and the civil and military administration of the Old City to be placed under an Arab authority. If the Saudis blinked first and lifted the embargo, he said, the Arabs who had joined them would accuse them of giving in to American pressure. There was only one clear solution, and that was for Israel to withdraw to its pre-1967 borders. Kissinger argued that it was impossible for the United States to take a position unfavourable to Israel, especially not before the start of peace negotiations. But if the embargo were lifted, he promised to devote American efforts to a 'just settlement' between Arabs and Israelis. Faisal had heard this from Americans before, and been disappointed. Unless Israel withdrew, the embargo stayed. There was nothing more to be said. Behind the courtesy lay confrontation.

After three hours with Faisal, Kissinger returned to his guest house. Prince Fahd, Faisal's younger brother and minister of the interior, and Omar Saqqaf came to see him. They told him not to take Faisal too literally. The Saudis were looking for a way out of this confrontation with the United States. They wanted the oil flowing again, but they needed a pretext, some sign that Nixon could orchestrate a settlement including Israel's withdrawal from Arab occupied territories.

Yamani made the same point in a message to Kissinger and a downbeat phone call to his deputy, Brent Scowcroft. He told Scowcroft that Faisal was still 'so terribly angry' with the United States. He had been ignored, belittled and played. His confidence in America's friendship had been drained. He hated that the relationship had turned so sour. But there had to be a price.

Kissinger left Riyadh the next morning, his mind already drifting home. He cabled Scowcroft, a brisk, self-effacing Air Force officer: 'Would you please see if Nancy can come down next weekend? I would also appreciate your having someone obtain tickets for the Redskins game on Sunday.'

Shortly after his return, Kissinger hosted a group of oil executives at the State Department. He was as brassy in Washington as he was deferential in Riyadh. Faisal was 'old and stiff-necked', and under so much pressure from Arab radicals, he was 'about to have a nervous breakdown.' It had been 'anguishing' to meet him. Fortunately, Kissinger had been assured by several of those closest to the king that he felt awful about the embargo, particularly its impact on the US armed forces which depended on Saudi oil, and was closer to easing it than he seemed.[18]

That same day, he was even blunter in a national security meeting in the White House. 'It is ridiculous that the civilized world is held up by 8 million savages.' Faisal, he believed, had initiated the embargo to get ahead of the radicals in his own country, and prove to them that he was no friend to the United States. But now he was stuck with nothing in return, and pleaded: 'Can't you help me? Can't you give me Jerusalem?' Kissinger said he told the king that it would look to the world as if America was giving in to Arab blackmail. But he promised help. 'Give us time and we will do it.'[19]

In Riyadh, Fahd told Akins that after Kissinger left, Faisal called a meeting of his family and senior advisers. They persuaded him to consider easing the embargo if there were a schedule for Israel to withdraw within its 1967 boundaries. Just a schedule. Even one that was only promised privately by Israel to the United States. But it had to include Israel's withdrawal from Jerusalem. That was non-negotiable. Nixon and Kissinger would then have to promise America would exert every effort to achieve a just peace in the Middle East. If Israel dragged its feet, or the United States stopped trying, the embargo would be reimposed.[20]

It was just a glimmer of a possible deal, but a glimmer nonetheless.

14

Choked with Oil

Golda Meir arrived swinging for a meeting of the Socialist International, a group of world socialist leaders in London. She had requested they meet at short notice after the European Economic Community issued a joint statement on the Arab-Israeli war. The statement, released on 6 November, called for Israel to withdraw from the land it took in 1967, and to recognise the 'legitimate rights of the Palestinians', as conditions for peace with the Arabs. It was the first time the EEC had issued such a unified statement on an important diplomatic matter. The Europeans needed Arab oil far more than the United States did, and were willing to abandon Israel and appease the Arabs to get it.

For fifty-five minutes, Meir berated socialist leaders from twenty countries gathered at the Churchill, a rackety old hotel near Marble Arch in London. She understood Europe's anxieties about oil. But this did not justify the joint statement, nor Europe's petty refusal to let American planes bringing supplies to Israel refuel at their continental bases. That day, 11 November, Egypt and Israel had formalised their October ceasefire at a ceremony at Kilometre 101 on the Cairo-to-Suez road. Achieving peace was hard and Israel had suffered terribly in the war. It had lost more than twice the number of men that the United States had lost in ten years in Vietnam. 'Israel is a small country and needs her friends,' she said. Europe had a 'Munich attitude,' appeasing the Arabs just as they had appeased Hitler in 1938 after he seized the Sudetenland. At the end of her speech, no one applauded, and no one wanted to respond.[1] Finally, a single voice rang out, suspected to be Harold Wilson, the resolutely pro-Israel leader of the British Labour Party. 'Of course they can't talk. Their throats are choked with oil.'[2]

Britain's problems were getting worse. As the value of their wages fell due to inflation, Britain's coal miners stopped working overtime shifts. Coal production fell by a half. Britain faced a miserable winter. Edward Heath would soon instruct that businesses could now only use electricity on three consecutive days each week. Television broadcasts stopped at 10.30 p.m.

As part of his tour of oil-consuming countries, Yamani arrived in London at the end of November to explain OAPEC's position. Britain's attitude to the Middle East remained proprietorial and patronising, coloured by its imperial history. The Foreign Office briefing on Yamani described him as 'of no mean ability . . . suave and shrewd', noting that he was reasonably well disposed towards Britain given he had three children at school there. He was 'Harvard educated, sophisticated and conceited, regarded as highly versed in Arab literature and culture. Not an intellectual or academic, he is sharp-witted, with a better grasp of politics than commerce. Theatrical, enjoys scoring points in debate . . . Highly ambitious both for himself and for the Saudi position in the Gulf and the Arab world.'[3] Some in the Saudi royal family were uneasy about a commoner of such ability and character representing them abroad, and Yamani was conscious of managing his profile. The British ambassador to Riyadh noted that when *Petroleum Intelligence Weekly* described him as the Henry Kissinger of Saudi Arabia, he asked its editor, 'Do you want to destroy me?'[4] Critically, he had Faisal's confidence. *The Guardian* called him the 'most menacing Eastern emissary to arrive in Europe since Genghis Khan.'[5] Shortly before Yamani arrived in London, Faisal bared his own fangs by questioning Israel's claim to Jerusalem, and the importance of the Wailing Wall to Jews. 'The Wailing Wall is a structure they weep against, and they have no historic right to it,' he told a Lebanese interviewer. 'Another wall can be built for them to weep against.'[6]

Yamani's message to Britain was clear, and unsentimental. The Arabs had been demanding that Israel withdraw from the territories it took in 1967, and the West had listened to them like people 'listening to a Sunday sermon': they forgot about it the moment they left church.[7] While the Arabs waited for a deal in the Middle East, the Americans had engaged China, pursued détente with the Soviet Union, and Europe had worked towards a union which would forestall the possibility of another world war. The Middle East had been ignored as too difficult and irrelevant to the rest of the world. The Arabs understood that the industrialised countries needed their oil. This was not the start of some escalating challenge to outlast each other. It was simpler than that. The Arabs would draw up a timetable for the phased increase in oil production once the Israelis drew up a timetable to withdraw.[8]

The foreign secretary, Sir Alec Douglas-Home, a Conservative aristocrat of the old school, tried to appeal to Yamani's sense of loyalty and honour. Home had renounced his hereditary earldom in 1963 to serve briefly as prime minister, and wore his power lightly. On a sunny morning in Luxembourg, before a meeting of the European Council of Ministers, he went into the British ambassador's garden and, in full view of the passing locals, removed his suit jacket, his tie, and finally his shirt, and lay out in a deck chair.[9] In retirement, he would write a book on his sporting life, *Border Reflections: Chiefly on the Arts of Shooting and Fishing*. Over lunch in the Foreign Office, he emphasised to

Yamani that in 1970, Britain had changed its policy to oppose Israel's occupation of the Arab territories, and eventually brought most of Western Europe along with it. And this was the thanks they got. When he visited his constituency, he said, people could not understand why the Arabs had cut off oil when Britain was in a stronger position than ever to deliver exactly what they wanted. At the very moment Western Europe should be focused on reaching a settlement on the Middle East, OAPEC had ensured 'we were all being distracted and compelled to look at whether we were going to be cold, unemployed, and poor.'[10]

Yamani offered the British scraps. As a friendly country, Britain would not be specifically targeted by further production cuts. It would continue to receive a volume of oil each month calculated as the average of the first nine months of 1973, or September 1973, whichever was greater. Any more would have to be taken from someone else's allocation, which would poison relations with that country. Britain would have to make do. One of Heath's senior advisers, Lord Rothschild, told him 'the party line should be, "Squeal, Fiddle, Ration" and carry on as before.'[11]

Jim Schlesinger, the defence secretary, was now urging serious consideration of a military operation to protect America's interests in Saudi Arabia. He believed that military power was essential to the United States' control of global events.[12] He envisioned the Marines swooping into the desert and seizing control of the oil installations. 'He is insane,' Kissinger told Haig, the White House chief of staff. 'These fellows in there at Defense – they are crazy.'[13]

But by late November, word had reached Faisal, who was rumoured to have instructed that all oil facilities in Saudi Arabia be set with explosives. If the Americans invaded, the mines would be detonated, and the US Army would seize control of an inferno. Word came back to the White House via the oil industry's friends in government, including George H. W. Bush, then chairman of the Republican National Committee, that Nixon needed to reassure the anxious Saudis that the talk of invasion was groundless.[14]

Unfortunately, it was not. The Pentagon's oil shortages were rapidly becoming so serious that it was considering standing down operational forces. Despite cutting oil consumption by one-fifth as the war in Vietnam wound down, the military still depended heavily on foreign refineries and their petroleum products.[15] In the Pacific, Singapore had cut off US access to its refineries, hoping to avoid the same fate as Rotterdam, the great Dutch refinery complex which had suffered due to the Arab embargo on oil sales to the Netherlands. This had a major impact on American military activity in Vietnam, Cambodia and Thailand. Exxon, the military's largest supplier in many parts of the world, had yielded to Arab pressure and cut back sharply on its deliveries. At many offshore refineries, the Department of Defense had to bargain for dwindling supplies of crude along with everyone else.[16]

Kissinger teased the idea of military action as a last resort. If the oil shortages threatened to break the US economy, he said he might consider a regional invasion, starting in Abu Dhabi.[17] He floated the possibility of invasion at a press conference on 21 November: 'If pressures continue unreasonably and indefinitely, then the United States will have to consider what countermeasures it may have to take.'[18]

Schlesinger was much less cautious. He told his NATO peers that the US 'did not – repeat – not intend to be driven to the wall in this situation,'[19] and asked them to stand up to the Arabs. In the UK, a cluster of Old Etonians stared at the problem, like cricketers looking up at the sky for rain. Lord

Cromer, the ambassador to Washington, advised the foreign minister, Sir Alec Douglas-Home, that Schlesinger's aggressive tone towards Lord Carrington, the defence minister, was more than sabre rattling. Schlesinger warned Cromer that the Europeans' 'overt acquiescence in Arab bullying' had left them vulnerable to more rough treatment in the future. The fact of the 'industrialized nations being continuously submitted to whims of the underpopulated, under-developed countries, particularly of the Middle East,' obliged the US to consider using force.

Cromer was a robust, pragmatic English aristocrat from the Baring banking family. King George V was the sponsor at his christening, and he had been the youngest ever governor of the Bank of England, at forty-two. Schlesinger's pomposity surprised him. The defence secretary asked why the British had not 'finished the job properly at the time of Suez,' and said Cromer's grandfather would have been mortified by Europe's spinelessness. The 1st Earl of Cromer had been Britain's consul general in Egypt at the end of the nineteenth century, and believed the inferior Arab world needed a good, hard civilising by the West. The 3rd Earl replied that this was no longer the nineteenth century 'when gunboats were in fashionable use.' He wrote back to London that he found Schlesinger's venom 'worrying'.[20] As a last resort, Cromer speculated, the Americans were considering landing two brigades, one in Saudi Arabia, the other in Kuwait, followed by a greater force capable of holding the oilfields for ten years.[21]

The threats of military action stiffened the Saudis' resolve. At the end of November, Yamani appeared on television in Copenhagen. Talking as gently as if he were reading a bedtime story, he said American military action would be 'suicide'. Saudi Arabia would simply blow up the most sensitive parts of its oil infrastructure. Rebuilding it would take years. 'You think Europe or Japan or the United States can survive with this?' Europe's economy 'will definitely collapse all of a sudden.' Saudi Arabia, meanwhile, could easily survive if its production was cut by 80 per cent. 'You know what will happen then? The barrel of crude, instead of being sold at, let's say, $3.50 or $4 from Ras Tanura, Saudi Arabia, it will be sold at $15 or $20. As a matter of fact, we'll get more income from a 20 per cent production than from our present level of production.' He paused and smiled. 'Law of supply and demand.'[22]

That winter, the United Nations peacekeepers appeared on the streets of Cairo, tall Scandinavian men in blue berets assigned to oversee and implement the ceasefire with Israel. Egyptians welcomed them as a sign that Egypt was finally being taken seriously by the world. Sadat's war had achieved its purpose.[23] In Washington, bravado was curdling into anxiety.

Kissinger's meeting in Riyadh convinced him that he could not allow the Saudis to link the lifting of the embargo to specific terms in the peace talks. The talks required the utmost sensitivity, not pressure from the religious radicals who influenced Faisal. But he had to give the king something, starting with an acknowledgement that the embargo had changed the course of events. The Arabs had shown their power. Kissinger also had to persuade him that his next best move was to win back the American public, who blamed the Arabs for the fuel shortages. America's friendship alone was worth ending the embargo.

This message had to be delivered directly to Faisal, and the most senior of his princes, Fahd and Sultan, the latter the minister of defence and aviation. Yamani lunched with the king more often than any member of the court,[24] but Kissinger considered him a 'ribbon clerk', transmitting messages sent by others.[25]

On 5 December, the ribbon clerk arrived in Washington. He

laid out the Saudis' position which had been explained to Kissinger now through multiple channels. They wanted Israel to withdraw from the territories occupied since 1967. The timetable for restoring production would correspond to a timetable for withdrawal. As for the embargo against the United States, the Saudis wanted the US to give them a reason which they could defend to the Arab public. A reason that did not smack of defeat to Israel.

Kissinger unloaded on him. 'You can get from the Europeans any amount of rhetoric you want, but they cannot deliver. The Europeans can make speeches, but cannot assure political progress in the Middle East.' Yamani had not mentioned the Europeans. 'Only we can give you a settlement.' He said that the United States' 'fundamental motive' for its military support of Israel was to prevent the Soviets from gaining dominance in the region. In any case, the US had already done the Arabs a huge favour by saving Egypt's Third Army from defeat, and forcing a ceasefire before Israel's imminent victory. Now he was doing his best to meet the Arabs' expectations of Resolution 242. If he said anything too concrete in public, he would rouse Israel's supporters in the United States and blow up the peace talks before they happened. He had given Faisal his word. So why, he asked, 'should we be blackmailed while we are in good faith trying to help meet Arab aspirations?' It was essential that America choose the timing for the peace, its terms and its implementation.[26]

Yamani said what Kissinger had not. That the reason for the embargo was America's overt military and economic support for Israel. What the Saudis wanted now was peace, and the 'fulfillment of the previous promises we received from the U.S.' 'But you never had promises in the past,' Kissinger replied. 'What you had were assurances of general objectives.' It was the kind of weaselly nuance which made people mistrust him. Yamani kept pressing on Resolution 242. How did the US interpret it? Kissinger pleaded for understanding by turning on a shared foe: Golda Meir, who had visited Washington in early November.

'When the Israeli Prime Minister was here, we had an unbelievably hard time. I spent three nights in this room with her. I can assure you if I have to spend three nights with a lady, I would rather not do it with her.' The Israelis craved security, the Arabs wanted the occupied lands back. This was going to be a long, difficult haggle, without the US making controversial commitments. But, he said, 'there is no dispute about the need for massive Israeli withdrawal.'

'We do not know what "massive Israeli withdrawal" means,' said Yamani.

'It involves the issue of establishing a final frontier,' said Kissinger.

Yamani had reason to feel disengaged from Kissinger's endless sophistry. During his travels through Europe, he had seen the effects of the embargo. People were losing their jobs and concerned about staying warm through the winter. Bicycle sales were up sharply. Sunday driving was banned in many countries. Italians made the best of their car-less days, digging out scooters, and roller skates. In Holland, people rode horses and had picnics on empty highways. But no amount of good cheer and making do could gloss over the fact that the continent was facing the worst recession since World War Two.

When Yamani was growing up in Mecca, Israel did not exist. When he left to study law in the United States, his interest was in commerce, and his country's economic development. He had founded the College of Petroleum and Minerals in Dhahran to teach young Saudis how to manage their greatest asset. The newspaper columns he wrote, which attracted the interest of

Faisal, were about the evolution of Saudi law to meet the needs of a modernising country. The prize he had always pursued was Saudi Arabia's economic security beyond oil. That meant investment and industrialisation, with the West's help. He could see the moment when the last reservoir went dry, and was determined that the Saudis not regret wasting their gift. It was a point that risked being lost in all the talk of frontiers, fighting and UN resolutions, but he had mentioned it almost in passing in an interview in Germany. If the West wanted Saudi Arabia to produce as much oil as it needed, there was a very simple answer. 'Industrialize Saudi Arabia. Then we will give you as much oil as you need.'[27]

The US Sixth Fleet, deployed in the Mediterranean, and the Seventh Fleet in the Western Pacific, were considered essential weapons of the Cold War. But they were running out of fuel. Frank Jungers was called back to Washington to visit the Department of Defense. The deputy secretary, Bill Clements, was a Texan and a former oilman. He asked Jungers if there was any way to persuade the Saudis to make an exemption for the navy. This could not be through an official, high-level negotiation. In public, America was calling for the consuming countries to stand together, and not go around cutting bilateral deals for oil. But this was a special case, which required special handling.

Clements raised the matter with Yamani while he was in Washington, and Yamani promised an additional 100,000 barrels per day, dependent on Faisal's approval. When he mentioned the shortages to the king, Faisal said the US Navy would get its oil along with everyone else when the boycott was lifted. Jungers went to see him to try to make the case more forcefully. The navy could not wait for the Israelis to change their policy in the Middle East. Faisal asked if this was coming from the oil companies. No, said Jungers, he was passing on a message from the US government. 'Well,' said Faisal, 'I really don't know how you are going to do this.' Jungers took his reply as a 'non-request of a non-event', a very Faisal way of saying do it at your own risk – and if you are caught, you are on your own.[28]

To confirm Jungers's read of Faisal's answer, Yamani went back and played to the king's hatred of communists. He said that if the Americans' fleet was not refuelled, they risked losing ground to the Soviets. Faisal said nothing. Yamani asked if his silence meant consent. Faisal said nothing. Yamani thanked him and ordered Aramco to proceed.

The operation had to be carried out in absolute secrecy. Neither the Israelis nor the other Arabs could know. On the Saudi side, only the king, Yamani, and his deputy Prince Saud were aware. Within Aramco, only one executive at each of Mobil and Exxon, the two largest shareholders, was informed. Yamani asked Jungers to tell only those who were needed to complete the operation. He asked Akins to make the same request of Washington. The slightest murmur to the press, Yamani warned, and the deal was off. He would lose his job, and any hope of lifting the embargo would be 'very seriously diminished.'[29]

Once everyone's silence was assured, Aramco arranged for a tanker to fill up with jet fuel at a non-Aramco terminal in Bahrain. Out at sea, it offloaded its cargo into another tanker, whose crew had no idea of their destination until the scheme was under way. This second tanker sailed on to a US Navy ship to bunker the oil for use by the Sixth and Seventh Fleets.[30] Faisal's non-requested non-event would keep them afloat a while longer.

15

The Czar

Big Sissy, Doggy Daddy and Dopey Diesel had had enough of the rising fuel prices and the threat of falling speed limits. It was impossible to make a living this way. They pulled their trucks to a halt on I-84, the busy highway running along the border between New York and Connecticut, and for ninety minutes on the afternoon of 3 December 1973 caused traffic to build up behind them. That night, River Rat ran out of gas in the slow lane of Interstate 80, in the middle of Pennsylvania. Another truck pulled up in the lane beside him. River Rat called the head of the independent truckers' association: 'Hey, we blocked the goddamn Interstate. A bunch of dumb truckers are going to shut down the country!' For the next forty-eight hours, truckers stopped in the middle of highways across the Midwest. One of the truckers explained: 'We figured if trucks could do without fuel, the country could damn well do without trucks.'[1]

American trucking was a profession of rituals, of thumbs-ups and palm jiggles to warn of cops or wrecks ahead, of lights flicked on and off in greeting as drivers passed in opposite directions. As they said goodbye at truck stops, the truckers told each other to stay between the fence posts and keep the rubber side down on the road. They communicated on CB radio using nicknames for each other, and their foes, on the open road. State troopers were 'Smokey Bears', 'bears in the air' were helicopters, and paying tickets meant 'feeding the bears'.

Most large trucks were made to cruise most efficiently at 60–70 mph. Driving at 50 mph, as Nixon was proposing, would cost them time, money and speeding tickets if they drove faster to meet their schedules. By December, the price of diesel had risen 15 per cent in twelve months, and was expected to go up at least another 30 per cent by January. Shortages meant the drivers had to keep moving from gas stop to gas stop to find whatever fuel they could. Talking to each other on their CB radios, they bemoaned this constant hunt for 'motion lotion'. It was humiliating for men who had come to see themselves as modern cowboys, riding the highways alone, and happy that way. They drove on caffeine, Benzedrine and speed, and kept a gun and a tyre billy for protection.

Around a third of truck drivers drove for large companies, and were members of the feared Teamsters Union. The rest were independent owner-operators who rented out their services to companies. Many of them were veterans, who recognised themselves in Nixon's 'silent majority', the opposite of the noisy counterculture generation of the 1960s. These were straightforward men who wanted to get up, go to work, and looked to no one else for help. The union drivers called them gypsies. Now they were caught by forces beyond their control. Their shipping rates were set by the Interstate Commerce Commission. As their costs had gone up, those rates had stayed the same as the government panicked about inflation. The Teamsters had the consolation of steady wages and a close relationship with government. Their contracts and bargaining power meant a rise in fuel prices, and a fall in speed limits would not affect them. But the independents, who were paid for each job rather than a salary, would suffer. They scrambled, forming dozens of ineffective quasi-unions to protest. They hated feeling so weak.

Between December and January, many of the independents stopped driving altogether, causing shortages of food and goods across the country, and emptying supermarket shelves. The truckers blockaded roads, and menaced the drivers who kept on working, slashing their tyres with ice picks, breaking their windscreens, and dropping bricks or firing bullets at them from highway overpasses. At least two drivers were shot and killed. A company in Cleveland hired a gang of Hell's Angels to provide security for their truck convoys. Happy Honky, Little Arab and Smokey the Pig were holding the country ransom.[2]

Nixon had already spoken of a 17 per cent shortfall of oil, but with Christmas looming, the number threatened to reach 23 per cent. By February, the eastern seaboard would be getting only half its usual flow of oil. Homes would go unheated. Israel, Egypt and Syria could take months to hash out their problems. If the embargo followed the same schedule as the peace talks, the consuming countries faced economic disaster. At home, the oil problem needed to be solved immediately. It could not wait for peace in the Middle East.

On the day of the first trucker protests, John Love, the intellectual force behind Nixon's vision for energy independence, resigned. His Office of Energy Policy had proposed a massive government gas-rationing programme, similar to one that had existed during World War Two. It was precisely the kind of government overreach that George Shultz did not want. Shultz preferred a gasoline tax to discourage consumption, and considered rationing a last resort. Bill Simon's aides called Love's initial proposals to deal with the embargo overdue, inadequate and 'pretty sad'.[3] Love returned to Denver saying he was 'battered, bruised but happy to be home'. He had been offered the meagre bone of the ambassadorship to Canada, but turned it down.[4] On 4 December, Bill Simon took charge of a new all-encompassing agency, the Federal Energy Office. He was now America's 'energy czar'.

Nixon told his Cabinet that Simon would have 'absolute authority' and made the unfortunate comparison to Albert Speer, to whom Adolf Hitler gave wide-ranging control of Germany's military efforts during World War Two. Like Speer, Simon would be encouraged to trample on government bureaucracy to get things done. Simon winced at the comparison. But he was walking into chaos. Energy policy was being determined by sixty bickering federal departments, offices and agencies. While all of them had seen the shortages looming for months, collectively they had failed to respond. Simon used the authority granted him by Nixon to assemble his own team, adding to his group at the Treasury with staff from the Department of the Interior who had been handling the misguided petroleum allocation passed by Congress, as well as energy data analysis and conservation issues. He and his 37-year-old deputy, John Sawhill, a former senior vice president of the Commercial Credit Company of Baltimore, chose eager young problem solvers, many with financial backgrounds, who had not yet been jaded by the bureaucracy.

They faced an enormous challenge. The new Office of Petroleum Allocation had a backlog of 15,000 enquiries from companies and individuals wondering how much oil they could buy. The New York office had taken to leaving their phones off to stem the flow of new calls.[5] Simon promptly ruled that industry could have as much oil as they used in 1972, assuming they could get it. Petrochemicals companies could have 20 per cent more than the year before. Homeowners could buy enough to keep their thermostats six degrees lower than 1972, around 68°F (20°C) for most. Refiners were ordered to prioritise industrial fuel and home-heating oil over gasoline for cars. People needed jobs, and to be comfortable at home more than they needed to drive. Simon pleaded with them to do their bit to conserve energy. He suggested gas-less Sundays, cooler homes and slower driving.

As Americans appreciated the severity of the embargo, they started heeding the government's pleas for conservation. Local radio stations organised car pools for their listeners. Office workers made sure to turn off lights when they were not needed. The government imposed a 50 mph speed limit for official cars, and dimmed the lights in its buildings. The secretary of the interior traded in his official Cadillac for a marginally less monstrous Plymouth Fury. Air Force pilots did more of their training in flight simulators to save jet fuel. Nixon ditched the back-up jet which trailed Air Force One, noting acidly that now if his plane crashed and there was no back-up to rescue him, at least Congress would be spared the trouble of impeaching him.[6] Colleges in the Northeast extended their winter breaks, to minimise their heating costs. Along Broadway, theatres dimmed their marquee lights as soon as their audiences had gone home. Coca-Cola ordered the lights switched off on its two giant signs at each end of Times Square, and other companies quickly followed, turning their billboards, and the mighty intersection beneath them, dark.[7]

General Motors and Chrysler said they would be shutting down their assembly plants for a few days at a time, and converting some of their production capacity to make the smaller, fuel-efficient cars which Americans now wanted. Mechanics reported a boom in tune-ups as drivers tried to make their cars as efficient as possible by cleaning their filters and replacing their spark plugs. Hardware stores stocked up on locking gas caps, as reports of siphon thefts increased. Television news programmes advised people to keep their curtains closed on cloudy days, and to pull them open when the sun shone, and that brown bread and baked beans offered nearly the same nutritional punch as a steak.[8] George G. Scott, the star of *Patton*, Nixon's favourite movie, recorded a television spot for the government's 'Don't Be Fuelish' conservation campaign. Sitting on a teacher's desk in a schoolroom, he said: 'There's a simple answer to the fuel shortage. We can continue to run our homes, our businesses and our cars the way we always have. Lavishly. All we have to do is close our schools.'

Simon had a simple prescription for the oil shortages: '[G]ive me a little higher prices, a little tax increase and a little rationing, and it [oil] will fly everywhere.'[9] It was a market man's solution. You stimulated supply by letting prices go up, and restricted demand with taxes and rationing, but nothing too drastic. A few gentle nudges, and the system would correct itself. Everyone would get what they needed. He was relentless about spreading his message, appearing endlessly on television and returning calls to reporters with a speed and openness rare in the capital. Love had managed to speak to Nixon only a few times in his months as energy czar. Simon spoke to him almost every day on the telephone, and frequently in person. As Nixon was subsumed by Watergate, Simon offered a rare source of light.

The day of his appointment, a journalist caught up with Simon's sister, Madeleine Becker, at her home in Florida. 'Bill has such great financial know-how and a certain something that puts him right up there in front,' she said of her brother, adding that the family called him 'Mr Magic'. He had evidently shared his Chicago school approach to markets with his family.

'Bill prefers to raise the price of gasoline, not ration it. Do you realize the cost of establishing a rationing committee? Millions of dollars – and Bill is too conservative for that.' She said that she and her husband, a periodontist, would be doing their bit for conservation by ordering a smaller station wagon, and not using their expensively installed outdoor lighting. But first, they would be burning up a little jet fuel by flying down to Puerto Rico, where her husband was chairing the Chi-Chi Rodriguez Golf Tournament for charity.[10]

Simon quickly found his rhythm. He arrived at the office at 7 a.m., his hair swept back, wearing horn-rimmed spectacles, button-down shirt, striped tie, a navy-blue suit and wing-tip shoes. He spent forty-five minutes drinking coffee, smoking extra-long cigarettes, and plotting the day ahead. Then it was straight into a sixteen-hour day.

All over Washington, people waited to ambush him, from special interests wanting special treatment as energy ran short, to Democrats hoping his failure would blow another hole in the already badly listing Nixon administration. But Evans and Novak, the *New York Post*'s Washington columnists, wrote, Simon's 'tough, quick response to challenges should give President Nixon one small comfort: he has finally picked a "czar" unafraid to crack heads in an Administration that badly needs it.'[11]

The Sunday after his appointment, Simon arranged a 10 a.m. conference call with the ten regional directors of his nascent energy agency. He spoke for fifteen minutes, outlining his plans and expectations, then passed the phone to Vice Admiral Eli Reich, a decorated submarine commander, who had come from the Navy to oversee the energy allocation programme. The admiral, his pride evidently wounded at having to answer to a

Wall Street slick, refused to take the phone, saying, '[Y]ou seem to have covered the subject yourself.'

Once the call was over, and the two men were alone with their aides, the admiral let rip. He was furious that Simon had spurned his choices for regional directors, removed them from his supervision, and worst of all not included him as one of his six top assistant administrators. He was humiliated by his slide down the organisational table. Simon couldn't care less. The nation was in crisis and this was no time for prima donnas. Simon had offered him the chance to prove himself, but it was clear that a working relationship was impossible. Reich was duly shunted back to defence.

The ideas emerging from Congress went from bad to worse. Price controls imposed earlier in the year meant that the market did not respond properly to the shortages caused by the embargo. Without controls, prices would have gone up further, people would have used less oil, and oil companies would have gone looking for more oil. But instead of deregulating the market, Congress, led by the delegation from New England, which imported more oil than other parts of the country, expanded the already baroque system of controls. The federal government now decided how much oil went to fuel oil dealers across the country. To encourage the drilling of new wells, while protecting the owners of old wells, it set different prices for 'old oil', from wells drilled before 1972, and 'new oil', from wells which began producing after 1972. The old oil was cheap, $5.25 a barrel, the new oil closer to the market price of $12 a barrel. But now the refiners with access to old oil had a huge cost advantage over those who could only buy new oil. To correct that, the government insisted that major producers of domestic oil subsidise smaller refiners with cheap oil. The system devolved into a perverse entitlement system. For buyers, there was only maddening inconsistency. You could find plenty of fuel in one county, and none in the next one, high prices at one end of a city, low prices at the other.

Through it all, Simon expected his staff to keep up with the long hours and bawlings-out. 'They don't mind it,' he said. 'I bust their balls, but they know I bust my balls, too.'[12] He ordered pizza and kept his people in the office late at night, and called them at 3 a.m. if a thought popped into his head. He churned through assistants. His colleague and successor, Frank Zarb, said Simon was 'tough, smart, high intelligence level, very focused, very intense, didn't suffer fools well, and in Washington that's a problem . . . You took the good with the bad, and there was a lot of good.'[13]

Simon was doing his best with the allocation programme passed by Congress, which offended every one of his economic principles. It was government micro-management at its worst, an arrogant, top-down attempt to deal with millions of slightly different everyday situations. 'What would the bureaucracy do about a poor family that heats a small, poorly insulated house with oil, while a wealthy neighbor heats a large, well-insulated home with gas?' he wrote. 'Or the Montana rancher who drives 600 miles a month versus the Manhattan apartment dweller who drives less than 100?' Let alone the inevitable black markets that would arise. All this to save Americans twenty cents a gallon at most.[14]

Members of Congress bombarded Simon with tales of woe, of people waiting for hours to fill up their cars, businesses unable to plan. An Oklahoma congressman called Simon into a hearing and complained that bee farmers could not fill up their trucks to take their bees from one site to another to pollinate. Simon explained the inefficiency of the allocation system imposed by Congress, but on his way out, murmured sarcastically to an aide,

'[W]hy don't they let the bees fly down?' A reporter overheard him and Simon's comment made the evening news, cueing rage in Oklahoma.

On 25 November, the residents of Block Island, off the coast of Rhode Island, began their day an hour ahead of Eastern Standard Time. While Congress was still debating the idea of putting the clocks back in order to conserve fuel, the mostly elderly and retired residents of Block Island decided to go ahead and do it. The first warden of the island's only municipality was asked what he would do if the rest of the country did not follow suit. 'Fooey on them,' he said. Electricity consumption on the island promptly dropped by 10 per cent.

More than two thousand letters arrived each day at the Federal Energy Office's correspondence office, housed in a former Civil War prison, from people with advice for Simon. Children sent in crayon drawings, engineers more detailed energy efficiency plans. Many suggested reducing the hours permitted for radio and television broadcasts. In some states, it was already permitted for cars to turn right on a red light, to cut the energy wasted as they sat idling. One legacy of the energy crisis was the widespread adoption of this practice across the United States. Several people had read the story of a man in England who was surviving the energy shortages by turning pig dung into fuel for his car and wanted to know if this could be more widely adopted. The correspondence office's favourite idea was that Americans turn off the lights while using the bathroom.[15]

Simon recognised that weaning Americans off oil was impossible. Treasury studies showed that even a doubling in the price of crude reduced consumption by just 15 per cent. Americans were 6 per cent of the world's population, but they were using a third of the world's energy and were used to living a certain way. In the depths of Watergate, conspiracy theories spread easily.

Perhaps the shortages were a scam, a manufactured national emergency to distract attention from Nixon's worsening legal troubles. People were furious, and Simon, with his slick look and Wall Street manners, made an easy target. The energy czar became a running joke for cartoonists. In Waltham, Massachusetts, they hanged him in effigy.

The threats against Simon and his family were serious enough to merit round-the-clock protection from the Secret Service. Bodyguards accompanied his family on shopping trips, to football games and on visits to McDonald's. Simon's daughter Mary was on a National Outside Leadership course, and once her instructor learned who her father was, he spent an evening attacking him and blaming him for the energy crisis.

At home, the family tried to set an example. They ate dinner by candlelight. Carol cooked energy-efficient casseroles, and left the oven door open afterwards to warm the kitchen. The children walked to the school bus stop, instead of driving, and the family unplugged all but one of their televisions.

On 14 December, Kissinger returned to Riyadh, confident, wheedling and devious. He sensed he was close to bringing Israel, Egypt and Syria into peace negotiations. All he needed now was for the Arabs to lift the embargo, and he and Nixon could declare victory. He told the king that Nixon's enemies were circling. Fuel shortages had made people angry and Congress was itching to retaliate. Faisal controlled the president's fate.[16] He suggested that the Arabs sheath the oil weapon for now, but bring it out later if the Israelis stalled the peace negotiations. Any blame for the consequences would then be directed at the Israeli side, not theirs.

Yamani had kept probing for cracks in the embargo, to find ways to mitigate its effects while keeping it formally in place. He wanted to help Belgium, which had suffered from the embargo on the neighbouring Netherlands. He wanted to provide fuel for America's military forces. He saw a possibility of using refineries in the embargoed countries, notably Rotterdam in Holland, and Portland, Maine, in the United States, to receive and refine oil, then ship it on to countries not subject to the embargo.[17] But Kissinger thought little of his efforts, and that the Europeans and Japanese paid him far too much respect. The Saudis in general he thought were behaving childishly, sneaking exports around the embargo, and kicking America to appease their own radicals.[18] He would reaffirm his contempt for the Saudis in a meeting with the German petroleum minister: 'There is no reason why seven million Bedouins should dictate to the industrialized world on a matter of such vital importance.'[19]

Faisal now told Kissinger that if the Americans wanted to announce an end to the embargo at the same time as they opened peace negotiations, they should call the talks 'one step in the implementation of 242, which stipulates total withdrawal' and 'to the realization of Palestinian rights.' Then, he said, the 'faucets would open again.'

'The difficulty,' Kissinger said, 'is that there are some things which are better not said.' He waffled about the need for 'quiet talk' rather than 'public declarations' and the strategic value of 'a certain vagueness' to keep his opponents off balance. As the meeting wound down, an underwhelmed Faisal said, 'Nothing would please me more than to say that tomorrow morning we will lift the embargo. But, as the American expression goes, it does take "two to tango."'[20]

The White House Christmas tree usually held hundreds of lights on its branches. This year, it had a single star at the top and eight floodlights circling its base. The decorations would use 80 per cent less energy than the year before. Nixon was fooling no one when he said that the spirit of Christmas was not measured by the number of lights in a tree, but the 'love that each of us has in his heart'. The strains of Watergate now stopped him sleeping, and he would rise long before dawn and play the piano for hours. His approval rating was down to 29 per cent. Investigators were focused on an eighteen-and-a-half-minute gap in the tape recording of a conversation between Nixon and Haldeman on 20 June 1972. It was when he told Haldeman to have the CIA obstruct the FBI's investigation of the Watergate burglary. Nixon's staff found him increasingly incoherent and indecisive.[21] One of his aides compared the mood around the White House to the final days in Hitler's bunker, a combination of backbiting and heavy self-medicating in the face of impending catastrophe.[22]

The shah had been urging the Arab countries to drop the embargo. He thought the oil weapon 'extremely dangerous' as it threatened the entire global economy. But as the OPEC ministers began arriving in Tehran for talks on 22 December, he was drooling over the prospect of even higher oil prices. At a recent auction, oil companies had bid $17.34 for Iranian oil, more than triple the going rate. If that indicated another price surge, he would soon have all the money he needed to fulfil his dream of making Iran one of the world's most developed countries within a quarter of a century.

Arriving at the conference, Yamani said that oil at $17.34 a barrel would 'ruin the existing economic structures of the industrial countries, as well as that of the developing countries.' He said in private that 'there just isn't that much money for oil in the world.'[23] Some were already facing ruin. Edward Heath had not slept for four days when he appeared on television in Britain to announce the country would face the toughest Christmas since the war. Electricity would have to be rationed in the New Year, companies could only use power on three consecutive days during the week, and non-essential shops would have to choose between opening in the morning or the afternoon. One minister suggested people brush their teeth in the dark. Candlemakers flourished and eighteenth-century watermills creaked back into operation. The Ugandan dictator Idi Amin mocked his former colonial rulers by setting up a Save Britain Fund and offering to send donations of fruit and vegetables.[24]

Yamani was not optimistic about the talks. He never trusted the shah, who was always open to backdoor deals, and resentful of the Saudis' influence in OPEC. The general expectation was that the ministers would move the posted price up from $5.11, set in October, to somewhere between $7 and $10. The calculations underlying OPEC's attempts to find the 'true' price of crude were less mathematics than politics and wishful thinking. But no one expected the price announced on 23 December, a more than doubling of the current price of Persian Gulf crude to $11.60 per barrel. Since October, it had risen nearly fourfold.

Slumped in a high-backed leather chair, and visibly exhausted, the shah told reporters 'The industrial world will have to realize that the era of their terrific progress and even more terrific income and wealth based on cheap oil is finished . . . They will have to find new sources of energy, tighten their belts. If you want to live as well as now, you'll have to work for it.'[25] The Arab world plus Iran produced 43 per cent of the oil used by non-communist countries. In two years, between 1972 and 1974, their earnings from oil would jump from $16 billion to $60 billion. The price rises would add $10 billion to America's bill for imported oil, $23 billion to Western Europe's and $8 billion to Japan's. Nixon wrote to the shah warning of 'catastrophic problems' for the international monetary system.[26]

Christmas brought more bad news for the Americans. The Arab producers of OAPEC met in Kuwait and decided to continue the embargo. They had not seen enough progress on peace between Israel and its neighbours, and despite America's pleas they were not going to lay down the oil weapon so easily.

16

A Handful of Desperadoes

Tony Barber, the British chancellor of the exchequer, looked like Monty Python's idea of a Tory minister: thin white hair swept back over his balding head, double-breasted suits, a rictus grin in the face of disaster. But he was also resolutely practical. During the war, he was a reconnaissance photographer, who flew a Spitfire at 30,000 feet across occupied Europe. In early 1942, he crash-landed on France's Channel coast and was taken prisoner by the SS. For three years, he tried escaping from several POW camps. He risked death by tunnelling under fences and once made it as far as the Danish border before being caught. Eventually, he settled into life as a prisoner and completed his law degree by studying books and exam papers sent to him by the Red Cross.

Peter Walker, the secretary of the Department of Trade and Industry, now came to him with an idea. Walker was a brisk, shiny-buttoned Conservative, who had been a successful insurance executive before entering politics. While other ministers were overcome by Britain's deepening malaise, Walker had bucked himself up and made deals to pull the country through. He had struck up a good, working relationship with the Iranians, trading British raw materials, machinery and equipment in return for oil. He proposed that he and Barber go and ask the shah for the oil that Britain so badly needed.[1]

Compared to Barber's wartime experience, asking for oil from the shah, humiliating as it was, held no fear. The chancellor and Walker gulped down what was left of Britain's pride, and on 24 January 1974 flew to see the shah during his three-week skiing holiday in St Moritz. They arrived at the resort shortly before lunch, wearing dark business suits. The British press feasted on the visit. *The Guardian* wrote that the 'Shah of Iran has snapped an imperial finger and two senior members of the British Cabinet are to come-a-running.'[2] When the ministers' plane landed at the local airport, the welcoming party consisted of the embarrassed British ambassador and a slovenly, minor Iranian official who arrived in a grubby Cadillac, and refused to tell reporters his name. The ministers checked into their hotel and waited to be told when the shah would meet them. That night the shah went to a party.

The shah had a strict routine in the mountains. He rose around 10 a.m., skied for several hours, then returned to his heavily guarded chalet several hundred feet up from the village, which looked 'more like an Edwardian convalescent home than a rich potentate's palace'.[3] He had a late lunch, a massage and a bath. He kept prostitutes at a nearby hotel. While he visited them, his SAVAK goons ostentatiously filled the lobby and reception. The shah considered paying for sex a triumph of virility, and liked his reputation known.

The next day, the shah skied until the early afternoon. The representatives of Her Majesty's government were told to wait for him at his home.[4] Once they had finished lunch, the shah asked to speak to Barber alone. He lectured him about Britain's decline. 'This man, who controlled SAVAK, one of the nastiest and most cruel secret services in the modern world, had the effrontery to talk to me about decadence in Britain,' Barber recalled.[5] The chancellor bit his tongue, posed for a ridiculous photograph with the shah and his entourage, he in his suit and overcoat, they in après-skiwear, and went home with boxes of Iranian caviar and a deal for enough oil to power Britain for months.

The *Daily Mirror* said the shah dealt with the British 'with the air of a millionaire distributing largesse.' But the largesse went both ways. The same newspaper reported that Kristine Sparkle, a young singer from Birmingham, who wore glittering short shorts and a skimpy matching waistcoat on stage, had recently flown out to sing for the emperor. The headline: 'What a sparkler for the Shah!'

Kissinger succeeded in turning the November ceasefire between Egypt and Israel into a formal disengagement. Egypt pulled its forces back west of the Suez Canal, and Israel retreated into the Sinai, leaving a buffer zone between them policed by the United Nations. More importantly, the two sides were now talking in a way they had not since 1948. The disengagement agreement was signed on 18 January, and now Kissinger turned his full attention to Syria, where the fighting of October had subsided into a series of violent scuffles over a 150-square-mile bulge of Syrian territory which Israel had occupied as it fought back. Menacingly for the Syrians, the Israelis' artillery could now reach Damascus.

The Syrians had gone to war with different motives from the Egyptians. They did not simply want the world's attention the way Sadat did. They wanted to fight to victory over their neighbour. Getting them to stop and disengage would require far more arduous rounds of diplomacy, but it would be essential for regional peace. The mystery for the Americans was how much progress they had to make before Faisal would lift the embargo.

In his brighter moments, Nixon still believed that he was just a couple of moves from rescuing his listing presidency. Kissinger now contacted the CIA station chief in Saudi Arabia, Raymond Close, an old-school State Department Arabist with the classic profile: the fourth generation of his family to serve in the Middle East as missionaries, teachers, businessmen and diplomats, and educated at the preppiest of schools, Deerfield, and then Princeton. In unusually solicitous terms, Kissinger asked Close to beg a favour of Faisal. Could Nixon say in his State of the Union address to Congress on 30 January that the oil embargo would soon be lifted? The president had so many problems that such an announcement would be a much-needed political coup, a reminder to Americans that Nixon remained a peerless international statesman.

Close went to see two of Faisal's sons, Saud and Turki. They spoke to Faisal, who said that Nixon could go ahead with his statement on two conditions.[6] First, he could say that 'friendly leaders' had assured him that there would soon be an urgent meeting about ending the embargo. Second, this should be explicitly linked to the implementation of Resolution 242.

Nixon duly said in his State of the Union that because of America's commitment to peace in the Middle East, based on the full implementation of 242, 'I can announce tonight that I have been assured, through my personal contacts with friendly leaders in the Middle Eastern area, that an urgent meeting will be called in the immediate future to discuss the lifting of the oil embargo. This is an encouraging sign.' But then came the kicker. 'However, it should be clearly understood by our friends in the Middle East that the United States will not be coerced on this issue.' Nixon and Kissinger could not bear the idea that Saudi Arabia had gained the upper hand.

*

'We have become a nation of energy wastrels, and this day is over because the day of cheap energy is over.' Bill Simon made his warning in late January, and that night, an ice storm swept through the Mississippi Valley, 4 inches of snow fell on Northern California, and Nixon once again refused to hand over the White House tapes demanded by the Senate Watergate Committee, on the grounds that it would be a violation of presidential confidentiality. Children now went to school before sunrise wearing fluorescent armbands, under a new energy conservation schedule of Daylight Savings. The press had declared a Second Dark Age in a country losing its way.

The nation's growing neurosis played out most vividly at gas stations. People used to abundance now had to wait in line to fill up their cars, like Soviets waiting for bread. As Bill Simon had feared, the allocation system turned out to be a mess. In Washington, his office allocated fuel to states, which in turn allocated it to gas stations. The states then introduced their own rules to manage supply and control panic buying. New York and New Jersey went furthest. Drivers with plates ending in an odd number could only buy gas on odd-numbered days of the month, even numbers on even days. Drivers with vanity plates without numbers had to treat the last letter as a number, based on its place in the alphabet, A for 1, B for 2 and so on. For months with thirty-one days, on the 31st, everyone could buy fuel. To stop people topping up, you could only buy gas if you had less than half a tank.

Commercial vehicles like buses and taxis were exempt, as were doctors and travelling salesmen. The disabled were not, and in New York they organised themselves and protested by stopping traffic on Sixth Avenue in Manhattan outside the governor's office. It was one of the first instances of disabled voters acting as a political force.

Post-war American life had been built around the car and the independence it offered. People no longer had to cluster around walkable communities or rely on public transport. They could spread out into the suburbs and the country, into bigger houses with lawns and neighbourhood pools. Connection to the world came through these joyous machines equipped with air-conditioning and soft seats which whipped you along to the sound of the radio. When the cars stopped moving, so did everything. It did strange things to people's minds.

Police in New York reported a surge in fights at gas stations. Walter Stack, the grizzled, beleaguered owner of an Exxon station at the corner of 42nd Street and 11th Avenue in Manhattan, said that with all the angry drivers, chauffeurs, pimps and street thugs converging on his pumps, 'it is like reenacting Custer's last stand every day, with me being Custer. Every day there are fights . . . It's living hell out there.'[7]

In Gary, Indiana, a man who skipped a gas line in search of air for his tyres ended up killing the station owner. In San Jose, California, an attendant sprayed gasoline on drivers who tried to force their way to the front of a long line.[8] In Seattle, teenagers pulled up to a pump in a closed service station late at night, to create the false impression that the pumps were about to open. Once a long line had stretched out behind them, they raced away. A station owner in Stamford, Connecticut claimed a woman offered him sex for $2 of gasoline.[9] Sweetly, in Concord, New Hampshire, the local library lent out record numbers of books as drivers looked for something to read while they waited.[10]

A psychiatrist in Honolulu told the local newspaper that 'until about three weeks ago, whoever had a real feeling of euphoria . . . watching the arrow on the gas dial creep slowly up past empty, quarter full, half full, right up to three-quarters full or, joy, beyond joy, full? Who ever got turned on by that a month ago?'[11] But it was also demeaning to have to wait for gasoline for hours. 'It drains the humanity out of you,' said a driver in New York. 'Out here in the line, we're no longer people, we're beasts.'[12]

The truckers had staged a series of short strikes through December, but in January, after Nixon introduced a national maximum speed limit of 55 mph, their protests intensified. Fuel prices kept rising, and the new lower speed limit squeezed their schedules and ability to make the most meagre living. Along Interstate 80 in Ohio, on the night of 28 January, five trucks were hit by bullets, one driver was shot, and two more were pulled from their bakery truck and beaten. At 12.01 a.m. on 31 January, the independent truck drivers of America, 'the gypsies', began a coordinated and indefinite protest.

Striking and non-striking drivers fought with their rigs, fists, tyre irons and guns at truck stops and highway entrances. Men lurked in the shadows of overpasses to drop cinderblocks or shoot into the cabins of drivers passing underneath. Housewives raided supermarkets before the groceries ran out, factories closed, employees were sent home, and livestock crowded into feedlots, as there were no trucks to take them for slaughter.[13] In Carson, California, a truck carrying frozen chickens was shot ten times from a large-calibre rifle. The unemployment rate moved steadily upwards, from 4.6 per cent in October to 5.1 per cent in January, as companies felt the economy fall out beneath them.

On the night of 3 February, police in Pennsylvania reported four shootings and forty-one incidents of rocks thrown at trucks driving on highways. The state's governor ordered 4,000 national guardsmen to stop the violence. Two days later, Claudie Nix, a 51-year-old truck driver for the Albany Felt Company, was heading north through Delaware when a man in a light-coloured Chevrolet pulled up alongside him and shot him in the chest. Nix collapsed on his steering wheel, and his truck swerved into a tree. He left behind a wife and six children.[14] On 6 February, a driver from Metuchen, New Jersey, stopped the morning traffic heading into Manhattan for hours after he drove his tractor trailer into the Holland Tunnel and jack-knifed it across two lanes.

The truckers' representatives nicknamed Bill Simon 'Simple', but on the night that Pennsylvania's governor called out the Guard, he came to meet them in the presidential room of the Mayflower Hotel in Washington DC. It was 9.30 p.m., a Sunday, and he was wearing corduroys and loafers rather than a suit and wingtips. He stayed for four hours to answer their questions. The root problem was America's dependence on foreign oil, he told the truckers, and higher prices were necessary to stoke domestic production and clear the path to self-sufficiency. Beyond the doors of the hotel, truck drivers were being shot, and Hell's Angels motorcycle gangs were escorting convoys to safety. The government was ready to negotiate, but only up to a point.

Four days later, the two sides had a deal. The government would allow an increase to the federally controlled shipping rates to compensate for the drivers' higher operating costs, and guarantee more diesel would go to truck stops.[15] It was enough to end the strike, but Nixon had squandered more of his reputation as a champion of the silent, American working man. He had called the truckers a 'handful of desperadoes'. 'The government doesn't give a damn about the little man, never has, never will,' wrote one driver to *Overdrive* magazine.[16] Another said that, '[W]hen the next shutdown comes around . . . I'm gonna take my goddamn truck and burn it on the goddamn White House lawn.'[17]

David Rockefeller, the chairman of Chase Manhattan and an eminence of American finance and politics, visited Jeddah in February with all the pomp of a head of state. Akins, reluctant to seem at the service of American plutocrats, refused an invitation to his hotel, but invited him to a small dinner at the embassy, along with Omar Saqqaf, the foreign minister.

Saqqaf and Akins had become good friends, and a formidable bridge pair, despite having very different personalities. Akins was intense and could be socially rigid, a scold to those around him. Saqqaf was more the bon vivant, eager for a Scotch and card game once out of sight of the local morality police. Akins refused to gamble on their games, offering various excuses, ranging from his miserable diplomat's salary to his Protestant guilt, which meant he would feel as awful winning as he would losing. When Akins chided Saqqaf that gambling was also against the rules of Islam, the minister warned him not to lecture him on his own religion.

During dinner at the embassy, Rockefeller talked about all the Arab leaders he knew, how much he admired King Faisal, and how saddened he was by the anti-Arab propaganda in America. When he finished, Saqqaf said, 'I've just read your statement that Chase is the greatest friend of Israel in all the banking community. Why don't you save your sweet words about us for the American market? Now *that* would impress us.'[18]

Kissinger's tone towards Faisal turned ugly after the State of the Union, from begging for the president to mention a possible lifting of the embargo in his speech, to threatening to stop the peace negotiations unless the oil started flowing again. Faisal asked the leaders of the other Arab producers if they would consider announcing an end to the embargo at a meeting of oil ministers later in February. With the exception of Egypt and Qatar, they refused. They did not trust the United States to keep Israel negotiating with its neighbours without the pressure of the embargo. The disengagement deal between Israel and Egypt was progress. But they wanted to see a similar deal with Syria. Syria's President Assad was far more difficult to engage with than the emollient Sadat, but that was the challenge.

When Saqqaf explained this to Akins, the ambassador channelled the desperation in the White House. He accused the Saudis of following one demand with another to keep the embargo tantalisingly out of reach. There were 'strong overtones of tragedy' in their decision to risk the entire peace process, and their relationship with the United States for such incremental gains. Saqqaf seemed disconsolate and tired. He shrugged away Akins's threats, saying 'so be it', or 'perhaps there must be another war anyway.'

The State Department's response to the Saudi position was vengeful and explosive. Unless the embargo was lifted immediately, the Americans would release the transcripts of Faisal's meetings with Kissinger, and his discussions of when and on what terms the embargo might be lifted. These would reveal the king's dishonesty and humiliate him before his fellow Arabs. As Akins read the cable out to Saqqaf, the minister grew so visibly angry that Akins worried he was going to have a heart attack. Saqqaf asked if the author of the message had lost his mind. It could not have come directly from Kissinger. It was so insulting it jeopardised America's interests in the entire Arab world.

Ever since the embargo began, said the minister, the king had been consistent. He wanted peace based on his understanding of

Resolution 242, with Israel retreating to its 1967 borders, including giving up Jerusalem. He understood this would take time, but had been willing to entertain Kissinger's and Nixon's badgering about lifting the embargo in return for making progress in the negotiations between Israel, Egypt and Syria. He had never been dishonest. He had simply tried to find a bridge between the needs of two sets of allies, the Americans and the Arabs. And this was the thanks he got from his high-minded friends: the threat of blackmail and public humiliation.

The Americans often accused the Arabs of acting irrationally, Saqqaf said. But this was beyond irrational. Did they not realise what they might lose? The Europeans were champing to take over the Americans' military and economic roles in Saudi Arabia. The moment the Saudis cut ties with Washington, it would simply turn to Europe and Japan. It would pull its swelling funds from American banks and terminate any deals with the American companies crawling over Riyadh pitching their technology, industry, and infrastructure projects. If the threat in the cable was real, Akins wrote in his memo back to Washington, it would be the final proof to the Saudis that the 'United States was even more totally enslaved to Israeli wishes and Zionist pressures than the Arabs had believed.'[19] Furthermore, Saqqaf had warned him, if the Americans did try to blackmail Faisal, the Saudis would release all the parts of these exchanges which the Americans left out, including all the pleading to save Nixon from his domestic problems.

Saqqaf knew what to expect when he read Faisal the cable. The king never responded well to threats. 'If this is Kissinger's final word,' Faisal thundered in a rare loss of temper, 'I will break all diplomatic, military and commercial relations with the United States, and no Muslim country can fail to follow my lead.'[20]

The next day, the House of Representatives authorised its Judiciary Committee to start investigating grounds for Nixon's impeachment. The committee now had full power to subpoena evidence and witnesses. There were immediate constitutional and legal questions. The last president to be impeached was Andrew Johnson in 1868, and it remained debatable what actions constituted the 'high crimes and misdemeanors' that justified sending a president for trial in the Senate, and possible removal from office. When Nixon met the Saudi ambassador in the White House Map Room the following afternoon, he was keen to de-escalate the situation with the king, but also to redirect blame for his political descent. He promised to work harder towards peace in the Middle East, but the embargo was not helping him with ordinary Americans. 'I understand it,' he said, 'but with lines at gas stations, and so on, I don't want our people to start blaming the Arabs.'[21]

17
A Quiet End

When Jim Akins spoke to the king and his advisers, he usually spoke Arabic. But this time, he spoke English, interpreted by the royal translator. He had arrived at the palace at 10 p.m. to drive home the American position once again.[1] The king had met the heads of state of Egypt, Syria and Algeria in Algiers, who had agreed in principle to lift the embargo. The final decision, however, would have to be made by the petroleum ministers who were not meeting for another two weeks, at the end of February. Perhaps by then, the king hoped, there would be progress on Israel disengaging from Syrian forces in the Golan. Without that, the embargo would likely remain in place. Nothing had changed.

Akins pushed. It came down to trust. Did the Arabs trust the United States and President Nixon to continue working towards a just and lasting peace in the Middle East? Nixon had promised it in his State of the Union and in his private communications. What more could he do? Akins repeated America's insistence that there would be no work on disengagement on the Syrian front without the lifting of the boycott. The administration was under pressure from pro-Zionist groups at home, and could not afford to do anything which looked like surrendering to Arab pressure. The American public more broadly was seething at the Arabs for the embargo, and there was no way Nixon would risk his own dwindling prestige on this issue. The embargo was a gift to the Israelis, who knew that as long as it was enforced, US support for Israel would not waver.

It was getting very late and Hume Horan, Akins's deputy head of mission, was staggered by Akins's bravado. He kept coming back to the need to end the embargo, brushing aside the king's refusals, making the same points again and again. Horan wondered how far Akins dared go. Faisal began to tire, and the interpreter began sweating under the stress of repeatedly translating Akins's message. But the king was clearly listening. Akins may have been moralistic and stiff in person, but he could be trusted. He had never tried to abuse his position for money, nor hesitated to tell the Saudis what he thought.

Eventually Akins stopped speaking, and neither the king nor his advisers responded. One of them played with his beads. Finally, Faisal said that it might be enough to agree on how the withdrawal of Israeli forces might occur, or at least say an agreement was imminent. But it would be helpful if Kissinger visited the region in the next few days to move the process along. As to Nixon's domestic challenges, Faisal said that he was confident God would come to his help.

After the meeting, Akins spoke to Prince Saud and the king's adviser Kamal Adham about how Saudi Arabia might unilaterally lift the embargo. The wall was beginning to crack. Later, Horan told Akins that he had been walking on such thin ice, it might as well have been water. 'They don't pay me to walk in and just show a piece of paper to the king, bow, leave, and get home in time for cocktails,' Akins told him. 'I'm Uncle Sam's attorney, and I'm paid to make the strongest case I can on his behalf.'[2]

Two days later, the Daytona 500 NASCAR race was held in Daytona Beach, Florida, its distance shortened to 450 miles to conserve fuel. But the weather was coming to Bill Simon's rescue. The winter had been warmer than feared, alleviating the effect of shortages in the North East, where many homes still ran on oil heating. Factories had for the most part kept running and schools stayed open. Conservation measures meant that there was still oil to spare if you looked, mostly in the inventories of oil companies. But drivers still waited in line at gas stations, exacerbating the sense of a nation in crisis.

Simon had inherited an allocation system, passed by Congress in November, whereby the federal government distributed oil to the states based on what it deemed they needed. It was precisely the kind of anti-market solution Simon had learned to hate, prone to corruption and inefficiency. Improving it seemed impossible. Eliminating it altogether was inconceivable as long as the embargo remained in effect. So, with Nixon's consent, Simon decided to overwhelm it, by over-allocating oil and gas to every part of the country, to flood the market. The oil was there. It was simply a question of turning the dribble of allocations into a gusher of availability, allowing supply to meet demand naturally, and hoping the crisis eased before the oil ran out.

As Simon and his colleague Zarb called governors and oil company executives to lay out their plan, caution slowly turned to enthusiasm. It was a gamble, but worth taking. 'We decided to demonstrate to the world that we weren't going to take any shit,' said Zarb. The strategy would only work if people believed that America could afford it beyond a few weeks. The long-term energy problems remained. But if Simon could cut the lines at the gas station, and relieve congressmen from the carping of their constituents, then perhaps his wife could snuff out their dinner candles and turn the lights back on in Virginia. He might also shut up the shah.

In a television interview in late February, the shah said that the shortages in America were a hoax, that in fact the United States was importing more oil than ever before, and that the oil companies were enriching themselves. In any case, depriving the wasteful Americans of oil was no bad thing, as oil was too valuable to be burned in homes and cars. It was much better used to make petrochemical derivatives.

Simon was called in to explain the shah's comments to the House Ways and Means Committee. On his way, he cracked the back of his head on the door frame of his government issued compact Chevrolet, a dismally small, fuel-efficient car, which had been confiscated from a drug dealer. He slapped a Band-Aid on his wound and spent five hours answering questions while his head throbbed. The shah had no idea what he was talking about, Simon said. IRS agents were monitoring ports and ships coming in and out to make sure there was no foul play. It was yet more reason why he preferred dealing with Yamani and the Saudis. Unlike the shah, they didn't try to make his life more difficult than it needed to be.

On 19 February, Saqqaf and the Egyptian foreign minister, Ismail Fahmi, visited Nixon in Washington to hammer out terms.[3] In public, there would be no connection between the process of Israeli and Syrian disengagement and the embargo, but in private this was the deal. Nixon would reiterate his commitment to peace in the Middle East, but not give any precise details or timetables. That was for the diplomats. He would say that he was actively committed to a disengagement in Syria, without being more specific, and that he would be sending Kissinger to the region as soon as possible to start talks. Coincidentally, the Arab producers, with the exception of Iraq and Libya, would lift the embargo. No one could accuse the United

States of succumbing to Arab pressure, nor the Arabs of giving in to America. Each would appear to have made their decisions independently.

The logic now brewing in the administration was that out of the chaos of the embargo, a new kind of US-Saudi relationship might emerge. There would still be the mood music of diplomacy towards a settlement in the Middle East, but it would now be accompanied by the more persistent and real thrum of economic interdependence. Europe would rely ever more on Saudi oil. But the goal in the United States was energy independence. Scowcroft wrote in a memo to Kissinger: 'Because our short-term economic self-interest in Saudi oil is much less than others, we may be in a unique position to broaden and deepen our economic relationship with the Saudis on a basis of mutual self-interest.' Nixon mentioned in a desultory way in a call with Kissinger that it was important for the Arabs to know that 'we look forward to working with them in their economic development – apart from oil. All that old jazz.'[4] It was the first thing Kissinger brought up with Saqqaf when he arrived in Riyadh on 2 March. The lifting of the embargo, the ministers agreed, was imminent. Kissinger had done his bit by coming to the Middle East. No official had spoken of any connection between his visit, progress on Syrian-Israeli disengagement and the embargo. Now it was time to discuss something else: a deeper economic relationship.

That afternoon, Kissinger was at his most ingratiating with the king.[5] 'We are prepared to begin talking about long-term cooperation in the military field, in the economic field, and in the scientific field, in each of which we would be prepared for substantial cooperation with His Majesty when he thought the time appropriate.' As Kissinger kept talking, unfurling his plans for a deeper US-Saudi relationship, Faisal's responses were like a religious incantation. 'We are fully prepared to move along this path with all our capability.' 'We will welcome this with the greatest pleasure.' 'These are our hopes for whose success we pray.'

Finally, on the matter of the embargo, Kissinger insisted that it was 'not an economic problem for us, but it is inconsistent with our dignity to be pressed by our friends.' It had also become a difficult personal challenge for Nixon. 'Let us hope the difficulties will end soon,' said Faisal, before sending Kissinger on his way with prayers for his success. Throughout the meeting, Faisal had looked straight ahead, not picking at the lint on his burnoose,[6] and in that non-committal phrase, 'let us hope the difficulties will end soon', he had indicated his intent.

Yamani had tired of the public theatre of the previous months, the endless press conferences and summits, the fighting between producers and consumers. He longed for two men from each of the US, Europe and Japan, representing consumers, and two men from each of Saudi Arabia, Iran and Algeria, representing producers, to lock themselves away in a mountaintop hotel and quietly thrash out a plan for energy and finance to cover the next decade.[7] But as Akins did the rounds of the senior ministers, including those closest to the king, he found them as 'close to euphoria as I could imagine them to be.' The prospect of a new US-Saudi relationship on every front meant the Saudis had no need for the French, the British or the Japanese to help them industrialise, and invest their growing oil earnings. The United States could do everything. The embargo was irrelevant now, an embarrassment being held in place by others. The Saudis were beyond it, thinking ahead to years of purposeful prosperity, supported by the Americans. Prince Fahd, America's closest ally in the court, said the king had praised 'our friend Dr. Kissinger, whose brilliance is matched only by his mobility.'[8]

For six months, Yamani and Belaid Abdesselam, the Algerian minister of industry and energy, had travelled relentlessly, bearing the bad news of the embargo. They had soaked up the bitterness directed at their leaders from countries which could not believe the revolution taking place. These were no bloodstained sans-culottes dragging aristocrats to the guillotine. Simply a couple of sober Arab men in their early forties, accomplished technocrats in three-piece suits and overcoats against the long European winter, threatening the demise of the industrial order and the overdue impoverishment of the West.

Now, they returned to Vienna to report back to their fellow OPEC ministers. Most of the major consumers had come round to the Arab understanding of UN Resolution 242, that Israel should withdraw entirely from the territories it had taken in 1967, and restore the rights of the Palestinians. Israel had been isolated and its expansionism condemned. The major European countries, with the exception of Holland, and Japan had all expressed support for the Arab position. There were even signs in America of the need to balance backing for Israel with greater sympathy for the Arab and Palestinian cause. Kissinger's efforts to achieve an agreement between Syria and Israel were indicative of America's strategic direction.

Faisal's anger at America had tempered. He realised that change in the Middle East would take time, far longer than he wanted to sustain the embargo, which had become less and less effective. After the initial shock, the oil companies had found ways to keep the oil flowing. They reassigned oil from other parts of the world to the embargoed countries, and sent Arab oil to the un-embargoed ones. The growing fleet of supertankers would leave their ports and disappear at sea, their untraceable cargoes vanishing to refineries and ports around the world. The Saudis might know where every drop of their oil was going, thanks to Aramco's diligent tracking, but they could not track the rest of the world's shipments. Faisal and his court had also achieved the objective of securing America's promise to help with Saudi Arabia's modernisation and development.

Kissinger waited eagerly for news from the Arab oil ministers' meeting in Vienna. He had been talking about an end to the embargo for months, as though his words and will alone could force the Saudis to give in. He checked in with Nixon before lunch on 18 March to tell him he expected news by mid-afternoon, the end of the day in Europe.

Around midnight, reporters gathered in the lobby of the Imperial Hotel in Vienna. The hotel had been built in the nineteenth century for Duke Philipp of Württemberg in the high Austro-Hungarian style, with marble hallways, classical statues and heavy chandeliers. Adolf Hitler had worked there as a day labourer while he was a struggling painter, and as Führer kept a suite following Austria's Anschluss with Germany. Yamani and Abdessalam took their seats on a couch beside a low table covered in microphones. Abdessalam said that before the embargo, the Arab countries had been disrespected and unappreciated. The embargo had forced the West to recognise their importance to the world's economies.[9]

Yamani said that Saudi Arabia would raise production by more than a million barrels a day immediately, provided there were any tankers available. The United States would start receiving 1 million barrels, and production would be increased to meet the full needs of West Germany and Italy. Both countries had recently called for Israel to withdraw to its 1967 borders. The full embargo on Holland would continue as long as it continued its support for Israel. Most European countries and Japan had been exempted from the embargo, but the overall rise in production would help meet any unmet demand. Syria and Libya refused to accept the decision.

At 6.28 p.m. in Washington, Kissinger called Nixon again: 'We finally got the official text.' The communique said: 'Israel alone will have to bear the heavy responsibility if subsequent developments lead to the adoption of more stringent oil measures, in addition to the enlistment by the Arab nation of other resources for use in the battle of destiny. Israel alone was responsible for the adverse effects suffered by those countries that were subjected to the embargo or the cutbacks in production, and remains responsible today for the maintenance of Arab oil production at a level which is below market requirements.' The embargo was lifted with the proviso that it would be discussed again at the next meeting of petroleum ministers on 1 June. If Sadat delivered on his promise to arrange the Syrian disengagement by the end of April, the embargo would stay lifted for good. Meanwhile, the Saudis and those more friendly towards the United States would work to kill the 1 June proviso altogether.

Walter Cronkite asked Yamani on *CBS Evening News* what might persuade the Arabs to reimpose the embargo. The minister was as disarmingly menacing as he had been since the crisis began. 'You stop your efforts . . . which you are making right now to bring peace to the area. This is the reason why we lifted the embargo. If you stop these efforts or if it is true that you are not serious enough to do it, then I think automatically we will reimpose the embargo.'[10]

Nixon addressed the embargo the next day at the National Association of Broadcasters in Houston, Texas. He was intentionally low-key. This was not a major victory for the United States, or any cause for celebration. It had become clear that it was 'in the interest of the countries that imposed it, as well as the United States, that it be lifted.' The goal in the Middle East remained 'permanent peace as an end in itself', not as a means to ending the embargo. The issues of oil and peace ran in parallel, reverberating off each other, but never intertwined. Nixon's lie preserved the dignity of both the United States and King Faisal.

The end of the embargo came just in time for Bill Simon. His gamble to flood the market with all the oil he could find had ended the panic buying and the lines at gas stations. But it could not be sustained unless Arab imports began arriving again.

Henry Kissinger could finally attend to other things. Nancy Maginnes was two and a half inches taller than Kissinger, blonde, cool and intellectual. She had been Kissinger's steady date for nine years, even as he had projected an image to the world as a rakish boulevardier, so convincing that some considered him a sex symbol. On 6 April, they made it official. They held a small reception for friends and family in the Madison Room at the State Department, then drove to Arlington to be married by a judge. From there they went to National Airport, where Nelson Rockefeller's plane waited to take them to Acapulco for a ten-day honeymoon. The television presenter Barbara Walters said Nancy would be a 'lovely, quiet stream in the turmoil' of Kissinger's life. But there was turmoil still to manage. Kissinger insisted that his assistant, Paul Bremer, come along and help with the non-stop flow of memos and cables. Bremer had been hoping for a break. As consolation Kissinger said he could bring his wife.[11]

PART III

18

Nixon in Jeddah

Ibn Saud was suspicious of asphalt roads. He worried that invaders would use them to take over his country. But as urban planners poured into Saudi Arabia from Europe, followed by American construction companies, its cities turned into grids of freeways, tunnels and flyovers. A country dependent on oil now fully embraced the car. Late at night, bored young men drifted their cars at high speed on roads which petered out into the desert. Bedouin camel-herders had long since switched to long-distance trucking. Their poetry and songs now spoke of Ford F-250s and Toyota Land Cruisers instead of dromedaries.

Bandar bin Srur was born in 1937 in the upper Nejd, a member of the Utayba tribe, the most powerful in central Arabia. He lived through the dissolution of the Bedouin by the Al Sauds. Ibn Saud was uncomfortable with Bedouin tribes roaming freely around his country, and forced them to settle in farms close to wells. His new state required homogeneity and subordination. In the 1950s, the government abolished the tradition of tribal lands, patrolled by the Bedouin. All land outside towns and villages now belonged to the state. The religious authorities imposed Islamic rules on Bedouin traditions, banning raiding, stealing cattle, and vengeance. The Bedouin believed that a man could avenge murder by killing the killer, or any of his male relatives, going back to his grandfather, and down to his descendants. In Islam, a crime is solely the responsibility of the person who commits it. With the disappearance of raiding, the Bedouin lost an important source of income and the last arena for displaying their traditional warrior qualities, of daring, speed, cunning and strength. Smuggling goods past the Saudi army in trucks was a poor substitute.

Each phase of modernisation robbed the Bedouin of chances to practise their three great virtues, known as the Three Whites. Respect for one's neighbour meant nothing when your neighbour was simply the person who lived next door, not someone you had grown up with or owed loyalty to. Respect for unexpected guests was impossible because no one ever showed up uninvited anymore. And respect for one's travelling companion was irrelevant. Before the tribal lands were abolished, travellers passing through had to pay a local tribesman for protection. No more tribal lands, no more travelling companions to protect from danger.

Bandar drove trucks around the Middle East, and died sleeping beside his truck in 1984. He wrote traditional poetry infused with the yearnings of his generation, who could remember just enough about their country before it was transformed by oil; a Bedouin version of American country music. His poems began with a few lines addressed to the messenger entrusted to take the poem to its recipient. Then came praise for the messenger's means of transport. Once it was a camel, ideally a swift, young, barren she-camel. Now it was a truck. He then described the journey facing the messenger and his steed, praised the recipient, and ended with a call to God.[1]

Kissinger and Nixon part ways after a crisis meeting at the White House to discuss the war shaking up the Middle East, October 1973.

No closer to lifting the embargo, the now notorious and celebrated Yamani leaves New York in his Cadillac, December 1973.

Moments before British ministers gatecrashed their annual ski trip, the shah of Iran and his family pose for a photograph in St Moritz, Switzerland, January 1974.

Bicycle sales soared across Europe, but a fed-up French cyclist asks for 'gasoline, please', November 1973.

When the Dutch government banned driving for a day at the height of the embargo, these men sought out alternatives, November 1973.

Britain's irrepressible trade minister, Peter Walker, launches a fuel-saving campaign, November 1973.

Protestors on bicycles blaze through Milan's Piazza del Duomo on Italy's first car-less Sunday, December 1973.

A controversially dressed German protestor drives his 'one-horsepower' Renault 16 in early 1974.

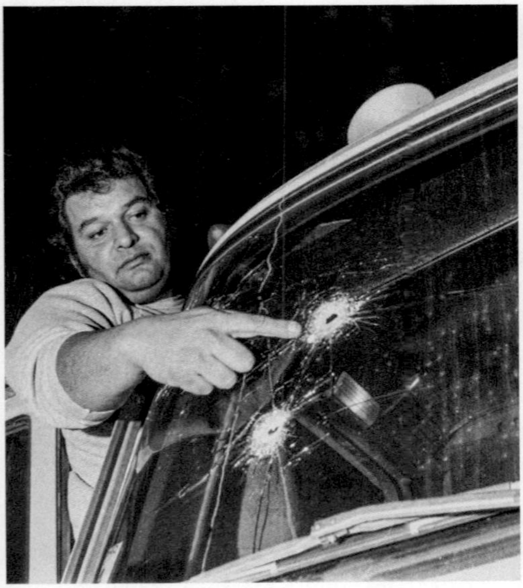

Mike Jarillo of Council Bluffs, Iowa, showing bullet holes in his windscreen during trucker strikes, February 1974.

As incidents of fuel theft rose, many Americans decided to take matters into their own hands, April 1974.

Presidents Sadat of Egypt, Boumediene of Algeria, and Assad of Syria discuss war and the embargo in Algiers, November 1973.

Men of few words: King Faisal in Riyadh with Frank Jungers, chairman and chief executive of Aramco, February 1974.

Journalists raced back from dinner to hear exhausted ministers announce the end of the embargo, Vienna, March 1974.

Just married: Henry and Nancy Kissinger on honeymoon in Acapulco, Mexico, April 1974.

After kissing so many Middle Eastern leaders, when Kissinger kissed Meir, she said, 'I never thought you would kiss a woman.' May 1974.

The 1970s were not all gloom for Nelson Bunker Hunt, whose filly Dahlia won the King George VI and Queen Elizabeth Stakes at Ascot, July 1974.

A pain-ridden and exhausted Nixon on his last foreign trip as president greets Faisal in Jeddah, June 1974.

Bill Simon and Zaki Yamani talk oil and petrodollars at a private dinner at Yamani's home in Taif, July 1974.

The interior minister and future king, Prince Fahd, became America's closest ally among the Saudi royals. Pictured at the March 1975 OPEC meeting in Algiers, he worked closely with Yamani but mistrusted him.

President Gerald Ford (centre) and his economic and energy advisers, (left to right) Bill Simon, Ron Nessen, Dick Cheney, Donald Rumsfeld and Alan Greenspan, December 1974.

As Yamani greets Kissinger in Riyadh, James Akins conceals his mistrust of the duplicitous secretary of state with a smile, March 1975.

Yamani with one of his Pomeranians entertains Joan Kennedy, Senator Edward Kennedy's wife, at his home in Riyadh, May 1975.

Kidnapped OPEC ministers are hustled onto a plane by the infamous Carlos the Jackal in Vienna, December 1975.

A new world order: foreign leaders, including Arafat, Sadat and Assad, attend Faisal's funeral in Riyadh, March 1975.

While fuel shortages hit the industrialised world, fortunes rise in Saudi Arabia. Jeddah, mid-1974.

Faisal's successor, his brother Khalid, with his preferred company, early 1970s.

O Mnir, take the Ford and collect the invoices; Take it
to the repair garage and have it checked.
Make sure gasoline pipes are clear; And for ignition,
make sure the spark plugs are working,
When it is ready to steal distances with speed; Such speed
as that of the peregrine chasing the bustard chick,
. . .
I yearn for the old chiefs who held Najd under their firm
grip, as if nailed to their hands
The chiefs of Najd's tribes who uprooted mighty armies
Have become docile and content to feed, like chicken,
on grain thrown out to them on dirt.

Bandar spoke for a Saudi Arabia hovering between centuries. By the mid-1970s, the country's ports were so busy that ships had to wait out at sea for five months for a loading berth. Construction materials were so scarce that helicopters flew out to ships to bring in huge, swinging bags of cement. Bankers descended on the kingdom in such droves that Aramco's executives could no longer meet with them one by one. Instead, they were hustled en masse into auditoria, where the executives took questions, like professional athletes after a game.[2]

Even as Saudi Arabia's treasury overflowed with oil money, the old ways persisted. The major police stations in the kingdom still employed men of the al-Murrah tribe to help solve crimes. These tribesmen could identify the faintest human and animal tracks in the desert sands. They knew the footprints of their camels, and the camels of their friends and enemies. They could look at a print and tell whether it had been left by a man, a woman, pregnant or not, or a child, young or old. When a crime was committed, they would examine any tracks left at the scene, then sit in the local marketplace watching people's gait to identify the perpetrator. Courts accepted their opinions as hard evidence.

In 1960, Saudi Arabia had been a poor, mostly nomadic country, incapable of drafting a budget to develop its economy and pay for the most basic social services. It still earned most of its money from pilgrims visiting Mecca. The government called the rapid changes financed by the oil boom 'tammiya', development. Others called it 'tafra', an explosion rather than a coordinated evolution. Nasser's former adviser Mohamed Heikal quipped that the 'thawra', the revolution of Arab nationalism, had been usurped by 'tharwa' (wealth).[3] During the embargo, the price of oil multiplied fourfold, and along with it the wealth of the Al Saud family. Faisal was now reckoned to be the richest man in the world. As ordinary Saudis received lavish government subsidies covering everything from housing to healthcare, they now spoke of 'tufush', the depression which accompanies boredom and helplessness. They had hours and days of free time, and little idea of what to do with it. There were few of the consumer distractions of entertainment, sports and shopping.

In the summer of 1965, crowds had gathered five deep on the streets of Jeddah to watch the first transmissions on Saudi television on the sets for sale in shop windows. The programming was limited. In the mornings, it was simply a test pattern. In the evenings, there was an hour's medley of readings from the Quran, music, photographs of the Kingdom, Mighty Mouse cartoons, and news read over still photographs. But the excitement was enormous, and the opposition from religious conservatives inevitable.

By the early 1960s, television was already widely available in Lebanon and Egypt, and to keep resisting on questionable religious grounds left Saudi Arabia in the dark ages. If the government could control it, Faisal believed, it could distract Saudis from the Arab nationalist radio broadcasts from Egypt which reached their homes and depicted the Kingdom as the enemy of progress. Good programming might contribute to a greater sense of Saudi identity, as the nation entered its fourth decade, still a brittle confection of regions and tribes.

To appease the religious authorities, Faisal promised that television would be used for religious purposes. One of the earliest and longest running shows on Saudi television starred Shaykh Ali Al-Tantawi, a scholar, who answered written questions in a warm, familiar way, connecting everyday situations to religious texts and traditions, in the way of an American televangelist. The original plan was to broadcast two hours of programming in the evening. But such was the demand that by the end of the first year, the two stations in Jeddah and Riyadh were broadcasting six hours a night. Those who could not afford their own television would gather in coffee shops and restaurants to watch.

Despite Faisal's pre-emptive efforts to appease the conservatives about introducing television, opposition remained. As the crowds clustered around shops to glimpse the first test pattern, a group marched on the television station in Riyadh, hoping to disable it. They failed. But in the aftermath, police followed one of the protestors home. Khalid ibn Musaid was a fringe member of the royal family. During a tussle with a policeman, he was fatally shot. Khalid's family demanded vengeance, but Faisal ruled that the policeman had done his duty.

Since Faisal became king in 1964, newspaper circulation had grown from 25,000 to 100,000; the number of radio listeners had risen from 200,000 to 2.5 million; and television now reached around 1.5 million of the country's 4.5 million people. The programming expanded to include American imports like *Gunsmoke*, *Lassie* and *I Love Lucy*, as well as men lecturing to the camera about religion.[4] Faisal wanted Saudi media to reach an international audience, which meant an end to the traditional Saudi way of timekeeping, based on the ever-changing hours of sunset. Now the time across the country was a consistent GMT+3.

Even as society grew richer, there was no way of climbing from one social or economic tier to the next, unless you had a personal connection or a stroke of dumb luck. The Al Saud were nicknamed the Al Shubuk, the fences, because they had criss-crossed their kingdom with wire fences, establishing property lines which had not existed before. Now this land was theirs to sell or use as rewards for those they favoured, as it rocketed in value. The family's princes were also given a piece of the country's oil production to sell. For those unfavoured, there was no mobility, and no point in ambition. All you could do was take what you got, and watch the people at the top grow ever richer.

In 1964, when Saudi Arabia was almost bankrupt and fighting with Egypt in Yemen, Crown Prince Faisal had spoken to a military rally at the Riyadh hippodrome, rousing them to save their own country. In April 1974, he arrived at the annual king's race at the same hippodrome in a convoy of limousines, sweeping along a wide, modern highway. Surrounded by the sprawling royal family, he watched five races of Arabian horses, followed by the royal camel race, 600 camels galloping across 9 miles of desert, a tradition going back to the earliest days of Islam.[5] The end of the embargo and the promise of a new, privileged economic and political alliance with the United States had invigorated the country.

For Nixon, it was a relief to travel to the Middle East, where people were curious to see this strange, tortured man, whose actions had had such effect on their lives. The House Judiciary Committee had begun formal impeachment hearings against him for his role in the Watergate cover-up. He was still refusing to hand over the original White House tapes, on the grounds that to do so would compromise the confidential activities of the presidency. He was exhausted and depressed by the looming ignominy of becoming the first president forced to resign.

He and his entourage of some 500 people in twenty planes flew from Cairo to Jeddah on 14 June. Nixon rode through the city in King Faisal's Rolls Royce, behind a fleet of armoured Jeeps, and red convertible Cadillac Eldorados, driven by the National Guard. It was the first time an American president had visited the Arabian Peninsula. Crowds lined the streets, and clambered up trees and street lights to get a glimpse of him. Their enthusiasm pierced the gloom which enveloped the travelling White House. Up close, Nixon looked like a waxwork, his face stiff and puce with make-up, his hair flecked with yellow dye to make him look less macabre for the cameras. His left leg was blue and swollen from phlebitis, and he had to wrap it in hot towels four times day and stay off it as much possible, to avoid a blood clot travelling up to his lungs and killing him.[6] Here in the Middle East, he could see what his presidency might have been without Watergate, a series of foreign policy triumphs without the stain of a two-bit burglary. Nixon had once been the most assiduous worker, but he no longer read the briefs compiled by his staff. In private, he was glum and ruminative. He asked his staff not to schedule anything for the middle of each day, as he wanted to have lunch alone with his wife, Pat.

The Al Hamra Palace in Jeddah had been built at great expense for King Faisal, who still lived in his ramshackle old residence in the city. His advisers felt he needed a home more befitting his wealth and influence. But when they showed it to him, Faisal refused to move in. He found it gaudy and excessive, suitable for his more sybaritic relatives but not him. It was repurposed as the government's guest house and the Nixons were its inaugural guests. Their bedroom and accompanying living room were each the size of a tennis court. In the president's dressing room, the Saudis placed twelve, one-litre bottles of eau de cologne, and in the first lady's, twelve similar bottles of perfume.[7]

That night, Faisal gave a dinner for Nixon in the Al Hamra's sprawling banquet hall. Akins asked to see a copy of the president's intended remarks. He was told the president drafted his own speeches, and then memorised them to appear spontaneous. There was no copy. After Faisal read his speech, Nixon rose and, as if extemporising, thanked the king for his welcome, then began listing his accomplishments: driving the Turks from Arabia; attending the Paris Peace Talks of 1919 with Lawrence of Arabia. Akins felt he was going to be sick. Nixon had confused his host with the Hashemite King Faisal, a leader of the Arab Revolt in World War One, and later king of Iraq. The Hashemite Faisal had died in 1933.

Fortunately, there was no simultaneous translation. Once Nixon had finished, Isa Sabbagh, the Americans' public affairs officer, rose to give the speech in Arabic. Sabbagh had been BBC radio's 'Golden Voice of the Arabs' during World War One, and was known throughout the Middle East. He was not only adept at capturing the finest nuances of both English and Arabic, but also stalwartly pro-American. Sabbagh veered expertly through the speech, editing as he went. He turned the story about driving out the Turks into an account of Ibn Saud's defeat of the Ottomans. He shaded Nixon's mention of the wrong Faisal's role at the Paris Peace Talks into a reference to his host's visit to France in 1919, when he was thirteen. By the end, the Arabic speakers in the audience had no idea of the president's mistake. They applauded noisily. As he was leaving, Akins ran into Prince

Saud, Faisal's son, a Princeton graduate, fluent in English. He asked him what he thought of Nixon's speech. 'Interesting you should ask,' said Saud, slyly. 'Actually, I was somewhat confused. But then Isa spoke and everything became clear.'

Nixon ended his speech with a reference to the issue which had so divided Saudi Arabia and the United States. 'Just to demonstrate that I am somewhat of a practical politician, let me say that while we will treasure most the wisdom that we will take with us after this visit, we, of course, will need the oil to carry us to our next stop. And, Your Majesty, I just want to make clear, we, of course, will pay the world price.'[8]

The next morning, he and Faisal met privately for an hour. Faisal talked as usual about the communist menace in the Middle East and the need for US resistance. He said it was no coincidence that Nixon was facing such trouble at home just as he was making such progress on peace in the Middle East. The Zionist/communist conspiracy, which Faisal saw lurking in every shadow, must be at work. Nixon mentioned that the Iraqis had sent a message to the United States saying that they were not, as everyone presumed, beholden to the Soviets. Faisal advised him to respond favourably, to give the Iraqis sight in one eye, at least, to see a path away from the communists. 'One eye is better than blindness,' he said. Nixon asked Faisal to intercede with his fellow oil-producing countries to lower the price of oil, to help stimulate investment in other sources of energy. Faisal said he would do what he could.[9]

While Nixon spoke to Faisal, Kissinger met a group of Saudi ministers led by Crown Prince Khalid. The conversation was light. They talked about their health and the challenges of negotiating with President Assad, who was notorious for keeping talks going well into the night. One night, Kissinger was preparing to leave after yet another long meeting, when Assad ordered a meal to be delivered and spent two and a half hours reciting Arabic poetry. Khalid joked about the eating habits of his ambassador to Washington, Ibrahim Sowayel. 'You should assign the Secret Service to Sowayel to force him to diet,' said Khalid. 'We will force him to cut from fifteen courses to twelve.' Khalid invited Kissinger to come out to the desert and hunt with hawks. Above all, the mood was relief. Kissinger said of Sowayel, 'During the embargo the Ambassador spoke in masterful ambiguity. No one knew what he was saying.'

'It was embarrassing for us,' said Sowayel.

'It was difficult for both of us,' said Kissinger. 'When traditional friends get into tension it hurts both.'

Just after the presidential party left Jeddah for Damascus, the Saudi chief of protocol summoned Akins. He asked if he remembered seeing the bottles of perfume and eau de cologne in the presidential suite. They were meant for the president and first lady to use while in Jeddah, but all twenty-four litres were gone. Akins burst out laughing. The Saudis should have made it clear they were not gifts. But that wasn't the worst of it. A finely worked silver table, 6 feet in diameter, had vanished from the president's living room. Akins sent a cable to Air Force One, and heard back within an hour. Nixon's overzealous valet, Manolo Sanchez, had assumed it was a gift, and packed it by mistake. It was promptly returned.

The significance of Nixon's visit was not stolen perfume, narrowly avoided diplomatic mix-ups, nor Faisal's familiar anti-Zionist, anti-communist paranoia. It was the change it brought about in US-Saudi relations.

The Saudis had been saying for years what they wanted: help industrialising and modernising their economy. They wanted trade, investments, construction, science, technology, and training in how to manage it all. They did not want to copy the shah and buy pointless amounts of military equipment. Nor did they just want to invest their money overseas and reap the financial rewards. They wanted to use the gift of oil and prepare Saudi Arabia for the day the wells ran dry. Now that the embargo had ended, an American embassy official in Riyadh said that 'every four-flushing mountebank in the world was at their door'. Hisham Nazer, the head of the central planning authority, said that he was being bombarded with schemes from 'bankers and thieves', and that he had trouble differentiating between the two. Jim Akins suggested the United States might start by simply helping the Saudis tell a good idea from a bad one.[10]

In return for the Americans' help, and progress towards peace in the Middle East, the Saudis were resisting the attempts of other OPEC members, led by Iran, to increase oil prices. They had even threatened to cut their own prices, raise production and pull back from OPEC to keep the other members in check. But Faisal could not keep doing this forever. He needed the Americans to pull harder on the line he had thrown them.[11] He was angry when details leaked of Yamani's talks about oil prices with American officials. Other OPEC members called Yamani an 'agent of the American imperialists', and he feared an attempt on his life.[12]

Shortly before Nixon arrived in Jeddah, a Saudi delegation led by Prince Fahd visited Washington to finalise the creation of a Joint Economic Commission between the US and Saudi Arabia, with working sub-groups on industrialisation, manpower and education, science and technology, and agriculture. Financial matters would be handled via a direct relationship between the US Treasury and the Saudi Arabian Monetary Authority, SAMA, which made decisions on investing the country's growing financial surplus.

The Saudis held a reception at their embassy to mark Prince Fahd's visit. The 1,400 guests pressed into the embassy to meet the Saudi delegation, and to see Kissinger with his new wife. Bankers, businessmen and diplomats skirted through tables groaning with strawberries and pistachio pastries. Fahd had reportedly been first into the pool at a party earlier in the afternoon, where every woman who jumped in got an Arabian dress. Bill Simon, who had succeeded George Shultz as treasury secretary in May, chatted with Zaki Yamani, and told a reporter from the *Washington Post* that the impending deal was simple: 'Here is help with our balance of payments. Here is a whole new market' for American goods and services which drive American growth. American companies needed no prodding to pursue the opportunities in Saudi Arabia.[13] 'Imagine it,' said a banker at the party. 'The great of the world coming to kowtow to the Arabs.'[14]

Nixon's visit concluded the opening round of the new US-Saudi relationship. But there were many more to come. The first and most pressing issue was what to do with all of that newfound Arab money. Yamani had warned of the impending problem. In 1969, he told an audience in Washington that Saudi Arabia would soon have to choose between investing its money in banks to earn interest, or leaving its oil in the ground to limit supply and raise prices. From a purely financial perspective, it made more sense to cut production and leave the oil where it was. But this would hurt consumers. A far better solution was to allow Saudi Arabia to invest in the marketing and distribution of its oil in the United States. This would be the first step to building an 'economic bridge' between the countries. America would pay Saudi Arabia for a steady supply of oil and Saudi Arabia would send its money back to America as investments. But the Americans had turned the Saudis down.

Now, banks in Europe noticed a growing daily pulse in

their short-term deposits as the oil price went up. Huge sums would appear in their accounts one day and vanish the next day, only to pop up elsewhere, like a mysterious sea monster occasionally surfacing for air.[15] Even this phenomenon was tainted by prejudices towards the Middle East. The chairman of Morgan Grenfell, the bluest of London's blue chip banks, boasted that the Arabs liked that 'we are effectively a non-Jewish bank.'[16] The reason for this constant ebb and flow of short-term deposits was that the Middle Eastern producers did not trust the Western financial system, and especially the American system after the acrimony of the embargo. When John McCloy was asked by a Senate subcommittee what he thought of Iran buying a controlling stake in General Motors, he said: 'Let them come in, then nationalize them. The Arabs learned that.'[17] The producers had every reason to worry that if they invested their money in the United States, they might never see it again. Instead, they chose to buy Eurodollars, a dollar-denominated currency held in London and Europe. Eurodollars had several advantages. They were dollar investments out of reach of the US authorities. They were not technically part of America's monetary system, nor subject to US banking regulations, but they tracked the fortunes of the American economy. The US government could not freeze these assets if there was another dispute with the producers. If it decided to devalue the dollar again, the Arabs could quickly withdraw their short-term deposits. Their priorities were liquidity and security, not the difference between interest rates on short- and long-term deposits.

The sums involved had bankers slavering and anxious. In 1972, the OPEC producers' combined surplus was $1.6 billion. In 1974, it was $60 billion. Saudi Arabia's surplus had risen from $2 billion in 1973 to $17 billion in 1974, and was still shooting up.

The sum of the United States' entire foreign investments, accumulated over decades, was $90 billion. David Rockefeller understated the matter when he said that the sudden shift of money from consumers to producers had thrown a 'monkey wrench' into the world economy.

Before the oil crisis struck, the developed countries of the OECD had been expecting to run a collective surplus of $10 billion in 1974. Now the price of oil had quadrupled, they were facing a deficit of some $30 billion. Italy had to borrow $12 billion against their gold holdings just to buy time and pay its bills, hoping oil prices would fall. France tried to balance its deficit by selling $4 billion of nuclear reactors to the shah. Every extra dollar consumers had to spend on oil meant a dollar not spent on other imports. Since the collapse of the Bretton Woods system, currencies now traded against each other in a system of 'dirty floats', a mix of market forces and government intervention. Economists warned that in order to cover their oil payments, countries might set up trade and capital restrictions, or start currency wars, racing each other to the bottom and wrecking the world economy.

Western politicians and diplomats wailed at the injustice of it all. Chester Cooper, a former senior diplomat in the Middle East, wrote: 'By the grace of Allah, a few Middle Eastern nations have become rich beyond even the wildest dreams of the fabled potentates of ancient Araby . . . The spice trade was but salt and pepper compared with commerce in black gold.'[18] A stereotype circulated of the treacherous sheikh, travelling the world with briefcases bulging with cash, intent on acquisition and domination. Maurice Adelman, one of the leading US experts on oil, carped that, '[T]he Persian Gulf states have a clean record; they have never yet failed to violate an agreement on oil. If they can rig the price higher, up it will go.'[19]

The conservative commentator William F. Buckley said OPEC's activities were 'justly viewed as a form of economic warfare'. Interviewing Bill Simon on his television show *Firing Line*, Buckley said, 'We are being taken advantage of.' Buckley had the eyes of a sadist and the smirk of a pickpocket and he weaponised both when he said that in America there was 'inhospitality to the idea that McDonald's hamburger stands should be owned by Sheikh Yamani,' which he pronounced 'Yammany'. To the Saudis, he said, the extra dollars meant nothing. Why should they care if America bought slightly less oil from them? It would not amount to even 'one less tent'.[20]

Western financial institutions and governments schemed to guilt the Arabs into handing over their money. Perhaps they could hand it over to the International Monetary Fund (IMF) to distribute it to countries struggling to pay for oil? Or to Western banks to invest it wisely, because what could these inexperienced, oil-flush countries know about the sophisticated use of capital? Mixed in with the patronising was straightforward fury and xenophobia. At Congressional hearings about the new waves of petrodollars, Representative Henry Gonzalez said: 'In the Mideast, the oil prices are 70 times the cost of production . . . The oil producers are engaged in economic warfare no less serious to the continued peace and prosperity of the world than armed warfare.'

The producers shrugged at the hypocrisy. Yamani said the Saudis were not going to send their money back to the West simply for the sake of the West's economies.[21] Nor were they going to feel guilty about not bankrolling the developing world, when the West had done so little for these countries in the past. Americans whined because they had to line up for gas to fill their cars. Farmers in the Punjab had it much harder. They had to wait days to fill oil tins to run their irrigation pumps. While the world ran short of fertiliser, Americans splurged it on front lawns and golf courses.[22]

Kuwait's oil minister, Abdel-Rahman Salem al-Atiki, said: 'This part of the world has been neglected for centuries and the wealth has been carried away by foreigners without giving it a hand for development.' Atiki believed that sustained demand for oil should drive its price even higher. 'I pay $21 for a Swiss-made shirt and $90 a sack for imported rice. So why is my barrel of oil the only thing supposed to be too highly priced?'

The Saudis began to explore alternatives. As the embargo wound down, they appointed an advisory group of bankers from Morgan Guaranty in New York, Flemings in London, and the Union Bank of Switzerland, and selected twenty-one financial institutions in Europe, Japan and the United States to direct their money into investments. The United States was far and away the largest economy in the world, offering the most investment opportunities. But the Saudis were concerned by the anti-Arab mood in the country, and had no interest in taking stakes in companies if they were going to be criticised or restricted. 'They would rather take their money home than be subjected to such calumny,' wrote Hume Horan from Jeddah.[23] They wanted to invest discreetly, freely, and with no tax on any profits reinvested in the United States.

The bloat of Eurodollars rewired the world in unexpected ways. Consumer governments began to borrow from the Euromarket to fund the deficits caused by the higher price of oil. They were effectively borrowing back the money they had paid to the producers, and paying interest on it. The Soviets were also quietly making a very un-communist fortune. The Middle Eastern producers were financing the purchase of Soviet arms by Egypt and Syria. The Soviets then invested their profits in the Euromarket, which were then borrowed by the Western governments to pay the producers. This roundabout of funds prompted Simon to differentiate between the real versus the financial consequences of higher oil prices on the consuming countries. 'Suppose that a landlord tells a tenant that he is tripling the rent but, to make sure that the tenant can make the payments, he will lend him the necessary money. The tenant may have his financing problem solved, but he nevertheless faces very real economic problems. For nations, the problem is not so much that they cannot make financial arrangements to cover higher oil costs as it is that they cannot afford them.'

In the early hours of 15 May, three members of the Palestinian Popular Democratic Front disguised as Israeli soldiers crept over the border from Lebanon and headed for the town of Ma'alot 6 miles into Israel. They killed five people as they made their way to an elementary school, where a large group of high-school students were staying on a field trip. When news of the hostage-taking broke, the defence minister, Moshe Dayan, flew up to take personal charge of the situation. The terrorists wanted their fellow PDF members released from Israeli prisons and sent to Syria by 6 p.m. The Israeli government decided to agree to the terrorists' demands in order to save the lives of the children. Dayan tried to keep the negotiations going throughout the day. But as he realised there was no way to meet the deadline, he prepared a military assault on the school to pre-empt any action by the hostage-takers. When the special forces stormed in, the terrorists murdered twenty-five of their 115 hostages with gunfire and grenades. Twenty-two were children. Thirty-one Israelis and all three terrorists were killed in just thirty seconds of fighting. The next day, Israel attacked suspected Palestinian terrorist training sites and bases in southern Lebanon, and killed many more.

The Ma'alot massacre prompted an emotional debate in the

Israeli parliament. Golda Meir had defended her government's decision to try to save the lives of the children by negotiating with the terrorists. When Dayan heard the government's opponents attacking its actions, he went to the podium at the heart of the Knesset. Dressed informally in a lightweight jacket and open-neck shirt, he said that rehashing Ma'alot was pointless. The questions now facing Israel were as profound as they had been when he spoke at the funeral of Roi Rotberg in 1956. How should it choose to live in a world of constant, violent threat? 'I saw pictures in the papers today of soldiers in helmets with gun belts posted on the roof of a yeshiva in Safad,' he said. 'Is that the kind of atmosphere we want to live in?'[24]

19
Riyal Politik

The Americans had tired of the shah's neediness, the demands for ever more military equipment, and the constant jangling of the threat of Soviet incursions into the Middle East. In a meeting with Abba Eban, Israel's foreign minister, Kissinger called the shah 'boring' and 'the most tiresome head of state'.[1] Yamani loathed him, and could not fathom why the Americans could not see that he was a deranged megalomaniac. He worried that any regime which followed him would be violently anti-American.[2]

While the shah tried to convince the West that he was a sophisticated, modern leader, his illiberal prejudices often burst out. He thought women inferior to men. Where, he asked, was the female equivalent of Michelangelo or Bach? Or even a great female cook, despite all the opportunities women had had working in kitchens? As for the few women leaders he could think of, Catherine de Medici, Elizabeth I, Catherine the Great and Lucrezia Borgia, all were evil schemers.[3] He had a similarly dim view of democracy, freedom of thought and permissiveness which he thought spelled the end of civilisation.

On his way to the Middle East in July 1974, Bill Simon stopped in Nice, France, where he gave an interview to the editor of the *American Banker* newspaper. Simon said that the main purpose of his trip was to influence the Arab nations on their investment policies, now that oil money was pouring in. Of Saudi

Arabia and Kuwait, he said he hoped to 'introduce calm and confidence into the process of investing their new oil riches and impart a sense of national self-interest in the preservation of orderly world financial markets.'[4] He was skipping Iran, though, because among other things 'the Shah is a nut.'

The explosion of oil prices had taken the shah's hubris to a new level. Between 1973 and 1974, the country's income from oil doubled, then quadrupled the following year ($4.6 billion to $17.8 billion). Its economy grew by 33 per cent in 1973, and 40 per cent in 1974. The shah read catalogues and magazines about military hardware the way others leafed through glossies at the hairdresser. Now he had the money to buy whatever he wanted, fighter jets from France, tanks, missiles and more fighter jets from the United States and Britain. In 1974, the United States sold $8.5 billion worth of military equipment, $5 billion of that to Iran. Iran was at war with nobody, yet the shah bought planes he could not fly and ships he could not sail.

For his own people, he promised free and compulsory elementary education, despite a shortage of teachers, and a daily glass of milk for every child, despite Iran's modest dairy industry. It was easier to build airports, and import flashy consumer goods, than to do the hard work of improving public health and education. To every challenge to his plans, he had a delirious solution. No teachers? Beam lessons into schools via satellite. No fresh milk? Import the powdered stuff. His latest five-year plan promised 2.1 million new jobs, even though there were only 1.4 million Iranians to fill them. He invited that epitome of moral vagrancy, the Harvard Business School, to guide the design and curriculum of the new Iran Center for Management Studies. It resembled HBS down to the horseshoe seating plan in the classrooms, and the professors, who came to Tehran from Harvard on sabbatical.

He also began flashing his wealth around the world's financial institutions, revelling in the topsy-turvy post-war world. He gave $700 million to the International Monetary Fund to help countries in financial need, and $300 million to the World Bank. To help trading partners like Britain and France, he made large down-payments on future imports.

Economists argued that different countries had different capacities to absorb their oil revenues, and would manage their finances accordingly. Saudi Arabia had a small population in relation to its revenues. It could not spend its surplus domestically, so it had an incentive to limit production and find sensible investment opportunities overseas. Indonesia had a large population in relation to its revenues, so wanted to increase production to fund its basic spending and growth. Simon did not believe that the absorption theory would lead the producers to make logical decisions about production and spending: 'I do not think there is any question about the ability of rich men to spend money.'[5] The shah's behaviour proved his point. Even his private excesses had reached a fever pitch. The court minister wrote that the shah's mood was affected by the fact that his 'groin and genitalia are inflamed with a nasty rash.'[6]

'He wants to be a superpower,' Simon told the *American Banker*. 'He is putting all his oil profits into domestic investment, mostly military hardware. Maximization of the oil price is in his best interests, as he sees it. But it is not in the Saudis' interest. It is crazy from their point of view. The Saudis helping keep oil prices high is making Iran, their natural rival, strong.'

Kissinger, en route to Saudi Arabia, cabled Simon to ask what he meant by calling one of America's closest allies a 'nut'. Simon explained that it was like calling someone a 'nut' about golf or tennis. The shah was simply very into oil prices. He pleaded that he thought he was speaking off the record, and that the remark had been taken out of context. Kissinger, having dealt extensively with the shah, saw the funny side. He cabled back: 'Just exactly how do you call the "King of Kings" a "nut" out of context?'

For all of his flaws, though, the shah was not so nuts that he couldn't see what was happening. When Admiral Moorer visited him shortly after the announcement of the US-Saudi Joint Commissions, the shah said, 'I see you have a new mistress'. He stroked an imaginary beard to indicate he was talking of Faisal.[7]

The stated purpose of Simon's visit to the Middle East was to educate its leaders in investing, using all of his 'influence and salesmanship'. He would need it as America was not leading by example. Its economy had slid back into recession, and the lifting of wage and price controls had sent inflation up to 11 per cent. When the Saudis first began collecting the revenue from higher prices in April, their first instinct was to bounce their money between commercial banks, trying to find the highest rate of return. The banks reacted by lowering their short-term rates to force the Saudis into longer term investments, and to look to the capital markets of Europe and the United States to soak up their fast accumulating cash. Simon, a bond trader to his bones, was excited by the possibility of the Saudis buying US government bonds, and was ready to package up billions of dollars' worth of intergovernmental securities. The Saudis could buy these securities in private transactions. If they tried to buy such volumes on the open market, they would immediately distort prices. This way, the US got to borrow more, and the Saudis got to tiptoe through the markets unseen. But this was just the start of the Saudis' long-term education. 'They have such newness and greenness,' said Simon, 'and such power.'

Jim Akins liked Simon. They had worked closely together in Washington. He arranged a lunch in Jeddah for about twenty of the city's top businessmen to meet the visiting secretary. Simon sat in the middle of a round table and did most of the talking. At one point he mentioned his father, and Akins asked him how he was. Simon replied in his brass hammer of a voice that he had recently moved him into a nursing home. He and his wife Carol visited him there twice a week. Akins noticed immediately that the Saudis were shocked. How could a man of such wealth and power do this to his own father? Afterwards, Akins called everyone who had attended the lunch to explain that Simon was not so callous. He had not banished his father to some squalid poor house, but to a luxurious retirement home, where he could retain some degree of independence. This was now common practice in America. He could tell the Saudis were unconvinced. It was yet more evidence of America's moral fall.[8]

Yamani and Simon had struck up a real friendship. Yamani spent a weekend at Simon's house in McLean following Prince Fahd's rollocking visit to Washington. He would spend many more over the years, and was always impressed by waking up, opening his curtains and looking out to see Simon already working through his papers in the garden. Simon embodied American energy and hard work.

When Simon's family joined him in Saudi Arabia, they stayed with Yamani at his house near Taif. Yamani organised a private dinner and a night of traditional entertainment. Simon explained to his children that any bad behaviour risked becoming an international incident. They should be especially careful not to compliment any of their host's possessions. If they did, the minister would be obliged to give it to them. 'If you like a painting on the wall, or the silverware or the carpet or his pencil or his shoes, just keep it to yourself, okay?' he said.

When the Simon family arrived, they passed a camel near the entryway. Yamani greeted them one by one. When he got to

Simon's son Billy, he piped up, 'Gee, we sure love your camel.' It took forty-eight hours of diplomatic manoeuvring to ensure the camel did not accompany the family back to Virginia.

The next day, Simon had meetings in Taif with Prince Musa'id, the minister of finance, Prince Fahd, the minister of the interior, and finally the king. He had been told that the Saudis did not want any formal discussions about finance. They did not want anyone thinking they needed the United States to help them manage their own money.[9]

Fahd emphasised that the new US-Saudi relationship would drive communism from the region, but that it was still fragile, based on trust in the future, rather than a past of cooperation. Yamani told a press conference that the Saudis were considering investing in special US government securities, and US stocks. They did not aspire to buy large portfolios of real estate or take over entire companies.[10] But he was intentionally vague, and in case anyone thought the US-Saudi relationship could now be taken for granted, he added that if Israel continued to refuse to withdraw to its 1967 borders, and the United States again supported them, then the embargo would be reimposed. Now that it had been brandished with such effect, the oil weapon should be feared more than ever.[11]

Behind the scenes, Simon made his case for the Saudis to buy US Treasury bonds. After his departure, they began to consider his proposal. He was offering to sell them Special Issue bonds at a fixed price, outside the usual auction system. This was a far more discreet way of investing than buying publicly traded shares, or entire companies. In September, Akins went to see Faisal to ask if he had made a decision.

It was less than a year since the king had imposed the embargo, and he was uncomfortable with the pace of change. Much as he wanted cooperation with the United States, he still had to deal with conservatives at home and in the region. He had two main concerns about buying US government debt. First, he had heard that Yitzhak Rabin, Meir's successor as prime minister of Israel, was on his way to the United States to ask for five times the aid they had received before the October war. Faisal did not want to give the United States money which went straight to Israel. Second was secrecy. He feared his Arab neighbours knowing what he was doing, and any bad publicity in America. He was insistent on this. If the Saudis felt cheated, Yamani warned, they could always cut production to increase oil prices. If the Arabs only produced enough to meet their own needs, the price of oil would triple.[12]

When the governor of the Saudi Arabian Monetary Authority (SAMA) told Simon that Faisal had agreed to buy Treasuries at a rate of $6 billion a year, half of them special issues, he 'forcibly emphasized' the importance of 'complete confidentiality of the amounts and types of the investments.' The Saudis' purchases would make up about 10 per cent of all the US federal debt held by foreign and international investors in the year they began their purchases. If they continued at that rate, they would quickly exceed 20 per cent. To conceal the flow of money from Riyadh, SAMA moved dollar deposits into Swiss banks, and from there into US banks in London, where they were safe from Congressional scrutiny.

When the idea of the Treasury purchases was first mooted earlier in the year, a Treasury official, Jack Bennett, wrote to Kissinger: 'The sine qua non for the Saudis in this arrangement is confidentiality, and we have assured them that we will do everything in our power to comply with their desires.'[13] When Simon appeared before the board of governors of the IMF in October, he did just that. He said that the 'U.S. Government offers no special subsidies or inducements to attract capital here.' It was exactly what the US government was doing for Saudi Arabia.[14] The lie would continue for decades.

'I hereby resign the Office of the President of the United States.' The one line letter was delivered to Henry Kissinger at 11.35 on the morning of 9 August. In his role as secretary of state, Kissinger initialled it, and with that Richard Nixon's presidency was over. By resigning, he avoided impeachment, but his corruption had been exposed. He had stopped the FBI investigation into Watergate and proposed paying off the men involved in the burglary. He had tapped the homes of journalists and officials suspected of leaking information related to his administration. And he had shown contempt towards Congress's attempts to subpoena evidence in their investigation. He had debased the presidency and now retreated mulishly to his home in California. Nineteen of his White House aides would serve prison terms, but Nixon received a pardon from his successor, Gerald Ford, which spared him criminal prosecution

Kissinger was left to carry the fraying banner of the Nixon Doctrine. At the United Nations General Assembly on 23 September, he quoted the economist John Maynard Keynes: 'Very few of us realize with conviction the intensely unusual, unstable, complicated, unreliable temporary nature of the economic organization.' Keynes was writing of Europe in 1919, comparing the strong, interconnected, pre-war global economy, with the prospect of impoverishment if the victors of World War One punished the defeated rather then helped them rebuild. Kissinger argued that after an excellent run following World War Two, the world was now similarly poised on the brink of economic collapse, brought on by 'unrestrained economic nationalism'.

Naturally, he blamed the oil producers, who had wrought such havoc on his quest for peace in the Middle East. 'The high cost of oil is not the result of economic factors – of an actual shortage of capacity or of the free play of supply and demand. Rather it is caused by deliberate decisions to restrict production and maintain an artificial price level.' He called on the producers to act in the interests of the world economy and to cut prices. 'What has gone up by political decision can be reduced by political decision.'

The delegates in the great hall of the General Assembly knew that no country in the world mixed economic with political decisions like the United States of America. And yet here was Kissinger proposing that America dictate the allocation of other nations' resources. Asserting that America would help the producers to industrialise, diversify their economies and invest their oil surplus. Declaring that America would determine the 'fair share' the producing countries should make from their own oil.

In February 1975, he proposed that the consumers band together and set a floor price for oil, to show the oil producers that they were serious about long-term stable pricing and to promote investment in cheaper alternatives. He also asked the consumers to contribute to a $500 billion fund over ten years to invest in nuclear power, synthetic fuels and other alternatives. He warned OPEC that they could accept the floor price now in return for long-term stability in demand, or risk sharp price cuts as alternatives came on stream. Consumers and producers yawned. The Europeans and Japanese said this was just an American scheme to get other countries to fund their investment in alternatives.[15] Milton Friedman wrote of Kissinger's latest laborious proposal, 'Henry, do stick to politics.'

In private, Kissinger continued to show his disdain for the Arabs. 'We've got to come up with ways to soak up their dough,' he told a meeting of Treasury officials including Bill Simon. 'If those Bedouins want to use all of their money to build soccer stadiums, that's fine with me.' All that mattered was to 'maximize their dependence on us.'[16]

In the spring, he came bustling back from meeting the shah proposing that the United States buy Iranian oil at a discount to OPEC prices, using bonds which the Iranians could redeem for American goods. The United States got cheap oil, Iran sold oil it could not sell because it was producing too much, and the money then came back to American companies which exported to Iran. Frank Zarb, the new energy czar, was given the sorry task of evaluating Kissinger's Rube-Goldberg proposal. Zarb was a no-nonsense New York banker, the son of Maltese immigrants, who had written his MBA thesis on training the owners of service stations. He had been one of the private sector fixers recruited by Simon in late 1973 and had little time for political convolutions.[17] He met the Iranian finance minister, and various oil officials, in Tehran, London, Paris and the south of France, the kinds of places oil people liked to meet. The main problem was the Jones Act, which required that when the American government buys anything from another country, it must ship it home on American ships. That would increase the cost of the shah's oil to fifty cents above the OPEC price. The plan may have satisfied Kissinger's grand geopolitical strategy, but it made no economic sense. Zarb and Kissinger went in to brief President Ford. When Ford heard Zarb's numbers, he said, 'No discount, no deal.' When they left the Oval Office, Kissinger called Zarb a 'nitpicking Talmudic scholar.' Zarb called a Jewish friend in New York to ask him what Kissinger had meant. He said, 'The scholar part and the Talmudic part is all right, but the rest is not so good.'[18]

The differences between Kissinger and Simon eventually erupted in a meeting on international trade. On the issue of protectionism, Simon said, 'We have to tell industry that we are working for an independent, open world trading order.' Kissinger shot back, 'This in a world with 123 dictatorships.'[19] For him, grand strategy and superpower pressure mattered far more than the horse trading, clamour, and brute logic of free markets. His approach was still framed by World War Two and its aftermath, when the winners reached down to help the losers, for a price. He valued consensus through control. Simon's hunger for competition was the way of the future.

The American diplomats in the Middle East who had to deal with Kissinger's stampeding shuttle now looked forward to when he travelled with Nancy. On trips to Arab countries, she brought Coca-Cola, which was banned because of its operations in Israel, for the embassy staff's rum and Cokes. Her husband pulled his usual stunts, barging into offices and barking unreasonable orders, but now Nancy would follow close behind and tell him he did not need to be so mean. Then as she ushered him out, she would turn and wink over her shoulder, as if to say don't pay any attention to him.[20]

20

God's Will

Rent-seekers and pencil-pushers had usurped a nobler breed of men in Saudi Arabia. Faisal shared this sense of loss, though he had done much to cause it. His country was running away from him, and he was losing the energy to rein it in. In the mornings he was still alert and sharp, but he now tired quickly, his speech and memory lapsing during meetings. The machinery of the Saudi monarchy was designed for impregnability, not speed. Oil money had gilded it into inertia, not lubricated it for change.

The next generation had none of Faisal's restraint. They were not trying to balance the old and the new, the traditions Faisal had experienced as a young prince, nor the explosion of wealth. They had not experienced the same hypocrisies, the belittlement of being dragged around in the cold, European rain, as a scrawny boy prince, followed years later by the snivelling embrace from old foes once he was the richest man in the world. They had not lived in Riyadh when it was still surrounded by gardens and orchards.

In the late summer of 1974, a private plane landed at Nice airport in France. It had flown from Riyadh, bringing Prince Fahd, and a retinue of family, friends, staff and bodyguards. The ringmaster of this jaunt was Adnan Khashoggi, an exuberant Saudi businessman close to the royal family. A fleet of black Cadillacs waiting next to the runway swept them off to the Hotel Majestic in Cannes. There they settled into a daily routine of trips on Khashoggi's yacht, followed by nights in the Palm Beach casino, where they were assigned the prime table, number 29, separated from the rest of the room by a balustrade. Ordinary gamblers had to pay cash for their chips and higher denomination plaques. Fahd just made a sign and the cashier brought him a stack of 5,000 and 10,000 franc plaques, roughly equivalent to $1,000 and $2,000 at the time.

The other players were mostly wealthy Italians, who had come to Cannes because the Italian authorities were swarming over Monte Carlo looking for tax evaders, to ease the government's financial problems; problems caused in large part by the soaring price of oil. The Italians were dapper, wearing smoking jackets and drinking champagne, and made a great show of each throw at the roulette wheel, crossing themselves and calling on divine help. The Saudis were informal and blasé. They wore light grey suits and open-neck shirts and seemed utterly indifferent to the scale of their bets and losses. They did not know the gambler's thrill of betting beyond their means, because their means were limitless.

After a month in Cannes, Fahd and his group resettled in the Hotel de Paris in Monaco. Here, they slept through the day, and started drinking whisky in the bar around 5 p.m., just as the principality's wealthy retirees were finishing tea. They spent their nights in a private room at the casino, decorated with cream stucco and pink lampshades, playing roulette, laughing, drinking, eating, and tipping heavily. Fahd could lose $12 million one night, nearly half the casino's annual take, and come back and win $4 million the next.

The private lives of Saudi Arabia's princes were an open secret at home and around the world. Unluckily for Fahd, this trip was scrutinised and reported on by the French news magazine,

L'Express.[1] Such 'gambling and wenching', as Jim Akins primly called it, fortified the religious conservatives back home. The reports of Fahd and his cronies tossing around thousand dollar gambling plaques as if dealing a cheap deck of cards reinforced the developing image of the Saudi elite as decadent, undeserving, and hypocritical. Religious conservatives at home, libertines abroad. Without Faisal in charge, Akins feared, 'there would be no figure in the Royal Family with the record of probity or the moral authority to check a rush to the trough.'[2]

As far as Kissinger was concerned, Faisal was a 'kook but a shrewd cookie' and he joked to Ford about his antisemitism. 'The first time I went, his speech was that all Jews are bad. They are cowards, who are mentioned unfavourably in the Koran. The second time I went, he pointed out he recognized the difference between Jews and Zionists. The third time, the foreign minister said he didn't consider me a Jew but a human being.'[3]

In early 1975, Kissinger returned to Riyadh, slippery as ever. On 15 February, he flew in from Jordan aboard his white and blue Air Force 707 jet, accompanied by his usual troop of adoring journalists. He intended to press Faisal on his plan to set a floor for long-term oil prices below the current $11 per barrel. He spoke to the king for ninety minutes towards the end of the day. Faisal was less interested in oil than the Israeli settlements encroaching into Arab neighbourhoods close to Jerusalem. Kissinger said they were 'nothing. They were moved in overnight and they will be moved out overnight.'

After Kissinger left, Faisal told Akins, '[I]f he believes that, he's a fool and I don't meet with fools. If he thinks I'll believe him, then he thinks I'm a fool and he could not be meeting me.' Akins tried to explain away Kissinger's flippancy. The secretary was tired, distracted and speaking without thinking. Of course,

Akins assured Faisal, the Israelis would address the settlements if they wanted peace. As he left Riyadh for Germany, Kissinger said that he had been 'enlightened' by the king's 'valuable views' on his continued mediation efforts. Yamani, who had also spoken to Kissinger, said, '[E]very time we meet our friend Kissinger we feel that he leaves among us a greater conviction of his ability and his efforts.'[4] It was as close to heavy sarcasm as the diplomatic Yamani would go.

On 19 March, Kissinger returned, having told a magazine interviewer that he had considered military action in the Middle East to avert the 'strangulation of the industrialized world' by high oil prices.[5] To many Arabs, Kissinger's threat sounded like America was saying it owned their oil. But Faisal had the measure of Kissinger's bluster, and of all their meetings this was the least fractious, bordering on warmth.[6] It was left to Akins to rant to a newspaper in Jeddah that those calling for war in Saudi Arabia were 'criminally insane'. Akins and Kissinger had accepted each other's differences in order to end the embargo. But ultimately, Akins could not bear the secretary's manoeuvring and sly deceits, and Kissinger found his ambassador intolerably pious. In an act of professional suicide, Akins wrote an Airgram back to the State Department, expressing his horror at Kissinger's idea of sending US troops to Arabia, titled, 'War for Oil: Armageddon As Fun City'.[7]

The Prophet's birthday is a holiday in Islamic countries, but on 25 March, Faisal stuck to his usual working schedule. At 10 a.m. he was to meet the Kuwaiti oil minister, Abdel Muttaleb al Kazimi, at the royal palace in Riyadh. As the Kuwaiti delegation, accompanied by a television crew, waited for Faisal outside his office, they were joined by Prince Faisal bin Musaid, aged twenty-six, one of the king's many nephews and a former classmate of Kazimi at the University of Colorado. Kazimi and the prince chatted.

As the Kuwaitis were ushered into the king's outer salon, the king greeted the minister, and appeared to recognise his nephew. As he acknowledged him, the prince pulled a small revolver from beneath his robe and shot the king once through the chin, once through an ear and once grazing his forehead. Kazimi froze, his head bowed to the king, while flashes went off around him.

The king's chief of protocol, Abdul Wahab, leaped on top of Musaid, and grabbed the arm holding the gun. Bodyguards rushed in, thwacking the prince with their sheathed swords and pulling out their submachine guns. Yamani screamed at the guards not to kill the king's assassin, who offered little resistance. The guards thrust Kazimi into a nearby room, and while Faisal lay on the floor bleeding they searched the palace for his personal physician. Yamani leaned down over him and Faisal murmured, 'Amrak' – God's will.[8]

Abdul Wahab called Frank Jungers, who was at home in Dhahran. 'Something terrible has happened. We need Aramco's help.' He would not tell Jungers any more, only to 'think of the most terrible thing you can imagine,' and to arrange for urgent medical care, including a surgical team, to fly to Riyadh immediately.[9] While the king fought for his life in hospital, his bodyguards drove Yamani back to his apartment. He was so pale and weak, they had to carry him inside.[10]

Within an hour, the head of Aramco's medical department and a fully-equipped surgical team were in the air. Within two hours, two ambulances and a limousine were hurtling towards the hospital in Riyadh where the wounded king lay in a critical condition. The doctors had massaged his heart and tried to pump him with enough blood to keep up with what was gushing from the artery in his neck. But it was pointless. The Americans were too late.[11]

Just after noon, a weeping announcer broke the news on Radio Riyadh. The king had died. His successor would be Crown Prince Khalid. The announcement interrupted broadcasts across the Arab world. Mourners filled the streets of Riyadh, and the army took up strategic positions in case of a coup. Every Arab government declared periods of mourning. President Ford described Faisal as a 'close friend of the United States' whose 'wisdom and stature earned the respect of the entire world'. Faisal's old adversary, Kissinger, called him an 'extraordinary personality' who had influenced 'both the moderates and the radical elements in the Arab world.' The Cairo paper *Al Gomhuria*, which had once thundered against Faisal, wrote: 'The Arab nation can never forget his heroic stand during the October war, or that he launched the oil battle in support of the fighters in Sinai and the Golan, or the moral and material aid that he gave without limit to the front-line states.'

Israel's prime minister, Yitzhak Rabin, deadpanned: 'There are surprises in the Middle East like the one that happened today. We have always taken into account that such a thing can happen in any of the Middle East countries.' A religious newspaper in Tel Aviv, *HaTzofe*, was more blunt: 'A Jew-hating Arab king has been removed from the stage.'

The first official announcements of Faisal's death said his assassin was 'mentally deranged'. Rumours began to spread that the murder was part of a broader conspiracy. In 1969, sixty air force officers had been arrested on suspicion of plotting to overthrow Faisal. Was this the culmination of their scheme? Perhaps Kissinger had had a hand in it, as revenge for Faisal's intransigence regarding Israel. The US was said to have instructed the Seventh Fleet to prepare to evacuate Americans from Saudi

Arabia, and to be spreading stories of unrest in Saudi Arabia to create a pretext for seizing the oilfields.[12] Maybe the Israelis had staged the murder to break the unity of the Arab states. As with any large family, there were always simmering rivalries and feuds. One of the most significant was between two of Faisal's younger half-brothers, Prince Abdullah, the commander of the National Guard, and Prince Fahd, the rising star of the family, considered the real power in the land. Abdullah happened to be outside the country, in Beirut, when Faisal was killed, fuelling speculation of his involvement.

Ten years earlier, Faisal had refused to prosecute the policeman who had killed Musaid's brother, Khalid, during riots over the introduction of television. The king had chosen the law over the pleadings of his own family. Musaid was reported to have set out to kill the king three times in the previous three months, but lost his nerve each time. Stories spread that his father was demented. He had once dressed up as a field marshal and demanded a full guard of honour when he disembarked from an airplane. One night in Paris, he had danced naked beside a fountain, waving a sword. Perhaps he had passed his madness onto his son.

Reports came in from the United States, where Musaid had been a student. He had dropped out of the universities of Berkeley and Colorado. He was described as pleasant, quiet and not much interested in his studies. He had been arrested in Boulder for selling LSD.[13] An old girlfriend surfaced, a former actress said to have appeared in a movie, *Bite of the Cobra*, and now the self-proclaimed 'only female auctioneer' in America. He had been a 'perfect gentleman' while they dated, she said, and if he had lost his mind, it must have been 'since he left the U.S.' There was a photograph of the two of them sitting on the grass in what appears to be a public park. Her blonde hair tumbles down her neck and she is kneeling in a short, low-cut, patterned dress, he in pants and a sweater, an ordinary American couple.

Immediately after Faisal expired, his family washed his body with hot water and soap, and wrapped him in a white sheet, and a brown shroud. Islamic law requires that the dead be buried as soon as possible. But in Faisal's case, the family delayed his funeral twenty-four hours to allow visitors to gather from around the world.

The new king was Faisal's half-brother, Khalid. Like Faisal, he had represented his father, Ibn Saud, from an early age in the family's dealings with tribes and foreign countries. But unlike Faisal, he had resisted formal roles and responsibilities. Faisal had to ask him several times to be his crown prince. But he was trusted by the most important factions in Saudi society, including the religious and security authorities, and well liked within his fractious family. He was a soothing choice for a suddenly traumatised country.

That evening, Khalid announced on the radio that Faisal had died, 'after a criminal attack at a time when we are in dire need of his leadership, wisdom and sound judgement. After he had worked with all his energy for the call for Allah and for the defense of his religion. After he had laid the foundations for our contemporary renaissance. And after he had put the Kingdom of Saudi Arabia on the level of the developed countries in all fields, preserving with determination our religion and our traditions.'

The following morning at 10 a.m., the great hall of the government palace opened to visitors. Thousands poured in, pressing up towards King Khalid, who cried as he greeted them. Fahd, whose high living in Europe had caused Faisal such embarrassment, was now prime minister and heir apparent. He was America's closest friend in the Kingdom and now he stood by

Khalid's side. Faisal's body lay at the Grand Mosque in the centre of Riyadh. As the prayers for the dead were recited, leaders from across the Arab world came and prostrated themselves before the dead king.

Jungers arrived on the morning of the funeral and took a seat on the bleachers outside the mosque in the spring sunshine, watching the foreign leaders and ambassadors gather. Idi Amin, the president of Uganda, came in his military uniform, with a holstered pistol at his side. His ten-year-old son walked beside him, dressed exactly the same, but with a toy pistol instead of the real thing. As the funeral procession emerged into the square, two military officers came up to Jungers and asked him to follow them. They hustled him to the centre of the square where he was invited to express his condolences to the king's sons, notably Prince Saud, the deputy minister of petroleum and soon to be minister of foreign affairs, and Prince Turki, soon to be head of Saudi intelligence. Both men were in tears.

Senator George McGovern, who happened to be visiting Saudi Arabia, attended the funeral on behalf of the United States, and the US Vice president, Nelson Rockefeller, arrived the following day, to pay his respects to the royal family. In 1966, Faisal had attended a lunch in Washington DC where journalists asked him repeatedly about Israel. He said, 'Jews of the world aid Israel . . . In our situation we consider those who aid our enemy as our enemy.' He tried to specify that he was criticising Zionists rather than Jews in general, but Rockefeller, then New York's governor, cancelled his planned meeting with Faisal. Now, here he was performing that most mundane of vice presidential duties, representing his country after the death of a foreign king, who had succeeded his grandfather, John D. Rockefeller, as the wealthiest oilman in the world.

After the funeral, six of Faisal's brothers carried his body, wrapped in black robes, on a board to a waiting ambulance, and accompanied it to the Al Oud cemetery on the edge of Riyadh. There they rolled him into a grave, filled it with dirt and left it unmarked, close by the grave of Ibn Saud. One of Faisal's brothers, and his eldest son, fainted at the graveside.[14] It was rumoured that Idi Amin insisted on accompanying the family to the cemetery, and had taken a shovel and helped to fill the grave. No one had the energy, will, or courage to stop this extraordinary intrusion.

The British had belatedly decided they needed more senior representation than their ambassador. The Royal Air Force sent a helicopter to pluck the defence minister, Roy Mason, a pipe-chuffing ex-coal miner and trade union official, from the deck of a Royal Navy frigate sailing off Portsmouth, and dispatch him to Riyadh. He rolled into town long after the ceremonies were over. The Saudi Royal Household, reported the British ambassador, appreciated the gesture, and Mason had endured the experience 'with equanimity'.

The traditional punishments for rejecting Islam ranged from exile and the amputation of a hand and a foot from opposite sides of the body, to public crucifixion and beheading.[15] Crucifixion could mean either being nailed to a cross and left to die, or 'gibbeting', being beheaded and having your corpse left out in public as a deterrent.

For several weeks, the Royal Cabinet debated Musaid's fate. If they decided he was deranged, he would spend the rest of his life in prison. If they ruled he was sane, he would be tried by a religious court and executed. King Khalid confirmed the verdict. Musaid had committed premeditated murder, and confessed to apostasy, rejecting Islam, a crime which alone would have justified his execution. Faisal was the most important voice in the world for the preservation and propagation of Islam, and Musaid hoped that by killing the king, he would stop people going to mosques to pray, and end religious practices such as fasting and pilgrimage.[16] The statement from the royal household said that the nation's loss of King Faisal could 'only be mitigated by those who carry the banner after him'. It cited a verse in the Quran: 'And regard not those killed for the sake of Allah as dead, because they are living at his side and enjoying His favour.'

On 18 June, shortly before noon, a call went out across Riyadh on the radio for people to gather at the mosque next to the Palace of Justice to hear prayers for the condemned. Dira Square, next to the palace of the governor of Riyadh, was closed off. At 4.30 p.m., before Asr, the evening prayer, Prince Faisal bin Musaid bin Abdulaziz was led out to the centre of the square and forced to his knees, his eyes blindfolded, his hands tied behind his back. An Alem, a Muslim judge, read him the verdict finding him guilty of murder, and asked for heaven's mercy. The executioner, dressed in yellow, swung down with his sword. The crowd shouted 'Allah is great . . . justice is done.'[17] Musaid's head was stuck on a wooden stake for the crowd to see, then taken away in an ambulance along with his body.[18]

Yamani could not eat or sleep for weeks after Faisal's death. His health worsened. 'A part of me died with him that morning,' he said.[19] He happened to be in the Palace of Justice delivering paperwork when the execution took place. From a window, he could see the fear in Musaid's face as he was led to the centre of the square. Despite claiming to hate the sight of blood, he stayed and watched the killing.[20]

21

The Jackal

The Zaki Yamani who arrived in Vienna for talks at OPEC's headquarters in December 1975 was very different from the young man who had caught Faisal's attention with his newspaper columns on modernising Saudi law. Six years earlier, when Yamani gave a press conference after an OPEC meeting, only one journalist showed up.[1] Now he was mobbed wherever he went as the face and voice of Arab oil. He entered middle age fabulously rich. Faisal had given him plots of land in and around Jeddah, which he had sold for hundreds of millions of dollars. During the 1960s, he had moved between a rented hotel suite in Riyadh, and a small house next to the royal palace on the Jeddah waterfront. Now he had homes in London, Switzerland and Beirut and his own plane to fly between them.

When he started advising Faisal, there wasn't even a Ministry of Petroleum. Now he held court from an office with walls of white marble. Visitors had to pass lines of armed guards. His anteroom thronged with visitors from around the world, begging for his time. His home at the Al Yamamah hotel near the palace was surrounded by palm trees and oleanders. Inside were silk carpets, wood panels and dim lighting. During the height of the oil crisis, an American newspaper claimed that he travelled with a personal troupe of belly dancers. The truth was more mundane. His only regular companion on his trips abroad was an aide from the ministry.

He had been the messenger of the poisoned choice presented to the industrialised world: Israel or oil. He had appeared on magazine covers and television shows around the world, pursued by the most famous reporters. A profile in *Newsweek* called him: 'Merely a Simple Bedouin'.[2] It was how he had described himself, despite being 'the complete international sophisticate right down to his neat Cardin suits and his mod black boots . . . a slick oil expert who knows his business cold.' Even his name was suggestive. Whose money? Yamani. When the Saudis raised oil prices, the headline wrote itself: 'Yamani or Your Life.'

He still kept a simple room on the second floor of the Grand Mosque of Mecca, where he would spend parts of Ramadan fasting and praying. But outside the Middle East, he was impeccably European. He particularly liked Vienna, where he could walk to the best opera in the world, and the Alps were close by. He had sent his two daughters to school in Switzerland, bought a chalet in Crans-Montana, and become an avid cross-country skier.

In September, Oriana Fallaci, the most celebrated magazine interviewer of the time, visited him in Taif.[3] She described him as 'fairly tall, plumpish, round-faced with a snub nose and Don Juan style pointed beard and whiskers. Only his eyes alert one to his true self: brilliant, darting, crafty. Eyes that know how to lie, to caress and pierce one with ruthlessness.' She found his lavish hospitality manipulative. Yamani gorged her with elaborate meals and saccharine moments with his young wife and children. She suspected he was trying to seduce her into complicity before he said a meaningful word. When they did finally speak on the record, Yamani was sure-footed and unrepentant.

The oil-consuming countries were begging for a cut in prices, but he was indifferent. He had heard it all now many times. 'Lower the prices of the goods you sell us, which you can since you have a monopoly in any field, and we'll behave accordingly,' he said. 'Do you know how much we pay for a barrel of mineral water? Double what you pay for a barrel of excellent crude oil.'

His confidence was hard and swollen after years of wrestling for control of Saudi Arabia's oil. Faisal's murder had been traumatising. Not only had he lost his patron and political ally, he was now exposed to the machinating Al Sauds, who had resented his proximity to the king, and his fame in the West. To Faisal's successors, he was and always would be an upstart Hijazi, a necessary evil and scold, with too much control over their money. When they thronged the casinos of Europe, Yamani opined that gambling 'rots the soul'.

Kissinger was jealous of Yamani, and the world's fascination with him. 'I had met him several times before the crisis made him an awesome figure fawned over in his global travels by eager votaries and journalists hanging on his every word.' In a different time, Kissinger said, Yamani might have led one of the 'tiny political parties on the moderate right or left whose influence depended not on size but on the intellectual integrity of the membership.' He conceded that Yamani had useful technical knowledge of the oil industry, but considered him 'far from the inner circle', based on the fact that Yamani said little at meetings in Saudi Arabia with the royal family present. 'I have often wondered whether Yamani's occasionally strident pronouncements did not reflect his insecurity in his own political hierarchy and his need to establish himself with key groups around the Arab world rather than the considered opinions of the Kingdom.'[4]

The Saudi royal family retained Yamani because he could

articulate and manage the realities of the oil industry. Unlike Kissinger, he understood economics. Saudi Arabia did not have to tolerate anyone's demands, whether it was the consumers squealing for cheaper oil, or the producers wanting to raise the price. It was the biggest exporter in the world and its oil cost less than anyone's to get out of the ground. If the Saudis wanted to punish oil buyers, they could simply cut production. If they wanted to crush their fellow producers, they could produce to their full capacity and put all the others out of business. As Yamani had once told the executives who challenged him on participation, he held the world's oil supplies in his palm like a glass. One squeeze, and he could shatter it. But that is not what Saudi Arabia wanted. It wanted the world economy to thrive and the producers to understand that they would be better off over the long term if they offered consistent supply and steady prices than if they hijacked the system for short-term price hikes.

The events of 1973 had exposed the fragility of the consumers' entitlement to cheap oil. They had put themselves in this position and were now spinning fantasies about how they would escape. Reserves beneath Alaska and the North Sea, perhaps even the Aegean, would yield enough oil to end the dependence on the Middle East. Nuclear power would render fossil fuels irrelevant. But the Saudis were sitting on at least a sixth of the world's oil. 'Unfortunately, the day when you can do without us is remote,' Yamani told Fallaci. By the time it came around, 'we'll be so wealthy that you'll need us for other things.'

The embargo had been intended as a political weapon, to punish countries which supported Israel against its neighbours and the Palestinians. And yet Yamani, who had expended extraordinary effort, spilled thousands of words, and wielded great influence on the Middle East conflict, had still never met an Israeli. The closest he had come was as a student at Harvard, when he had seen Israel's then ambassador to Washington, Abba Eban, across a library.

It was a grey, slushy, winter's day on 21 December. Vienna was dusted with snow. There were several empty chairs inside the meeting room in OPEC's offices. The ministers from Qatar and the United Arab Emirates had grown bored and left the night before for London, leaving their aides behind. But Yamani felt obliged to stick around. More than anyone, he lent credibility to the circus. His relationship with Aramco had settled after the contentious negotiations over prices and participation. He arrived in Vienna on one of its fleet of Gulfstream jets, which would wait and fly him to London, where he had to give a speech the next day. After that he had a few days off to recover from a trying year.

He was listening to the Iraqis lying. OPEC negotiated the price of oil as a group. Unity was their power. If one member snuck around selling its oil for less, as the Iraqis had been, it not only undermined OPEC's influence, it also reinforced the widespread view that its members, though blessed with oil, were short on wisdom and self-restraint. Of course the Iraqis would deny it.

Yamani had grown used to this, the raised voices, table-pounding and stagy walkouts; the accusations of skullduggery, and the protestations of innocence. The guilty countries were like soccer players rolling around on the grass, pretending to have been fouled. There was always some dubious explanation, a technical problem or a pricing issue lost in the thickets of differentials, buy-backs and all the other tangled accounting terms which enveloped the oil markets. There was always an ambitious leader, desperate for money, who tried to skirt OPEC's rules, and it was usually Yamani who had to play referee. In the corridors outside the meeting, other OPEC members were threatening to raise production to overwhelm Iraq's entire pricing structure.[5] The last OPEC meeting in September had been especially toxic, 'violent' Yamani had called it. Since then, the Iranian oil minister had accused him of being an American stooge and flat out lying.[6] It was all in a few months' work.

Later that morning he was listening to the Algerian minister of industry and energy demand that the Iraqis stop their secret discounts, when he heard shots outside the meeting room. Two men holding guns, their faces covered, appeared in the doorway. Yamani's first thought was that they must be Europeans furious about the soaring price of oil, or yet another gang of whey-faced psychopaths funded by Gaddafi to incite worldwide revolution. There were plenty of those in Europe at the time. He dived under the table, crouched among his fellow ministers, and repeated a verse from the Quran reassuring men facing imminent death that heaven awaited them: 'To the righteous soul will be said: O thou soul, in complete rest and satisfaction! Come back to thy Lord, well content thyself and well-pleasing unto Him! Enter thou, then, among thy devotees! Yea, enter thou my Heaven!'

When the shooting stopped, he heard an explosion, and a voice nearby, a non-Arab speaking Arabic: 'Put down the explosives.' Another voice said in English, 'Have you found Yamani?' The minister from Gabon, crouching nearby, glanced pityingly at him. A man in a beret and leather trench coat, with a scraggly beard, peered under the table, inspecting the ministers one by one. When he saw Yamani, he smirked and saluted.

The terrorists ordered the ministers and their aides to stand up, and searched them. They divided them into three groups: Saudi Arabia, Iran, Qatar and the United Arab Emirates; Iraq, Libya, Algeria and Kuwait; the non-Arab members of OPEC, Ecuador, Venezuela, Nigeria and Gabon. The OPEC staff were separated out, and its British members let go. A young woman, slim and boyish, with dark bangs, entered the room and boasted to the leader of the gang, 'I killed two.' She asked if they had found Yamani. The man in the beret pointed him out.

One of the terrorists took out two packets of explosives and placed them on the floor. He attached two wires to the explosives, sat down, pulled them around his neck and held them up. One touch would close the circuit and blow up the room. The leader of the gang told the Arab hostages in Arabic that they were Palestinian commandos; Palestinian extremists had long said that the oil producers of the Gulf, with the exception of Kuwait, were not being tough enough on Israel. The terrorists' targets were Saudi Arabia, and Iran, which was represented by Yamani's old negotiating partner, Jamshid Amouzegar. If everyone cooperated, no one would be killed. He took the Venezuelan minister aside and began talking to him in what seemed a much friendlier manner. Watching them, Yamani twigged. The man in the beret and trench coat must be Carlos, a Venezuelan mercenary, nicknamed the Jackal by the British press, after a reporter claimed to have seen a copy of Frederick Forsyth's thriller, *The Day of the Jackal*, in an apartment where Carlos stashed weapons. In June, the French police discovered Carlos had drafted a detailed plan to kill Yamani. He had been tracking the minister's family for months and knew everywhere they went. Yamani murmured more verses from the Quran to calm himself down.

Yousef Ismirli, a Libyan civil servant, burst out of a room where he had been hiding and lunged at Carlos, grabbed the machine gun from his hand, and knocked him to the floor. Carlos was overwhelmed but managed to pull out one of several pistols in his coat and shoot at Ismirli's hand. Ismirli dropped the gun. Carlos fired at his knees, and killed him with a final mercy bullet.[7]

At 3 p.m., Carlos told Yamani to come into one of the smaller rooms next to the meeting room. Yamani looked at the ministers around him, and could tell they were thinking the same thing. This was how it worked. Terrorists took their hostages one by one into a separate room, and killed them out of sight of the others.

The room was dark and Carlos spoke calmly, admiringly of Yamani. He told him he would be killed. He hoped that a man of Yamani's brilliance would understand why, and not feel bitter. Yamani was mystified. He asked Carlos, 'How can it be that you tell me that you will kill me and then ask me not to feel bitterness toward you? You must be trying to force me to do something..' Carlos laughed. The only pressure he was applying was on the Austrian government to read a communique explaining his actions on Vienna Radio by 5 p.m., and to provide a plane to fly the kidnappers and their hostages out of the country. He planned to release the Libyans, Algerians and the non-Arab delegations, except the Iranians, in Tripoli; the Iraqi and Kuwaiti ministers in Baghdad; and then fly on to Aden where he would execute Yamani, and Amouzegar. If the Austrians did not meet Carlos's demands, Yamani would be executed there and then as a display of intent.

As the afternoon ticked by, Yamani had time to consider who might have hired Carlos to kill him. There were plenty of people with a motive. Saddam Hussein wanted higher oil prices to fund a war on his neighbour Iran. But the Saudis were keeping prices down, to develop and sustain long-term demand. Gaddafi resented the Saudis' emergence as the leading voice among the Arabs, a role he wanted for himself. The Palestinians felt the Saudis had betrayed them by developing their economic and military relationship with the United States, Israel's greatest friend. Israel itself was capable of such a strike, but this was not Mossad's style. Powerful figures within the Saudi royal family hated that Yamani, a non-royal, had wielded such influence over their oil, and achieved such global renown. Any one of them might have recruited Carlos to kill him. As 5 p.m. approached, Carlos reminded him of the consequences if the Austrians denied his requests. The terror Yamani had been feeling all afternoon subsided. He wrote a farewell letter to his family and asked one of his colleagues to deliver it to them after his death.

Five o'clock passed. Vienna Radio stuck to its regular broadcasting. Zaki Yamani waited to die.

Outside the OPEC building, Austrian commandos and police closed off the streets. Austria's chancellor, Bruno Kreisky, returned by helicopter from a skiing holiday in Lech to take charge. He faced a similar choice to the one he had faced during the Schönau kidnapping on the eve of the Yom Kippur war. Do you make a deal to save lives, or do you stick to the principle of never negotiating with terrorists? This time, the hostages controlled half of the world's oil.

Fortunately for Yamani, Carlos's statement was broadcast shortly after the deadline. It denounced the Arab countries which had succumbed to American imperialism and accommodated Israel. The Iraqi chargé d'affaires, Riyadh Al-Azzawi, volunteered to mediate between the terrorists and the Austrian authorities. 'We are revolutionaries, not criminals,' Carlos told him. 'We are the Arm of the Arab Revolution.' Al-Azzawi said that he did not look like an Arab. 'We are working for the revolution all over the world,' Carlos replied. He could not help it that he had a 'Jewish appearance'.[8] His team of five mercenaries included two West Germans, a Lebanese, a Syrian and a Palestinian.

Al-Azzawi arranged for sandwiches and fruit to be sent up, but the attackers sent them back, saying they could not eat pork. The secretary general of OPEC had been planning to serve a banquet that night. Al-Azzawi had that delivered instead. As the negotiations continued through the night, Kreisky mobilised the entire Austrian government, joined by diplomatic representatives of the OPEC countries and their ambassadors in neighbouring countries. The Algerians assured Kreisky that if he gave the terrorists a plane, they could fly to Algiers and continue their negotiations there. The problem would be out of Austria's hands. At 2 a.m., the prime minister emerged to say he had an agreement.

At 7 a.m., a light green bus, with curtains drawn across its windows, pulled up to the OPEC building. The Austrians and the OPEC staff living in Vienna stayed behind. The terrorists and the rest of their hostages, including Yamani, drove to the Schwechat airport, where they boarded an Austrian Airlines DC-9. Shortly after 9 a.m., they departed for Algiers.

The Aramco flight crew waiting for Yamani had prepared their plane for a quick take-off in case he and his staff were released. After talking to Jungers, the pilot discreetly followed in the terrorists' wake, listening to their communications.[9]

When the plane took off, Carlos relaxed. He did not strike Yamani as a revolutionary. He boasted to him about how crime had funded his life of high living. Yamani noted the high quality of his leather jacket.[10] When they landed in Algiers, Carlos stepped out to talk to the Algerian foreign minister. Inside the plane, the terrorists trained their guns on the hostages and on the rear door in case they were attacked. Carlos soon returned. The Algerians had nothing to offer, and he was sticking to his plan and flying to Tripoli.

Once they were back in the air, the terrorists opened the

window shades and served food. Yamani asked Carlos if he expected trouble in Libya. 'On the contrary,' he said. 'The Prime Minster shall be present to receive us.' The Libyans were going to give him a plane to fly to Baghdad, and then on to Aden. That had been the plan all along. Algiers had been a diversion in order to get out of Austria.

But when they landed, Prime Minister Jalloud was not there. He arrived an hour and a half late, and insisted he would only negotiate with an Arab. Carlos sent Anis Naccache, a Lebanese militant, who operated under the alias Khalid. Khalid returned after an hour with Jalloud, who now spoke at length to Carlos, and assured Yamani and Amouzegar that they would not be killed. Once Jalloud left, Carlos told the hostages that the Libyans had promised him a Boeing 737 which could take them all the way to Baghdad without refuelling. But it was stuck in Tobruk due to a storm. The Libyans were trying to find them a replacement. As the hours passed Carlos grew frustrated and decided to return to Algiers to see if he could find a 737 there.

They arrived back in Algiers in the middle of the night and Carlos spoke again to the same officials he had spoken to a few hours earlier. Yamani and the other ministers waited. Carlos's moods veered from smug and self-satisfied to angry and threatening, while the Algerians juggled his demands with offers from the countries whose ministers he held hostage. Yamani sat in his seat 'waiting for evil things to happen'. At one point Carlos told him he would be released, then later that he would be executed at daybreak. If for any reason the Algerians stopped him, Carlos vowed to pursue Yamani for as long as it took to kill him. Finally, in late morning, Carlos told the hostages that he and the terrorists would leave the plane, and they should follow a few minutes later. The Algerian authorities escorted all of them, kidnappers and hostages, to the same room in the airport. Khalid lurched threateningly towards the ministers. The Algerian foreign minister stood in his way, and offered Khalid a glass of juice, which he drank down. It was just enough time for security guards to step in. When they searched him, they found a pistol hidden in a shoulder holster. He said angrily that he wanted to 'carry out the death sentence against the criminals,' but the guards had 'prevented me from doing so.'

Two days after the terrorists burst into the OPEC conference room, the hostages were released. Amouzegar returned to Tehran. Yamani boarded the Aramco plane which had been waiting for him. He flew to Switzerland to see his family, then to Jeddah for a hero's return.[11]

As soon as the hostage-taking was over, the rumours began to spread like an elaborate game of Telephone. The leading theory was that Gaddafi paid Carlos millions of dollars up front and promised millions more on completion of the mission. A lawyer in Stuttgart told the West German Federal Criminal Police that the Kuwaiti oil minister, who had been at the OPEC meeting in Vienna, had discussed the hostage-taking at a New Year's reception given by an American oil company in Kuwait. He said that Carlos had come across as rational, motivated by money rather than politics, and that the Libyans had paid him for the OPEC attack.[12] But Gaddafi denied any role in the kidnapping and the Austrian authorities found no evidence that he was involved.[13]

Saddam Hussein was the other obvious suspect. The weapons for the attack had arrived from Baghdad. Saddam was angry at both the Saudis and the Iranians. The shah, along with the United States and Israel, had been assisting the Kurds in their fight for autonomy against the Iraqis. The shah offered to stop if Iraq gave Iran access to the contested Shatt al-Arab waterway which led out of the Persian Gulf. Saddam agreed.

The shah stopped the Kurds from escaping over the border into Iran, and the Iraqis massacred them. But Saddam resented the public spectacle of having to shake hands and exchange kisses with the shah. It felt like defeat. He wanted to wage war on Iran, but to pay for it he needed higher oil prices, which the Saudis were resisting. By hiring Carlos to execute Yamani and Amouzegar, went the theory, Saddam would terrify OPEC into submission.[14]

By using the front of an armed Palestinian group, Gaddafi and Saddam could supposedly send their message without being directly accused of sponsoring terrorism. But in Carlos, they chose a perpetrator bound to enrapture the press, and one easily swayed. Before he released the hostages in Algiers, Carlos was rumoured to have accepted $20 million from the Saudis. He remained active and at large until 1994, when the French arrested him in Sudan, extradited him and sentenced him to multiple life sentences.

It was barely nineteen years since Crown Prince Faisal had summoned a young Hijazi lawyer and asked him to be his legal adviser. Now the king was dead, and for Yamani, the days of travelling with a single aide were over. For the rest of his life, he was accompanied by a team of British ex-soldiers who provided round-the-clock security. Murder and kidnapping were the price they paid for Saudi Arabia's oil.

22

Running for the Storm Cellars

Shortly after the Yom Kippur invasion, the novelist and historian Robert Graves wrote to *The Times* from his home in Mallorca.[1] He recalled that in 1919 he had befriended T.E. Lawrence at Oxford. Graves was pursuing an undergraduate degree which had been delayed by his service in World War One. Lawrence of Arabia had returned from the Paris Peace Conference, where the British and French had reneged on his promise to the Arabs that they would have their own state after the war. Embarrassed and embittered, he had retreated to a research fellowship at All Souls' College. One morning, Graves found Lawrence 'talking to an oilman whose name I disremember.' The oilman asked if it would be 'both possible and lucrative to help the poor sheikhs at the top of the Persian Gulf to drill oil there.' Lawrence said: 'Possible, yes, and lucrative, probable, but it would eventually lead to political disaster. Leave them alone!' The oilman shook hands and left, looking disappointed. Lawrence, Graves noted, 'had been famous among Palestinian Arabs for his second-sight.'

When OPEC met again three months after the kidnappings, the bullet holes in the conference room had still not been repaired. In the 1960s, the organisation had been ignored and kicked around. A few years later, its ministers were coveted by the world's most notorious terrorists. Their capture gripped the world. The embargo, price rises, nationalisations and participation agreements had changed how the producing countries were treated. Algeria's President Boumediene said they should be wary now of the consumers' needy enticements: 'In the past we spoke and nobody listened. We shouted and heard no echo. We called for help and the wind drowned our voices . . . We must be careful not to fall into the trap which has been laid for us. We should refuse to talk with the industrialized countries simply in our capacity as oil producers.'[2]

Jim Akins wrote in 1973: 'With the possible exception of Croesus, the world will never have seen anything like the wealth which is flowing and will continue to flow into the Persian Gulf.' It was happening more quickly than even he had predicted. At the simplest level, the embargo was about an essential commodity and the disruption of a market. But it was also about the price of loyalty, and the cost of sudden, exorbitant wealth. It forced the industrialised powers to decide between their economies and a state born out of the greatest atrocity in history. It was a moment of extreme tension in the Arab countries, between religious conservatives, nationalists and the prospect of dizzying economic and social progress. A few decades earlier, Saudi Arabia had been created by a warrior chief at the head of armies of wild-eyed fanatics. Now the most powerful industrialists and financiers jostled for its king's attention.

At the start of the 1970s, the market for oil was controlled by a few Western companies in collaboration with the producing countries. Prices and supply were steady, and contracts mostly predictable. There was little frantic buying and selling to address sudden shortages or spikes in demand. But as the producer countries asserted their rights to pricing and ownership, the number of buyers and sellers proliferated. OPEC replaced the oil majors as the industry's dominant force, and the market became much freer, seething with new participants.

Prices settled more naturally at the intersection of supply and demand. A world of long-term contracts signed by jowly men in thick-carpeted offices was replaced by a bazaar of moment-to-moment traders. The amount of oil bought and sold for immediate delivery on the spot markets rose from 5 to 50 per cent, reflecting this new dynamism.

Commodity trading up to then had been dominated by agricultural products, metals and minerals. Its leading firms tended to be traditional, conservative and secretive. Ludwig Jesselson, the head of Philipp Brothers, which was founded in Germany at the turn of the twentieth century, bemoaned the vulgarity of the booming oil trade: 'The world changed in 1973. The old ways of trust were gone. Everybody started breaking contracts. Prices were changing too quickly for people to keep their word . . . Everybody got greedy.'

The new breed of oil traders praised each other for their 'tomatoes', balls big enough to take risk, and they lived as extravagantly as they worked. A visitor to the leading oil-trading firm of the time, said, 'You never heard businessmen say "fuck" so much in your life.'[3] Its traders once held a competition for who could spend the most on a prostitute in Taiwan. The winner paid to drink monkey brains straight from the skull to enhance his libido.

The embargo awakened the wider world to oil's stranglehold on the global economy. The ninth James Bond film, *The Man with the Golden Gun*, featured a triple-nippled villain, Scaramanga, who stole the Solex Agitator, a device capable of capturing the sun's energy. He intended to make a fortune by auctioning it off to buyers from all over the world. As Bond observed, the Arabs would pay a fortune just to hide it away and preserve oil as the world's main energy source. The Arab sheikh became an ugly stereotype, often depicted as a decadent hypocrite, vulgar and dripping in cash, conservative at home, libertine abroad.

The best-selling car in America in 1973 was the Chevy Monte Carlo, which did 9–12 mpg in the city. Other popular gas guzzlers on the market included the Buick Riviera, the Cadillac Eldorado, the Chrysler Cordoba, and the Oldsmobile Toronado, 'the car with pull for the men with push'. None managed much more than 10 miles to the gallon. After the oil crisis, the Detroit executive Lee Iacocca said, '[T]he world had turned upside down . . . Small, fuel efficient, front-wheel drive cars were the wave of the future.' The American passion for bigger, longer, heavier cars, with tyre bumps and front-row seats as wide and soft as a living-room couch, had been quenched by expensive gas. Congress approved new restrictions on emissions in 1974, which killed the huge V8 engine and the kind of land yachts it powered. Henry Ford II had always resisted making small cars, saying 'mini cars mini profits', but as he saw the rising popularity of more efficient European and Japanese cars, he pushed for the creation of the small Fiesta. While American manufacturers struggled to build fuel-efficient cars, and make money from them, the Japanese and Europeans stole into their market. Americans were 'running for the storm cellars', Iacocca said, and looking for Honda's Civics, Toyota's Corollas and Volkswagen's Beetles, Golfs and Rabbits to save them money.

In the consumer countries without large domestic sources of energy, the changes were even more profound. In Britain, Edward Heath's Conservative government lost its majority in parliamentary elections in February 1974, and could not form a ruling coalition. In Germany, Willy Brandt resigned as chancellor that May, under pressure from the economy and a spy scandal. In Italy, extreme austerity measures could not stop inflation from soaring over 30 per cent. Oil executives and politicians were caught in a bribery scheme, trying to fix prices and stop the development of alternatives. The strains of the embargo had exposed the disunity of Europe's Economic Community. Each of the major countries had pursued their own means to survive the embargo, striking bilateral deals with producers. They had proved to be no more measured than the Bedouin children who scrambled after the coins King Saud used to throw from the window of his Rolls Royce. When oil became scarce, it was each for his own.

Under the slogan 'No oil, No coal, No choice', France built fifty-six nuclear reactors in fifteen years, based on American technology, to meet its electricity needs. Japan increased its civil nuclear power programme sixfold during the 1970s, and shifted its economy away from energy-intensive steel and shipbuilding, to electronics and car-making.

In Alaska, engineers learned how to build a pipeline carrying hot oil across 800 miles of frozen ground without destroying the fragile permafrost. In the most delicate areas, they ran the pipeline above ground, protecting it from avalanches, moose and inquisitive musk oxen. On the afternoon of 1 August 1977, nine years after oil was discovered on the North Slope, the *ARCO Juneau* became the first tanker to leave the terminal at Valdez, carrying 800,000 barrels of oil south to Cherry Point, Washington. By the second half of 1979, the daily flow of oil from Alaska exceeded Saudi exports to the United States. Even so, American dependence on foreign oil rose from 35 per cent in 1973 to 45 per cent in 1979. Rather than pulling inwards to become more energy independent, the United States grew more confident in its ability to spin the world in its favour, and more reckless about its own consumption.

Yamani remained as Saudi Arabia's oil minister until October 1986. New sources of oil in the North Sea, Alaska, Mexico and the Soviet Union, as well as attempts by OPEC to maintain its market share by increasing production, meant that prices collapsed. King Fahd had never much liked Yamani and used the crash to remove him. Yamani remained a suave, self-deprecating authority on energy. When he spoke in the United States, he would sometimes hold up his worry beads, and joke that each bead represented one of his wives.[4]

Nelson Rockefeller tried to get a share of the new oil money by announcing the creation of a new development bank, a joint venture between the Rockefeller family and the Saudi royal family, the two greatest oil dynasties of the twentieth century. His plan was to build a giant fund of Arab oil money and invest it in projects in the developing world. It would be a rival to the World Bank. In the spring of 1977, the former vice president travelled to Israel, Egypt and Jordan, where he was received as a statesman. But in Riyadh, where the money was, he was made to wait for two days. When he finally got to pitch his new $20 billion bank, Crown Prince Fahd listened and politely sent him on his way. The son of John D. Rockefeller had no leverage with the new kings of oil.[5]

Bill Simon had far more success. He teamed up for a while with the Olayan family, one of the Saudi families who made their fortune in transportation and construction starting in the 1960s. In the 1980s, he made hundreds of millions of dollars through leveraged buyouts, borrowing large amounts of money to buy and sell companies in quick succession. He burnished his record as a fixer by taking on the presidency of the United States Olympic Committee in 1981, and turning the 1984 summer games in Los Angeles into a major financial success, by rejecting public funding and maximising corporate sponsorships and television rights. He was close to Ronald Reagan, and used his access, his talents and his money to promote the ideas he had developed during the energy crisis, and the woeful last months of Nixon's presidency: the limits of government bureaucracy, the hopelessness of elected representatives, and the curative power of free markets.

Kissinger got his revenge on Jim Akins. Akins had returned to Washington in July 1975 so that his daughter, Mary Beth, could undergo a painful operation to treat her spine, which was twisted by scoliosis. Early one morning, he received a call from one of his former colleagues in Jeddah, who asked if he had read that day's *Washington Post*. Akins fetched it from outside his front door, and read that Kissinger had decided to fire him. He received calls from Bill Simon and James Schlesinger telling him not to worry. There was no way Kissinger could sack someone so important to American policy in the Middle East. The next day, he discovered that was exactly what Kissinger was doing. Akins would not be reassigned. His diplomatic career was over.

One of his last assignments was to accompany Kissinger to Taif in September when he came to ask for the Saudis' approval for his latest Egyptian-Israeli settlement. Kissinger had been making these steps for a while now, and as far as the Saudis were concerned he was still a long way from the destination they had in mind. After they saw the secretary off at the airport, Prince Saud asked Akins to drive back with him. He asked why Kissinger thought the Saudis would believe him when he told lie after lie. Akins said they should have stopped him and told him he was lying in the meeting. Saud laughed and said that wasn't the Saudis' style. Akins told him that, deplorable as it was, Kissinger was probably telling his travelling press pack right now that the dumb Bedouins had believed him.[6]

The shah proved to be a Potemkin emperor. Nature gave him vast resources, which spared him the hard work of developing his country according to any sensible logic. He hosed the money away on vanities: the latest military aircraft from America and France – even though he had few pilots to fly them; tanks without tank drivers; chemicals for factories which had not been built yet. When the price of oil fell, his dream of lifting Iran into the ranks of the world's industrialised superpowers died with it. His reign ended violently in 1979, undone by religious conservatives. The fundamentalist Ayatollah Khomeini returned from exile in France to become Iran's new supreme leader. The shah became the world's most famous drifter, a toxic guest, wandering from country to country, until he died of cancer in 1981.

Saddam Hussein and Muammar Gaddafi grew into bywords for pathological dictatorship, and ended up toppled by Western interventions. After the Americans invaded Iraq in 2003, Hussein was found cowering in a hole in the ground near Tikrit, the town where he spent his miserable childhood. He was tried and sentenced to death by the new Iraqi government. As he stood on the scaffold, taunted by his captors, he murmured the first pillar of Islam: 'There is no God but God, Muhammad is the messenger of God.'

In Libya, rebels supported by NATO chased Gaddafi from power in 2011 and found him in a drainage ditch in Sirte, the town on the Mediterranean coast where he had grown up, and where he often retreated when his moods overcame him. The men who found him could scarcely believe that this filthy, bloodied, frightened wretch was the man who had tyrannised their country for so long. They dragged him through the streets, beating and humiliating him while he begged for mercy, then shot and killed him.[7]

When Nasser died in September 1970, the Americans cobbled together a delegation to attend his funeral. Nixon and Kissinger were both on major state visits to Europe. There were no diplomatic relations with Egypt at the time. The group consisted of Donald Rumsfeld, then director of the Office of Economic Opportunity in the White House, Elliot Richardson, then deputy secretary of state, Bob Murphy, who had been ambassador of North Africa during World War Two, John McCloy, and Dick Cheney, Rumsfeld's aide.

Cheney was twenty-nine but had never left the United States and did not have a passport. He travelled on a letter signed by an official in the White House. The party stayed in Shepheard's Hotel in Cairo facing Gezira, an island in the middle of the Nile. Nasser's body was flown in by helicopter for a funeral procession which was supposed to start on Gezira, then move across the Nile to the Arab Socialist Union headquarters. Women ululated as the helicopter flew in low over the city. Millions of mourners lined the route. The procession had only gone a quarter of a mile, when the police began beating people in the crowd who pressed in, reaching for the coffin. The attending dignitaries who had begun the procession walking behind the gun carriage carrying the coffin had long since dropped away, frightened of the chaos. Forty mourners died in the crush. Cheney watched all this from his balcony at Shepheard's. 'I always remember sitting up on that balcony watching them as they came across the bridge, people were being pushed off the bridge into the Nile because the crowds were so intense.' It was his first foreign experience.

Two decades later, when Iraq invaded Kuwait, and the Saudis begged America to intervene, the young politicians who operated on the fringes of the oil embargo were now in charge. George H. W. Bush, then head of the Republican National Committee, was now president. Dick Cheney, one half of the White House duo who had crafted Nixon's disastrous price control plan, was now secretary of defence. Cheney became CEO of the giant oil services company, Halliburton, before returning to Washington as vice president under George W. Bush, while Rumsfeld came back as secretary for defence. The years passed, but the characters remained the same, men who had emerged at a dire moment for the United States. They had lurked offstage while Nixon lurched towards resignation, Gerald Ford tried to control an economy beset by inflation and uncertainty, and the world wondered what American leadership meant anymore. They began their political rise when people lined up to fill their cars, and truckers killed each other over the price of fuel. They witnessed the financial dark arts which bound the United States and Saudi Arabia together, and how dangerously this contradicted America's relationship with Israel. They heard the most senior actors in government describe Arabs as savages and blackmailers, who deserved military strangulation, and served a president, Nixon, who could be grossly antisemitic in private, and resolutely behind Israel in public. They were there for the tying of this tortuous knot.

Then they were in charge on 9/11. They authorised the first flight out of the United States following the attacks: a plane carrying members of the Saudi bin Laden family, heirs of the Yemeni contractor who had won Faisal's respect by building a road up the steep mountains from the plains of Mecca to Taif, switching back and forth across bridges and through tunnels. Instead of being welcome guests from an important ally, they were now the frightened relatives of the fundamentalist who had organised the attacks. America's violent responses to Iraq's invasion of Kuwait in 1990 and Osama bin Laden's attacks in 2001 were led by men with deep roots in the oil business. Even if they denied that their reaction was about oil, oil was a world they knew far better than most.

When Gaddafi died on 20 October 2011, the baseball World

Series was being played in the United States. Three nights later, George W. Bush threw out the ceremonial opening pitch at Game 4, hosted by the Texas Rangers, the team he had once owned. The crowd roared its delight. It had been forty years since Gaddafi humiliated the American oil companies, threatening to nationalise their assets unless they paid more for their oil. But memories in the oil business are long, and its leading players vindictive. It might take decades, but eventually one side ends up dead in a ditch, while the other plays ball.

Many of the Aramcons loved how the desert sorted the essential from the superfluous, and found it hard to leave. The work suited a certain kind of personality. The men who had grown up in the American West and Midwest in the first decades of the twentieth century found a familiar experience in the oil industry of Arabia, one that rewarded men in shirtsleeves, holding a wrench and a pencil, solving difficult problems in unthinkable heat. When the time came, some of them had to be forced into retirement. Syd Bowers, who joined Aramco in 1949 and rose to be chief geologist, bought an apartment in Las Vegas. No one in Vegas came from Vegas, and that reminded him of his community in Saudi Arabia. It was a city of runaways and strangers. When he visited friends, he moved from motel to motel several times during the same trip, unable to treat his restless fidget. His body could not accept that there was no more fieldwork to do. His final wish was to be buried in Dhahran, in the cemetery the Aramcons called 'the reclamation yard'.[8]

Oil had determined the nature of modern American life, how far cities should sprawl, the distances people should drive, the cars they bought, and the kind of homes they lived in. The car had created the suburbs, and most of what was in them. Gasoline and petrochemicals underlay all of it. Oil's addicts had got a lot from their addiction, but they showed little appreciation.

As prices rose in 1973, the oil companies made record profits. Exxon's profits increased by 60 per cent over 1972. Appearing before a Senate committee investigating the crisis, one of Exxon's executives said he could not recall the amount of the company's latest dividend to shareholders. One of the senators telephoned his stockbroker there and then for the correct figure. The oil executives complained they were being treated like criminals.[9] They were also suspected of being in cahoots with the Arabs. Senator Charles Percy of Illinois accused the Arabs of constant 'nibbling' at price and ownership agreements. 'As I look at them, they have done a credible job, a tremendous job, a skillful job; they have employed everything in the book. Of course, they have been at this for centuries before we were; we were babes in the woods. Sometimes I think we look like it.'[10]

Yamani's counterpart at Exxon during the crisis was its CEO, Cliff Garvin, a strait-laced Eagle Scout and process engineer, who liked birdwatching and golf. The more cosmopolitan Yamani would call him any time of day or night, and appreciated his rugged straightforwardness. Garvin could not understand the hostility directed towards his industry. 'The American is a funny person,' Garvin said. 'He worships the results of things that are big, economies of scale, mass production, but he hates anything that is big and powerful, and the oil industry is seen as the biggest and most powerful industry.'

The environmental movement had been growing rapidly before the oil crisis, but afterwards it fell back. Concern for the environment came to seem like something ordinary Americans could not afford. Ambitious politicians like Ronald Reagan equated environmentalism with all the other woolly ideologies of the counterculture, which Republicans blamed for holding back American progress. The broader conservative line was that the crisis resulted from America forgetting its self-interest. It had been caused by heavy-handed economic interventionism, and an excessive trust in dangerous foreigners, then solved by letting markets operate freely and acting in American interests first. All of Kissinger's talk of interdependence between nations, and thawing relations with existential enemies had left America exposed. It would take the rest of the 1970s for America to stagger through ever more economic misery, and foreign policy humiliations under President Jimmy Carter, for the country to learn its lesson.

But one could equally well understand the crisis of 1973–4 in more personal and emotional terms, of resentment and distrust. The Arabs and Persians felt mistreated and undervalued, personally and economically, by the West. The Israelis never felt secure within their own borders, constantly under threat of extinction. The fading imperial powers of Europe could not take being pushed around by people they had once ruled. The United States and the Soviet Union saw the world only through the distorted lens of the Cold War. And there to complicate this tangled play was the incalculable treasure of oil.

Perhaps the only clear thinkers in all of this were the executives at Aramco. They lost their ownership of Saudi oil, but not their access to it, and ultimately supply was all that mattered. For all the globe-spanning drama of oil, the invasions and negotiations, the chokepoints and price hikes, what people want of oil is quite mundane: the pumps to flow, the lights to switch on, the heating to heat, and the machines to whirr. The lesson of the embargo was that anyone meddling pointlessly at this basic level of human need risks oblivion.

*

In 1906, the year Faisal was born, Riyadh was more a fortification than a town, a small knot of human life surrounded by thick, mud walls. Riyadh meant 'the Gardens', for the gardens beyond the city walls, in the rich land fed by water from the Wadi Hanifa. Ibn Saud's growing band of children played among the orchards and deep, stone wells, boys and girls together, their long hair loose, nothing to cover their heads or veil their faces. They watched their fathers trap and train falcons for hunting, and mimicked them with small, fierce sparrow hawks, which they caught as they flew south across the Arabian Peninsula during winter. They rode bareback on swift Hamdani mares through the desert, and challenged each other to jump into the dark wells, not knowing when their feet would touch water.

The games in the orchards offered the boys a break from school, where they learned to write by drawing Arabic letters in the sand, and memorised the 114 chapters of the Quran through endless recitation. Once the emir's sons completed their studies, they were put on a horse and paraded around town, cheered by crowds who sang and waved their swords. Their education prepared them for a warrior's life of stern faith, fighting and austerity, governed by the laws of Islam. Sooner than later, the emir wanted his sons to ride with him into battle, to lead his patchwork tribal armies as they flew across the sand on horses, or kneeling in the saddles of jolting, galloping camels.

In the eighteenth century, the Al Sauds had allied with Muhammad ibn Abd al-Wahhab, a conservative Muslim determined to restore Islam to its supposedly pure state, when the Prophet and his immediate descendants were alive. Ibn Saud's most feared warriors were a near monastic corps of Wahhabis, the Ikhwan. They wore white robes and turbans, and staged terrifying raids, a shimmering, ghostly, delirious force, riding at their enemies and slaughtering them with swords and lances.

Despite the soft pleasures of the Gardens, with its carpeted tents and perfumed harems where the emir spent his evenings, the Al Saud was a family at war.[11]

In 1924, when Ibn Saud led his army into the Hijaz, the Ikhwan veered off to attack Taif, and the people of Mecca, terrified that they would be next, sent a desperate telegram to the British government: 'The Wahabites, instead of simply occupying this unfortunate town, have acted methodically in the most ferocious manner, and have not left undone any manner of atrocity against the citizens and strangers found in it . . . They killed the people, respecting neither young infants nor the aged.'[12] The British ignored the plea, and when Ibn Saud took Mecca, the Hijazis were shocked by his half-dressed forces, who looked more like bandits than soldiers.[13] But appearances apart, he was now their king, and Faisal would become their viceroy.

This was the world to which Faisal was born, a world before Well No. 7 changed everything for him, his family and their country. When he died, he was the richest man in the world, and the Saudis had the world on a string, thanks to oil and the embargo which they orchestrated. Faisal's younger brother and successor, Khalid, ordered himself the longest Cadillac ever built, 25 feet 2 inches long in navy blue, a car fit for the world's most powerful king. The 'Khalidillac' had custom insulation and air-conditioning to tolerate the desert heat.[14]

Khalid loved to hunt even more than Faisal did. By 1973, the houbara had become scarce in Arabia, so the royal families of the region travelled to south-west Balochistan in Pakistan, where the Pakistani government assigned them hundreds of square miles for their sport. The Saudis took land in Chaghi and Khalid commissioned a Swiss car designer to convert a Mercedes G-Wagen into a 6x6 falcon-hunting machine, with hydraulics specially engineered for the desert. The front passenger seat could go up and down through the open roof, and swivel 180 degrees. Khalid used his falcons to hunt bustards, oryx and gazelle. He could slide into a rough, Bedouin Arabic, and far preferred the company of tribesmen, with whom he would compete to drink the most camel milk, to oil executives.[15]

But the final links to the old world of the Al Sauds would soon be cut for good. Members of the royal family travelled in fleets of planes, carrying falcons and falconers, customised vehicles, water tanks, communication centres, armed security forces, all that was needed to build small, tented cities in the flat deserts of Balochistan. Falcons were given names like Dollar and Petrol, as well as traditional names like Mansour and Shabib.[16]

Arabian hunters had once tracked the houbara on camels, slipping noiselessly through the early light to come close enough to launch a falcon in pursuit. Now they tracked their prey by radar and infrared lights all day and night. An elegant dance between men and birds became a bludgeoning.

Acknowledgements

When *The Daily Telegraph* sent me to New York in 1998, my broadly defined brief was to bring the city to British breakfast tables. Send home a few weekly marmalade droppers. New York is more than generous to such a mission. But before I left London, one of Fleet Street's gargoyles took me aside: 'We know you can do the soft stuff, Philip. But can you do the hard stuff?' The hard stuff came hurtling through the sky on 11 September 2001, and started me thinking about the questions that led eventually to this book.

Robin Lane Fox opened my eyes to the different ways history can be approached. His intellectual verve and subversiveness are infectious. I first travelled to the Middle East while his student, with money provided by New College, Oxford. Having spent all that money, I read T. E. Lawrence's *The Seven Pillars of Wisdom* on the roof of a hostel in Amman, surviving for three days on the gift box of pastries I had bought for my long-suffering parents. At Harvard Business School, I learned to think about the world differently from how I had as a journalist, in terms of companies, industries, the economic competitiveness of nations, supply chains and flows of capital. Michael Porter's and Felix Oberholzer-Gee's classes were profound.

Steve Schwarzman founded a company, Blackstone, which has its own view of the world derived from its vast array of investors and investments. For all that he has going on in his life, Steve is the most prompt and thoughtful connector. He introduced me to the Saudi ambassador to the United States, Her Royal Highness Reema Bandar Al-Saud, a granddaughter of King Faisal. When we met on a rainy afternoon in Washington DC, she lit up at the mention of Nejdis, Hijazis, and Well No. 7, and encouraged me to explore a story dimly known in the West. James Akins's daughter Mary Anne Colvill spoked devotedly of her father, who had an essential role during the months of the embargo, and shared her father's unpublished memories of his time in Saudi Arabia. Bill Simon's son, Peter, helped me to understand his larger-than-life father.

Tina Bennett is a wonderful agent and friend. Her craft, intelligence and warmth make the world a brighter place – and if you're feeling blue, she will leave cookies on your doorstep. Robert Messenger and Rowan Borchers were good enough to acquire this book for publication, and Rowan and Priscilla Painton have been excellent company on the jaunty ride to market. Among the many who have seen me through the writing are: Margret Frame, Victoria and Luke Bridgeman, Tom Rhodes, Vanessa Bismarck, Sasha Cutter, Jo Johnson, Milly Gentleman, Anda Rowland, Charlotte Edwardes, Jill Furman, Antonia Apps, Hugh and Sandra Lawson, James Lyle, Paul Hardart, Dorrit Morley, Christopher Coleridge, Julian Large, Victoria Kader, Barnes Martin, Heather Lindsey, Sebastian Mallaby, and Florian Amereller, whose Al Moudira Hotel in Luxor is an astonishing place to rest awhile and think of Egypt. Thank you also to the staff at the American Academy in Rome and the New York Society Library.

The universe sometimes sends people into your life at precisely the right moment. Caroline Schmidt's astonishing energy, laughter and occasional reprimands – 'I'm going to assume you're working much harder than you seem to be' – propelled me along. Her devotions, self-belief, and refined intuition set a standard I felt impelled to meet. They also made me very happy.

My sons, Augie and Hugo, are the Well No. 7 of my life. Augie flows downhill with an enviable gift for friendship, fun and hard work. Thank God, he still laughs at my jokes. Hugo is twenty-one now, and has experienced violent, daily seizures since he was seven. He is the most decent, empathetic, funny, dog-loving person, and the sheer fact of his life renders other dramas pale.

Select Bibliography

BOOKS

Aburish, Said K., The Rise, Corruption and Coming Fall of the House of Saud (London: Bloomsbury, 1994).

Aburish, Said K., Saddam Hussein: The Politics of Revenge (London: Bloomsbury, 2000).

Alam, Asadollah, The Shah and I: The Confidential Diary of Iran's Royal Court (London: I. B. Tauris & Co., 1991).

Almuhanna, Ibrahim, Oil Leaders: An Insider's Account of Four Decades of Saudi Arabia and OPEC's Global Energy Policy (New York: Columbia University Press, 2022).

Al-Rasheed, A History of Saudi Arabia (Cambridge: Cambridge University Press, 2002).

Ammann, Daniel, The King of Oil: The Secret Lives of Marc Rich (New York: St. Martin's Press, 2009).

Armstrong, Karen, Islam (New York: The Modern Library, Random House, 2000).

Ascheim, Daniel, Kreisky, Israel, and Jewish Identity (New Orleans: University of New Orleans Press, 2022).

Ashford, Emma, Oil, the State, and War: The Foreign Policies of Petrostates (Washington: Georgetown University Press, 2022).

Atkinson, Neville, Death on Small Wings: Memoirs of a Presidential Pilot (Librario Publishing, 2006).

Bamberg, James, British Petroleum and Global Oil, 1950–1975: The Challenge of Nationalism (Cambridge: Cambridge University Press, 2000).

Bancroft Library, Regional Oral History Office, American Perspectives of Aramco, the Saudi Arabian Oil Producing Company, 1930s to 1980s (University of California, Berkeley, 1995).

Barber, Anthony, Taking the Tide: A Memoir (London: Michael Russell, 1996).

Barr, James, Lords of the Desert: Britain's Struggle with America to Dominate the Middle East (London: Simon & Schuster, 2018).

Beling, Willard A. (ed.), King Faisal and the Modernisation of Saudi Arabia (London: Croom Helm, 1980).

Ben-Ami, Shlomo, Scars of War, Wounds of Peace: The Israeli-Arab Tragedy (Oxford: Oxford University Press, 2006).

Bénard, André, Le Hasard et l'opiniâtreté: De la Royal Dutch Shell au Tunnel sous la Manche (Paris: L'Harmattan, 2016).

Benoist-Méchin, Jacques, Fayçal, Roi d'Arabie (Paris: Albin Michel, 1975).

Bergman, Ronen, Rise and Kill First: The Secret History of Israel's Targeted Assassinations (New York: Random House, 2018).

Bini, Elisabetta; Garavini, Giuliano; Romero, Federico (eds), Oil Shock: The 1973 Crisis and Its Economic Legacy (London: Bloomsbury, 2016).

Bird, Kai, The Chairman: John J. McCloy & the Making of the American Establishment (New York: Simon & Schuster, 1992).

Blandford, Linda, Oil Sheikhs: Inside the Supercharged World of the Petrodollar (London: W. H. Allen, 1977).

Blas, Javier; Farchy, Jack, The World for Sale: Money, Power, and the Traders Who Barter the Earth's Resources (New York: Oxford University Press, 2021).

Burrough, Bryan, The Big Rich: The Rise and Fall of the Greatest Texas Oil Fortunes (New York: Penguin Books, 2009).

Chermack, Thomas J., Foundations of Scenario Planning: The Story of Pierre Wack (New York: Routledge, 2017).

Coll, Steve, Private Empire: Exxon Mobil and American Power (New York: Penguin Books, 2012).

Commins, David, Saudi Arabia: A Modern History (Yale University Press, 2025).

Copetas, A. Craig, Metal Men: How Marc Rich Defrauded the Country, Evaded the Law, and Became the World's Most Sought-After Corporate Criminal (New York: G. P. Putnam's Sons, 1985).

Dallek, Robert, Nixon and Kissinger: Partners in Power (New York: HarperCollins, 2007).

Dayan, Moshe, Moshe Dayan: Story of My Life (New York: William Morrow, 1976).

De Bellaigue, Christopher, Patriot of Persia (London: The Bodley Head, 2012).

De Gaury, Gerald, Faisal, King of Saudi Arabia (Louisville: Fons Vitae, 2007).

Dobson, Christopher; and Payne, Ronald, The Carlos Complex: A Study in Terror (New York: G. P. Putnam's Sons, 1977).

Ferguson, Niall; Maier, Charles S.; Manela, Erez; Sarjent, Daniel J. (eds), The Shock of the Global: The 1970s in Perspective (Cambridge: The Belknap Press of Harvard University Press, 2010).

Ferrell, Robert (ed.) Inside the Nixon Administration: The Secret Diary of Arthur Burns 1969–74 (Lawrence: University Press of Kansas, 2010).

Garten, Jeffrey, Three Days at Camp David (New York: HarperCollins, 2021).

Ghattas, Kim, Black Wave: Saudi Arabia, Iran, and the Forty-Year Rivalry that Unraveled Culture, Religion, and Collective Memory in the Middle East (New York: Henry Holt and Company, 2020).

Golan, Matti, The Secret Conversations of Henry Kissinger (New York: Quadrangle, 1976).

Haykel, Bernard; Hegghammer, Thomas; Lacroix, Stephane, Saudi Arabia in Transition: Insights on Social, Political, Economic and Religious Change (Cambridge: Cambridge University Press, 2015).

Heikal, Mohammed, The Road to Ramadan (London: William Collins, 1975).

Hope, Bradley; and Scheck, Justin, Blood and Oil: Mohammed Bin Salman's Ruthless Quest for Global Power (New York: Hachette Books, 2020).

House, Karen Elliott, On Saudi Arabia: Its People, Past, Religion, Fault Lines – and Future (New York: Vintage Books, 2013).

Hurt III, Harry, Texas Rich: The Hunt Dynasty from the early Oil Days through the Silver Crash (New York: W. W. Norton & Company, 1982).

Iacocca, Lee, Iacocca: An Autobiography (New York: Bantam, 1984).
Indyk, Marting, Master of the Game: Henry Kissinger and the Art of Middle East Diplomacy (New York: Alfred A. Knopf, 2021).
Isaacson, Walter, Kissinger: A Biography (New York: Touchstone, 1992).
Jacobs, Megan, Panic at the Pump: The Energy Crisis and the Transformation of American Politics in the 1970s (New York: Hill & Wang, 2016).
Jobert, Michel, Mémoires d'Avenir (Paris: Éditions Grasset & Fasquelle, 1974).
Jungers, Frank, The Caravan Goes On: How Aramco and Saudi Arabia Grew Up Together (Surbiton: Medina Publishing. 2013.
Kalb, Marvin; and Kalb, Bernard, Kissinger (New York: Dell Publishing, 1974).
Kaplan, Robert, The Arabists: The Romance of an American Elite (New York: The Free Press, 1993).
Kapuścińksi, Ryszard, Shah of Shahs (New York: Houghton Mifflin Harcourt, 1985).
Kepel, Gilles, Jihad: Expansion et Déclin de l'Islamisme (Paris: Éditions Gallimard, 2000).
Kinzer, Stephen, All the Shah's Men: An American Coup and the Roots of Middle East Terror (Hoboken: John Wiley & Son, 2003).
Kissinger, Henry, Crisis: The Anatomy of Two Major Foreign Policy Crises (New York: Simon & Schuster, 2003).
Kissinger, Henry, Years of Upheaval (New York: Simon & Schuster, 1982).
Klagsbrun, Francine, Lioness: Golda Meir and the Nation of Israel (New York: Schocken Books, 2017).
Klein, Hans-Joachim, La Morte Mercenaries: Temoignage d'un Ancien Terroriste Ouest-Allemand (Paris: Éditions du Seuil, 1980).
Lacey, Robert, The Kingdom: Arabia & the House of Saud (New York: Avon Books, 1981).
Menoret, Pascal, Joyriding in Riyadh: Oil, Urbanism, and Road Revolt (Cambridge: Cambridge University Press, 2014).
Merrill, Karen R., The Oil Crisis of 1973–74: A Brief History with Documents (Boston: Bedford/St Martin's, 2007).
Mitchell, Richard P., The Society of the Muslim Brothers (Oxford: Oxford University Press, 1993).

Monroe, Elizabeth, Philby of Arabia (Reading: Ithaca Press, 1973).

Monroe, Elizabeth; and Mabro, Robert, Oil Producers and Consumers: Conflict or Cooperation (New York: American Universities Field Staff, 1974).

Moorer, Admiral Thomas Hinman, The Reminiscences of Thomas Hinman Moorer, USN (Ret.) vol. III (Annapolis: US Naval Institute, 1984).

Mosley, Leonard, Power Play: Oil in the Middle East (New York: Random House, 1973).

Norton-Smith, Richard, On His Own Terms: A Life of Nelson Rockefeller (New York: Random House).

Rubino, Anna, Queen of the Oil Club: The Intrepid Wanda Jablonsky and the Power of Information (Boston: Beacon Press, 2008).

Sadat, Anwar El, In Search of Identity (New York: Harper & Row, 1977).

Sampson, Anthony, The Seven Sisters: The Great Oil Companies and the World They Shaped (New York: The Viking Press, 1975).

Schulze, Reinhard, A Modern History of the Islamic World (London: I. B. Tauris & Co., 2000).

Scott Cooper, Andrew, The Fall of Heaven: The Pahlavis and the Final Days of Imperial Iran (New York: Picador, 2018).

Scott Cooper, Andrew, The Oil Kings (New York: Simon & Schuster, 2011).

Seale, Patrick, Abu Nidal: A Gun for Hire: The Secret Life of the World's Most Notorious Terrorist (New York: Random House, 1992).

Seale, Patrick, Asad: The Struggle for the Middle East (London: I. B. Tauris & Co., 1988).

Sharon, Ariel, with Charnoff, David, Warrior: An Autobiography (New York: Simon & Schuster, 2001).

Shavit, Ari, My Promised Land: The Triumph and Tragedy of Israel (New York: Spiegel & Grau, 2013).

Shawcross, William, The Shah's Last Ride (New York: Simon & Schuster, 1988).

Sheehan, Edward, The Arabs, Israelis, and Kissinger: A Secret History of American Diplomacy in the Middle East (New York: Reader's Digest Press, 1976).

Sherrill, Robert, The Oil Follies of 1970–80 (New York: Anchor Press, 1983).

Simon, William, A Time for Reflection: An Autobiography (Washington: Regnery Publishing, 2004).

Simon, William, A Time for Truth (New York: Reader's Digest Press, 1978).

Sparrow, Bartholomew, The Strategist: Brent Scowcroft and the Call of National Security (New York: Public Affairs, 2015).

Terzian, Pierre, OPEC: The Inside Story (London: Zed Books, 1985).

Thesiger, Wilfred, Arabian Sands (London: Penguin Books, 2007).

Thomas, Evan, Being Nixon: A Man Divided (New York: Random House, 2016).

Thompson, Helen, Disorder, Hard Times in the 21st Century (Oxford: Oxford University Press, 2022).

Unger, Craig, House of Bush: House of Saud (New York: Simon & Schuster, 2004).

Upton, Roger, Arab Falconry (Hancock House Publishers, 2002).

Vassiliev, Alexei, King Faisal of Saudi Arabia (London: Saqi Books, 2012).

Venn, Fiona, The Oil Crisis (New York: Routledge, 2013).

Walker, Peter, Staying Power (London: Bloomsbury, 1991).

Wight, David M., Oil Money: Middle East Petrodollars and the Transformation of US Empire, 1967–1988 (Ithaca: Cornell University Press, 2021).

Yallop, David, Tracking the Jackal: The Search for Carlos, the World's Most Wanted Man (New York: Random House, 1993).

Yamani, Mai, Cradle of Islam: The Hijaz and the Quest for Identity in Saudi Arabia (London: I. B. Tauris & Co., 2009).

Yergin, Daniel, The New Map: Energy, Climate, and the Clash of Nations (New York: Penguin Press, 2020).

Yergin, Daniel, The Prize: The Epic Quest for Oil, Money and Power (New York: Simon & Schuster, 1990).

Wright, Lawrence, The Looming Tower: Al-Qaeda and the Road to 9/11 (New York: Vintage Books, 2007).

Ziegler, Philip, Edward Heath: The Authorized Biography (London: HarperPress, 2010).

The *Foreign Relations of the United States* series, maintained by the Department of State is an invaluable historical resource. The volumes which I consulted most frequently were:

1969–1976, Volume XV, Soviet Union, June 1972–August 1974, eds. Douglas E. Selvage, Melissa Jane Taylor (United States Government Printing Office, 2011).

1964–1968, Volume XXI, Near East Region; Arabian Peninsula, ed. Nina Davis Howland (Washington: United States Government Printing Office, 2000).

1969–1976, Volume XXV, Arab-Israeli Crisis and War, 1973, eds. Nina Howland, Craig Daigle (Washington: United States Government Printing Office, 2011).

1969–1976, Volume XXVII, Iran; Iraq, 1973–1976, ed. Monica L. Belmonte (United States Government Printing Office, 2012).

1969–1976, Volume XXXI, Foreign Economic Policy, 1973–1976, ed. Kathleen B. Rasmussen (Washington: United States Government Printing Office, 2009).

1969–1976, Volume XXXVI, Energy Crisis, 1969–1974, ed. Linda Qaimmaqami (Washington: Office of the Historian, 2011).

1969–1976, Volume XXXVII, Energy Crisis, 1974–1980, ed. Stephen G. Galpern (Washington: United States Government Printing Office, 2012).

1969–1976, Volume E–4, Documents on Iran and Iraq, 1969–1972, ed. Monica L. Belmonte (Washington: United States Government Printing Office, 2006).

1969–1976, Volume E–9, Part 2, Documents on the Middle East Region, 1973–1976, ed. Paul Hibbeln (Washington: United States Government Publishing Office, 2017).

1969–1976, Volume E–15, Part 2, Documents on Western Europe, 1973–1976, Second, Revised Edition, ed. Kathleen B. Rasmussen (Washington: United States Government Publishing Office, 2021).

I am also grateful for having had access to the following libraries and archives: the Foreign Affairs Oral History Collection, maintained by the Association for Diplomatic Studies and Training; the Amherst College Archives and Special Collections; the William E. Simon

Papers held at Lafayette College; W. R. Poage Legislative Library, Baylor University; the Saudi Aramco Publications Collection at Georgetown University; the Richard Nixon Presidential Library; the Gerald Ford Presidential Library; the George H. W. Bush Presidential Library; the United States National Archives and Records Administration; the diplomatic archives of France's Ministère de l'Europe et des Affaires Étrangères; the UK National Archives; the British Library; the King Fahad National Library; the King Faisal Foundation; the Middle East Centre Archive at St Antony's College, Oxford; the American Academy in Rome; the Arabian Gulf Digital Archives; and the peerless New York Public Library.

Notes

PROLOGUE: HAWKING SEASON

1. Marianne Alireza, 'The Late King Faisal: Life, Personality and Methods of Government', in *Kingdom of Saudi Arabia in 100 Years, Studies and Researches*, ed. Dr Fahd Al-Semmari (Riyadh: King Abdul Aziz Foundation, 2008), 399.
2. 'Faisal's Character', Aramco profile, Saudi Aramco Publications Collection, GTM-20230816. Georgetown University Manuscripts.
3. Wilfred Thesiger, *Arabian Sands* (London: Penguin Books, 2007), 288–95.
4. Telcon with Liza Minnelli, 19 October 1973, Series IV: Telephone Conversation Transcript Copies, Box 195, Folder 4, Henry A. Kissinger Papers, Part III (MS 2004), Manuscripts and Archives, Yale University Library.

CHAPTER 1: BETRAYAL

1. H. St.J. B. Philby, *Arabian Jubilee* (London: Hale, 1952).
2. Major R. E. Chesman, *In Unknown Arabia* (London: Macmillan, 1926), 167–73.
3. Humphrey Bowman, 'Arab Mission to England', UK Document. 252.
4. 'Faisal's Character', Aramco profile from Georgetown archives.
5. Gerald De Gaury, *Faisal: King of Saudi Arabia* (London: Arthur Baker, 1966), 34.
6. 'Monarch, Statesman and Patriarch: 1905–1975', *Aramco World*, July/August 1975.

7. 'Hijaz-Nejd Mission to Europe', File 61/28 (D85), Qatar Digital Library.
8. 'Fish to Jedda', *Time*, 19 February 1940.
9. William Eddy, *F.D.R. Meets Ibn Saud* (New York: American Friends of the Middle East, 1954).
10. Captain William Eddy account of Ibn Saud meeting FDR.
11. The Minister in Saudi Arabia (Eddy) to the Secretary of State, Jeddah, 22 February 1945. Foreign Relations of the United States, Diplomatic Papers, 1945, The Near East and Africa, Volume VIII.
12. Nubar Gulbenkian, *Portrait in Oil: The Autobiography of Nubar Gulbenkian* (New York: Simon & Schuster, 1965), 214.
13. Dean Acheson, *Present at the Creation: My Years at the State Department* (New York: W. W. Norton 1987), 177.
14. Dean Rusk, interviewed by Richard Rusk and Thomas Schoenbaum, April 1985. Dean Rusk Oral History Collection, University of Georgia Libraries.

CHAPTER 2: ARAMCONS

1. Details of early Aramco, Michael Sheldon Cheney, *Big Oil Man from Arabia* (New York: Ballantine Books, 1958), 58–83.
2. James H. Bahti Oral History, interviewed by Charles Stuart Kennedy, Foreign Affairs Oral History Collection, Association for Diplomatic Studies and Training, Arlington, VA, adst.org.
3. Tom Barger, 'Myth or Man', *Aramco World*, September/October 1969.
4. Idries Shah, *Destination Mecca* (London: Octagon, 1969), 101.
5. Bahti, ADST Oral History.
6. Cheney, *Big Oil Man from Arabia*, 245.
7. Cheney, *Big Oil Man from Arabia*, 178–9.
8. David Holden, *Farewell to Arabia* (New York: Walker & Company, 1966), 125.

9. Bancroft Library, Regional Oral History Office, *American Perspectives of Aramco, the Saudi Arabian Oil-Producing Company, 1930s to 1980s* (Berkeley: University of California, Berkeley, 1995), 560.
10. 'Faisal, Rich and Powerful, Led Saudis Into 20th Century and to Arab Forefront', *New York Times*, 26 March 1975.
11. Leonard Mosley, 'Aramco is not so much a company as it is a country within a country', *New York Times*, 10 March 1974.
12. De Gaury, *Faisal*, 138.
13. Ministry of Information, Kingdom of Saudi Arabia, *Faisal Speaks*, 17.
14. Ibid., 38.
15. Ibid., 17.
16. Edward Sheehan, 'Mastermind of Mideast Oil', *Reader's Digest*, September 1974.
17. Jeffrey Robinson, *Yamani: The Inside Story* (New York: Simon & Schuster, 1988), 54.
18. Eugene H. Bird, interviewed by Charles Stuart Kennedy. ADST Oral History Collection.
19. Katrina Thomas, 'America as Alma Mater', *Aramco World*, May/June 1979.
20. Bancroft, *American Perspectives of Aramco*, 257.
21. Richard Nixon interview with Frank Gannon, Part 3, 27 May 1983, Walter J. Brown Media Archives & Peabody Awards Collection, University of Georgia.
22. Gordon Gaskill, 'Saudi Arabia's Modern Monarch', *Reader's Digest*, January 1967.
23. Alireza, *The Late King Faisal*, 400.
24. Ibid., 402.
25. 'Faisal's Character', Aramco profile, Saudi Aramco Publications Collection, GTM-20230816. Georgetown University Manuscripts.

CHAPTER 3: JERUSALEM SYNDROME

1. Report on the State Visit of King Faisal to the United Kingdom by George Brown, UK Foreign Secretary, 22 June 1967.
2. Bahti, ADST Oral History Collection.
3. Bancroft, *American Perspectives of Aramco*, 501–3.

4. Ibid.
5. Telegram from Embassy of the United States in Saudi Arabia to the Department of State, Jeddah, 23 June 1967, National Archives and Records Administration (hereafter NARA), RG 59, Central Files 1967–69, POL 27 ARAB-ISR.

   Foreign Relations of the United States, 1964–1968, Volume XXI, Near East Region; Arabian Peninsula, Document 297. https://history.state.gov/historicaldocuments/frus1964-68v21/d297
6. The National Archives of the UK (TNA): FCO 8/1169: King Faisal: Impression of his Rule. Inside King Faisal. Memo from D. J. McCarthy, Arabian Department FCO, British Embassy, Jedda 2 April 1969.
7. TNA: FCO 8/1169 King Faisal, by D. J. McCarthy, FCO Arabian Department, 14 October 1969.
8. TNA: FCO 8/1169 Saudi Arabia: Internal. W. Morris, FCO Arabian Department, 1 November 1969.
9. Ibid.
10. Conversation with Shaikh Mohammed Ali Reza, by W. Morris, FCO Arabian Department, 16 November 1969.
11. TNA: FCO 8/1170 Arrests connected with plot to kill King Faisal, A Plot in Saudi Arabia, FCO Memo, 9 September 1969.
12. Dana Adams Schmidt, 'Saudis Hold 200 in Plot on Regime', *New York Times*, 9 September 1969.

CHAPTER 4: THE GADDAFI EFFECT

1. Ethan Chorin, *Exit the Colonel: The Hidden History of the Libyan Revolution* (New York: PublicAffairs, 2012), 38.
2. Department of State to Henry Kissinger, 'Qhadafi Resignation Reported in Libya', 27 September 1971, National Security File, Country Files, Middle East, Box 739, Richard Nixon Presidential Library and Museum.
3. John Bonar, 'Life in Libya Under Gaddafi', *The Observer*, 24 January 1971.
4. Warren Clark, interviewed by Charles Stuart Kennedy, ADST Oral History Project.

5. Edward Sheehan, 'Colonel Qadhafi Libya's Mystical Revolutionary; So Much Oil Money, and So Little to Spend it On', *New York Times*, 6 February 1972.
6. Kai Bird, *The Chairman: John J. McCloy & The Making of the American Establishment* (Simon & Schuster, 2017), 743.
7. Robert Kaplan, *The Arabists: The Romance of an American Elite* (New York: The Free Press, 1993), 200.
8. John Tigrett, *Fair and Square: A Collection of Stories from a Lifetime Among Friends* (Nashville: Spiridon Press, 1998), 202, 290.
9. Edwin Shrake, 'Standing Knee Deep in Clover', *Sports Illustrated*, 21 June 1976.
10. 'Libya Pumping Up Profits', *Time*, 24 February 1967.
11. Ann Rubino, *Queen of the Oil Club: The Intrepid Wanda Jablonski and the Power of Information* (Boston: Beacon Press, 2008), 245.
12. Henry Tanner, 'Qaddafi, Libya's Shy Power Broker', *New York Times*, 4 February 1974.
13. US State Department Telegram 2934 from Tripoli, 8 October; ibid., Central Files 1967–69, PET 1 LIBYA

    Information Memorandum Prepared in the Bureau of African Affairs, Washington, 13 May 1970.

    Foreign Relations of the United States, 1969–1976, Volume XXXVI, Energy Crisis, 1969–1974, Document 45. https://history.state.gov/historicaldocuments/frus1969-76v36/d45
14. Senate Subcommittee on Multinational Corporations.
15. Melhuish to Brant, 'Negotiations between the Libyan Government and the producing companies on posted prices', 19 May 1970, FCO 67/432.
16. Foreign Relations of the United States, 1969–1976, Volume XXXVI, Energy Crisis, 1969–1974, Document 55. https://history.state.gov/historicaldocuments/frus1969-76v36/d55
17. Yamani told Akins in September 1971 that 'Saudi Arabia would leave the running to Libya and Iraq' on national participation. If they went first, 'Kuwait and Saudi Arabia could not be seen to be lagging far behind.' Jedda telegram (745) to FCO, 19 September 1971, FCO 67/561; 'OPEC Countries Plan to Negotiate with Oil

Companies on Participation and Monetary Changes', *Middle East Economic Survey*, 14/48 (1971, 1–7).

CHAPTER 5: TEHRAN

1. Robert Graham, *The Illusion of Iran* (New York: St Martin's Press, 1980), 77–92.
2. Frances Fitzgerald, 'Giving the Shah Everything He Wants', *Harper's*, November 1974.
3. Ibid.
4. 'Iran: Oil, Grandeur and a Challenge to the West', *Time*, 4 November 1974.
5. Harrison Smith, 'Ardeshir Zahedi, flamboyant Iranian ambassador who advised the shah, dies at 93', *Washington Post*, 20 November 2021.
6. William Shawcross, *The Shah's Last Ride* (New York: Simon & Schuster, 1988), 339.
7. Richard D. Lyons, 'McCloy Testifies He Took the Oil Companies' Case on International Talks to President Kennedy', *New York Times*, 7 February 1974.
8. Telegram 218 from the Embassy in Iran to the Department of State. Tehran, 14 January 1971. National Archive, RG 59, Central Files 1970–73, Pet 3 OPEC.

   Foreign Relations of the United States, 1969–1976, Volume E–4, Documents on Iran and Iraq, 1969–1972, ed. Monica L. Belmonte (Washington: United States Government Printing Office, 2006), Document 109. https://history.state.gov/historicaldocuments/frus1969-76ve04/d109

   Multinational Petroleum Companies and United States Foreign Policy, Hearings before the Subcommittee on Multinational Corporations of the Senate Committee on Foreign Relations, 93rd Congress, 28 January 1974 (statement of Henry Schuler), 84.
9. Multinational Petroleum Companies and United States Foreign Policy, Hearings before the Subcommittee on Multinational

Corporations of the Senate Committee on Foreign Relations, 93rd Congress, 31 January 1974 (statement of Henry Schuler), 122.
10. Peter Martin, 'The Brother Colonel is on maneuvers again', *The Times*, 24 July 1973.
11. Peter Hillmore, 'Libya Opposed to Five Year Pact', *The Guardian*, 25 March 1971.
12. 'Oil Pact Is Hailed in Libya as a Victory for the People', *Reuters*, 3 April 1971.
13. Dick Cheney interview with Timothy Naftali of the Richard Nixon Presidential Library, 19 December 2007.
14. U.N. Sec. Council, Prof. Verbatim Rec., S/PV.1610, 9 Dec. 1971. Cited in, G. Winthrop Haight, 'Libyan Nationalization of British Petroleum Company Assets', *The International Lawyer* 6, no. 3 (1972): 541–7. http://www.jstor.org/stable/40704761.

CHAPTER 6: I WILL USE MY POWER

1. 'Report of Meeting Held in Geneva at Intercontinental Hotel', John J. McCloy (AC 1916) Papers (MA-00035), Box 28, Folder 16, Archives and Special Collections, Amherst College.
2. This section draws on a speech Yamani gave at the American University of Beirut on 7 February 1967, *Islamic Law and Contemporary Issues*.
3. Gulbenkian, *Portrait in Oil*, 96.
4. Bancroft, *American Perspectives of Aramco*, 441.
5. Bancroft, *American Perspectives of Aramco*, 460.
6. William D. Smith, 'Spotlight', *New York Times*, 6 October 1972.
7. Frank Jungers, *The Caravan Goes On* (Surbiton: Medina Publishing, 2013), 171.
8. Bancroft, *American Perspectives of Aramco*, 441.

CHAPTER 7: OPEN FLOW

1. Jack Keever, 'Texas Wells Given Full Go Ahead', *Abilene Reporter News*, 17 March 1971, 17.

2. Jan Jarboe Russell, 'Meaner Than a Junkyard Dog', *Texas Monthly*, April 1991.
3. Robert N. Jones, 'Close-ups of the Oil Industry', The *Texas Observer*. 7 July 1967.
4. David Harris, 'The Crisis', *New York Times*, 27 February 2005.
5. Intelligence Note RNAN-18, Prepared in the Bureau of Intelligence and Research. National Archives, RG 59, Central Files 1970–73, POL 23–28 Iran.

   Foreign Relations of the United States, 1969–1976, Volume E–4, Documents on Iran and Iraq, 1969–1972, Document 203. https://history.state.gov/historicaldocuments/frus1969-76ve04/d203
6. Telegram 4789 from Embassy in Iran to the Department of State, 10 August 1972. National Archives RG 59, Central Files 1970–73.

   Foreign Relations of the United States, 1969–1976, Volume E–4, Documents on Iran and Iraq, 1969–1972, Document 217. https://history.state.gov/historicaldocuments/frus1969-76ve04/d217
7. 'Gunmen Kill 24 at Airport in Tel Aviv', *Washington Post*, 31 May 1972.
8. 'Belly Dancer Sits on Kissinger's Lap', UPI, 30 May 1972.
9. Foreign Relations of the United States, 1969–1976, Volume XXVII, Iran; Iraq, 1973–1976, ed. Monica L. Belmonte, (United States Government Printing Office, 2012), Document 28. https://history.state.gov/historicaldocuments/frus1969-76v27/d28
10. William W. Lehfeldt, interviewed by William Burr, ADST Oral History Collection.
11. Jack Anderson, 'Shah Link to Nixon Campaign Hinted by Jack Anderson', *Washington Post*, 10 June 1974.
12. Said Aburish, *Saddam Hussein: The Politics of Revenge* (London: Bloomsbury, 2000), 101.
13. John Kifner, 'Baghdad's Strongman', *New York Times*, 15 July 1982.
14. Aburish, *Saddam Hussein*, 67.
15. Jim Hoagland, 'Iraqi Victory on Oil Seen', *International Herald Tribune*, 24 July 1972.
16. 'Iraq Declares Low Crude Price Offers are "Unauthorized"', *PIW*, 11 December 1972.
17. 'Fuel Bridge, Across the Middle East – Israel, Iran and the Eilat-Ashkelon Oil Pipeline' by Uri Bialer, *Israeli Studies*, Vol. 12, No. 3,

p. 54, quoting from *My Life Story* by Yaakov Nimrodi (Tel Aviv, 2003), p. 315, and from Israel government records, Abba Eban to Spain, 23 August 1968, ISA 5256/4.

18. Yossi Melman, 'The Story of Iranian Oil and Israeli Pipes', *Haaretz*, 11 October 2007.
19. Edward Sheehan, 'Mastermind of Mideast Oil', *Reader's Digest*, September 1974.
20. Pierre Terzian, *OPEC: The Inside Story* (London: Zed Books, 1985), 152. 'Western Oil Units Get Faisal Warning', *New York Times*, 17 February 1972.
21. 'Saudi Arabia Warns Companies, Reassures Consumer States', *PIW*, 17 July 1972.
22. National Archives, Nixon Presidential Materials, NSC Files, Box 1287, Saunders Files, Saudi Arabia, 1972.
23. 'Yamani Urges Responsible Use of New OPEC Power', *PIW*, 30 October 1972.

CHAPTER 8: THE RAPIDS

1. Thomas Chernack, *Foundations of Scenario Planning: The Story of Pierre Wack* (New York: Routledge International, 2017), 1–17.
2. Ibid., 62–3.
3. Ibid., 72–5.
4. Minutes of the Secretary of State's Staff Meeting, Washington, October 26, 1973. FRYS, 1969–1976, Volume XXXVI, Energy Crisis, 1969–1974, Document 229.
5. Joseph Kraft, 'Those Arabists in the State Department', *New York Times*, 7 November 1971.
6. Ibid.
7. Many of the details that follow are from William Simon's memoir, *A Time for Reflection: An Autobiography* (Washington: Regnery Publishing, 2004).
8. Simon, *A Time for Reflection*, 89.
9. George Stigler, 'A Personal Reminiscence by Milton Friedman', *Journal of Political Economy*, Vol. 101, October 1993.

10. Milton Friedman, 'Oil and the Middle East', *Newsweek*, 26 June 1967.
11. Marian Christy, 'He has his playful side, Treasury's Simon insists', *Boston Globe*, 9 November 1975. B1.
12. William D. Smith, 'Peterson Assures Oil Industry U.S. Will Act on Energy Needs', *New York Times*, 15 November 1972.
13. James Akins, 'The Oil Crisis: This Time the Wolf is Here', *Foreign Affairs*, April 1973.
14. Documents diplomatiques français. 1967, Tome I, 1er janvier-1er juillet / Ministère des affaires étrangères, Commission des archives diplomatiques. [sous la direction de Maurice Vaïsse]. 2008. Compte Rendu. 'Entretien entre le général de Gaulle et le Roi Fayçal d'Arabie Saoudite', 2 June 1967, 243. https://gallica.bnf.fr/ark:/12148/bd6t53270772
15. CIA Weekly Summary Special Report on France's policy towards the Middle East, 7 March 1969.
16. 'French-Saudi Summit May Foreshadow Closer Oil Ties', *PIW*, 21 May 1973.

CHAPTER 9: TRIPS OF THE FOX

1. Ariel Sharon with David Charnoff, *Warrior: An Autobiography* (New York: Simon & Schuster, 2001), 239–43.
2. Ibid., 247–62.
3. RAND Corporation, 'International Terrorism 1968–1974', March 1975.
4. Ibid.
5. Memorandum from the Chairman of the Interdepartmental Group for Near East and South Asia (Sisco) to the Chairman of the Review Group (Kissinger) 21 November 1969. Source: National Archives, Nixon Presidential Materials, NSC Files, Box 1319, NSC Secretariat, Unfiled Material, 1969.
6. Memorandum from the Chairman of the Interdepartmental Group for Near East and South Asia (Sisco) to the Chairman of the Review Group (Kissinger) Washington, 21 November 1969.

   FRUS, Foreign Relations of the United States, 1969–1976, Volume XXIV, Middle East Region and Arabian Peninsula,

1969–1972; Jordan, September 1970. 133. ed. Linda W. Qaimmaqami Adam M. Howard (Washington: United States Government Printing Office, 2008).

7. Wanda Jablonski, 'Prince Saud Spells Out Arabia's Oil Policy Goals', *PIW*, 20 November 1972.
8. 'At Least 15 Killed in Raid on Lebanon', *New York Times*, 22 February 1973.
9. 'Israelis Down a Libyan Airliner in the Sinai, Killing at Least 74', *New York Times*, 22 February 1973.
10. James Akins, private memoir.
11. Robinson, *Yamani*, 41.
12. Oriana Fallaci, 'A Sheik Who Hates to Gamble', *New York Times*, 14 September 1975.
13. Oriana Fallaci, *Interview with History* (New York: Houghton Mifflin Harcourt, 1977), 123–39.
14. Memo for the President's Files by Deputy Assistant for National Security Affairs Scowcroft. 23 February 1973.
15. Eugene Bird, interviewed by Charles Stuart Kennedy, ADST Oral History Collection.
16. Alfred Leroy Atherton Jr, interviewed by Dayton Mak, ADST Oral History Collection.
17. Anwar Sadat, *In Search of Identity* (New York: Harper & Row, 1977), 238.
18. Yigal Allon, 'The Case for Defensible Borders', *Foreign Affairs*, October 1976.
19. Arnaud de Borchgrave, 'Anwar Sadat's Uncertain Trumpet', *Newsweek*, 9 April 1973.
20. Abba Eban meets Kissinger in Washington. Nixon Presidential Materials, NSC Files, Kissinger Office Files, Box 135, Country Files, Middle East, Rabin/Dinitz Sensitive Memcons, 12 May 1973.

    Foreign Relations of the United States, 1969–1976, Volume XXV, Arab-Israeli Crisis and War, 1973, eds. Nina Howland, Craig Daigle (Washington: United States Government Printing Office, 2011), Document 55. https://history.state.gov/historicaldocuments/frus1969-76v25/d55
21. Memo of Conversation, Zavidovo, 7 May 1973. National Archives, Nixon Presidential Materials, NSC Files, Kissinger Office Files,

Box 75, Country Files, Europe, USSR, Kissinger Conversations at Zavidovo, 5–8 May 1973.

Foreign Relations of the United States, 1969–1976, Volume XV, Soviet Union, June 1972–August 1974, eds. Douglas E. Selvage, Melissa Jane Taylor (United States Government Printing Office. 2011), Document 109. https://history.state.gov/historicaldocuments/frus1969-76v15/d109

CHAPTER 10: WAR IS COMING

1. Nixon/Gannon Interviews, 12 May 1983, part 4. Nixon-Gannon Interviews Collection, University of Georgia Libraries Oral History Collections.
2. Gannon interviews.
3. Susanne Schattenberg, *The Making of a Statesman* (London: I. B. Tauris, November 2021), 343.
4. Evan Thomas, *Being Nixon: A Man Divided* (New York: Random House, 2016), 169.
5. Thomas, *Being Nixon*, 443.
6. Henry Kissinger, *Years of Upheaval* (New York: Simon & Schuster, 1982), 297.
7. Memorandum for the President's File by the President's Assistant for National Security Affairs (Kissinger), 1.

   San Clemente, 23 June 1973. National Archives, Nixon Presidential Materials, NSC Files, Kissinger Office Files, Box 75, Country Files—Europe—USSR, Brezhnev Visit Memcons, 18–25 June 1973.

   Foreign Relations of the United States, 1969–1976, Volume XV, Soviet Union, June 1972–August 1974, Document 132. https://history.state.gov/historicaldocuments/frus1969-76v15/d132
8. Thomas, *Nixon*, 457. Julie Nixon Eisenhower, *Pat Nixon: The Untold Story* (New York, Simon & Schuster, 1986), 373.
9. Memorandum from Director of Central Intelligence Schlesinger to Nixon, 20 April 1973. National Archives, Nixon Presidential Materials, NSC Files, Box 51, Presidential Daily Briefings Eyes Only for the President.

Foreign Relations of the United States, 1969–1976, Volume XXXVI, Energy Crisis, 1969–1974, Document 178. https://history.state.gov/historicaldocuments/frus1969-76v36

10. Telegram from the Embassy in Saudi Arabia to the Department of State. Jeddah, 27 March 1973. From Ambassador Nicholas Thacher. National Archives, RG 59, Central Foreign Policy File.

    Foreign Relations of the United States, 1969–1976, Volume E–9, Part 2, Documents on the Middle East Region, 1973–1976, ed. Paul Hibbeln (Washington: United States Government Publishing Office. 2017), Document 83. https://history.state.gov/historicaldocuments/frus1969-76ve09p2/d83
11. Bird, ADST.
12. Memorandum of Conversation, 17 April 1973. National Archives, Nixon Presidential Materials, NSC Files, Box 1027, Presidential/HAK Memcons, Memcons, April–November 1973.

    Foreign Relations of the United States, 1969–1976, Volume XXXVI, Energy Crisis, 1969–1974, Document 176. https://history.state.gov/historicaldocuments/frus1969-76v36/d176
13. NLN-NSC-1298-4-113-5. Memo from Harold H. Saunders to Dr. Kissinger, 30 July 1973.
14. Bancroft, *American Perspectives of Aramco*, 126–33.
15. Juan de Onis, 'Faisal Gives U.S. Subtle Warning', *New York Times*, 29 July 1973.
16. President's Monday Briefing, 4 August 1973, NLM-NSC-1298-3-98-4.
17. Notes for Backchannel message from Ismail to Kissinger, 20 March 1973. National Archives, Nixon Presidential Materials, NSC Files, Kissinger Office, Box 131, Country Files, Middle East, Egypt/Ismail, Vol. IV 24 February–19 May 1973. Foreign Relations of the United States, 1969–1976, Volume XXV, Arab-Israeli Crisis and War, 1973, Document 41. https://history.state.gov/historicaldocuments/frus1969-76v25/d41
18. Fedayeen Seizure of Saudi Embassy in Paris, 11 September 1973, Report by Bureau of Near Eastern and South Asian Affairs, US State Department.

19. Interview with Prince Amr ibn Mohammad al-Faisal, Faisal's grandson, *Frontline PBS*, 1 October 2019.
20. Eric Pace, 'Saudi Government, Ever Wealthier, Maintains Firm Grip and Slow Pace', *New York Times*, 18 February 1971.
21. Oriana Fallaci, *Interviews with History and Conversations with Power* (New York: Rizzoli, 2011) 140–51.
22. 'Saudis React Coolly to Libya's Oil Nationalization', *Petroleum Intelligence Weekly*, 10 September 1973.
23. Ibid.
24. Hurt, *Texas Rich*, 321.
25. *PIW*, 13 August 1973.
26. *Middle East Economic Survey*, 14 September 1973.
27. *Petroleum Intelligence Weekly*, 28 May 1973.
28. Ashraf Abd al-Hameed, 'The Nubian military code that helped Egypt win 1973 war against Israel', *Al-Arabiya English*, 9 October 2017.
29. Abraham Rabinovich, *The Yom Kippur War: The Epic Encounter that Transformed the Middle East* (New York: Schocken, 2004), 230.

CHAPTER 11: VOLCANO

1. L. Paul 'Jerry' Bremer, interviewed by Charles Stuart Kennedy, ADST Oral History Project.
2. 'Terrorism: Blackmail in Vienna', *Time*, 8 October 1973.
3. https://thomas-riegler.net/2017/09/24/das-geiseldrama-von-marchegg-und-die-bislang-unbekannte-rolle-der-ddr-staatssicherheit/
4. Daniel Ascheim, *Kreisky, Israel, and Jewish Identity* (New Orleans: University of New Orleans Press, 2022).
5. David Yallop, *Tracking the Jackal: The Search for Carlos, the World's Most Wanted Man* (New York: Random House, 1993), 160.
6. Memo of Conversation, Department of State, 17 October 1973. Arab-Israeli Conflict. Kissinger with foreign ministers of Saudi Arabia, Kuwait, Morocco, and Algeria.

   Foreign Relations of the United States, 1969–1976, Volume XXV, Arab-Israeli Crisis and War, 1973, Document 195. https://history.state.gov/historicaldocuments/frus1969-76v25/d195

7. Faysal Replies to Kissinger Plea for Help in Middle East. King Faysal to Kissinger, Scowcroft. 6 October 1973, Library of Congress, HAK-206-8-2-2 https://www.cia.gov/readingroom/docs/LOC-HAK-206-8-2-2.pdf
8. National Security Council Memo for Kissinger, from William Quandt and Donald Stukel, WSAG Meeting – Middle East, 6 October 1973. Source: NPMP, National Security Council Institutional Files, Box H-94, WSAG Meeting, Middle East 10/6/73 7:30 pm., folder 1. https://nsarchive2.gwu.edu/NSAEBB/NSAEBB98/octwar-15.pdf
9. Minutes of WASG, 7 October 1973. National Archives, Nixon Presidential Materials, NSC Files, NSC Institutional Files (H-Files), Box H-117, WSAG Meetings Minutes, 1973. Foreign Relations of the United States, 1969–1976, Volume XXV, Arab-Israeli Crisis and War, 1973, Document 121.
10. Mitch Ginsburg, 'Dayan pushed PM Meir to consider using nuclear weapons in 1973 war', *The Times of Israel*, 3 October 2013.
11. State. 'Oil Company Officials' Meeting With Deputy Secretary October 10'. Wikileaks Cable: 1973STATE202689_b. Dated: 1973, October 12, 18.26. https://wikileaks.org/plusd/cables/1973STATE202689_b.html
12. State. 'Vienna Oil Price Negotiations'. Wikileaks Cable: 1973STATE203180_b. Dated: 1973, October 12, 22.30. https://wikileaks.org/plusd/cables/1973STATE203180_b.html
13. André Bénard, *Le Hasard et l'opiniâtreté: De la Royal Dutch Shell au Tunnel sous la Manche* (Paris: L'Harmattan, 2016), 103–12.

CHAPTER 12: WHAT DO WE DO IF THE OIL IS CUT OFF?

1. Frank Zarb Interview, for Richard Nixon Presidential Library and Museum. 2007-10-04 ZAR.
2. Robert Ferrell (ed.), *Inside the Nixon Administration: The Secret Diary of Arthur Burns* (Lawrence: University Press of Kansas, 2010), 97.
3. Kissinger, *Years of Upheaval*, 202.
4. George Lardner Jr, 'Nixon defended envoy's groping: 1972 tapes

also reveal talk of a Justice Dept. "full of Jews" ', *Washington Post*, 1 March 2002.

5. 'September 13, 1971: The President and Haldeman, 4.36-5.05 pm., Oval Office', Stanley Kutler (ed.), *Abuse of Power: The New Nixon Tapes* (New York: Free Press, 1998), 31.
6. Timothy Noah, 'Nixon's Jew Count: The Whole Story!' *Slate*, 26 September 2007.
7. Robert Dallek, *Nixon and Kissinger: Partners in Power* (New York: HarperCollins, 2007), 170.
8. Kissinger, *Years of Upheaval*, 202.
9. William Safire interview with Timothy Naftali, Director of the Richard Nixon Presidential Library and Museum, for Richard Nixon Oral History Program, 27 March 2008.
10. Henry Kissinger, *Diplomacy* (New York: Simon & Schuster, 1994), 786.
11. Admiral Thomas Hinman Moorer, USN (Ret.) *The Reminiscences of Thomas Hinman Moorer, USN (Ret.)* vol. III (Annapolis: US Naval Institute, 1984), 1128.
12. Henry Kissinger, *Crisis: The Anatomy of Two Major Foreign Policy Crises* (New York: Simon & Schuster, 2003), 252.
13. Walter J. Boyne, 'Nickel Grass', *Airforce Magazine*, December 1998.
14. Military Airlift Command History Office, Heist, Harry, Lt. Col. USAF, memoirs.
15. Minutes of Washington Special Actions Group Meeting, 16 October 1973. National Archives, Nixon Presidential Materials, NSC Files, NSC Institutional Files (H-Files), Box H-117, Minutes Files 1969–1974. Foreign Relations of the United States, 1969–1976, Volume XXXVI, Energy Crisis, 1969–1974i, Document 217. https://history.state.gov/historicaldocuments/frus1969-76v36
16. Multinational Corporations and United States Foreign Policy, Hearings Before the Subcommittee on Multinational Corporations of the Committee on Foreign Relations, United States Senate, 31 January, 1 and 6 February 1974, 236.
17. Terzian, *OPEC*, 173.
18. Rabinovich, *The Yom Kippur War*, 472.
19. Jedda/Akins, 'Saudi Minister of Petroleum's Account of Kuwait Arab Oil Meeting'. Wikileaks Cable: 1973Jeddah04615_b.

Dated 1973 October 20, 14.15. https://wikileaks.org/plusd/cables/1973Jeddah04615_b.html
20. Frank Jungers, *The Caravan Goes On* (Cowes: Medina Publishing, 2013), 154.
21. Bancroft, *American Perspectives of Aramco*, 134.
22. Ibid., 436.
23. Allan T. Demaree, 'Aramco is a lesson in the management of chaos', *Fortune*, February 1974.
24. 'Poison warning to children who stole sweets', *The Times*, Monday 29 January 1973.
25. TNA: PREM 15/1845, Letter from Frank McFadzean to the Prime Minister, 23 February 1973.
26. TNA: PREM 15/1838, Cabinet Office note of a meeting held at 10 Downing Street on Wednesday 17 October 1973 at 5.30 p.m.
27. Memorandum of Conversation, Washington, 24 October 1973. Ford Library, National Security Adviser, Memoranda of Conversation, Box 2. Secret.
28. Telegram 212618 From the Department of State to the Embassy in the Federal Republic of Germany, Washington, 27 October 1973, 2249Z.

    Department of State Secretary's Meeting with FRG Ambassador Von Staden, 26 October 1973. NNO 969046.

    Foreign Relations of the United States, 1969–1976, Volume E–15, Part 2, Documents on Western Europe, 1973–1976, Second, Revised Edition, ed. Kathleen B. Rasmussen (Washington: United States Government Publishing Office, 2021), Document 274. https://history.state.gov/historicaldocuments/frus1969-76ve15p2Ed2/d274
29. Dallek, *Nixon and Kissinger*, 523.
30. Lt. F. C. Miller, 'Those Storm-Beaten Ships, Upon Which the Arab Armies Never Looked', *Proceedings of the US Naval Institute*, March 1975, Vol. 101/3/865.
31. Moorer, *Reminiscences*, 1378.

CHAPTER 13: THE SHUTTLE

1. Jeddah. 'Views of Saudi Petroleum Minister: Oil as a Political Weapon, The Stick'. Wikileaks Cable: 1973Jeddah04768_b.

Dated: 1973, October 30, 14.51. https://wikileaks.org/plusd/cables/1973Jeddah04768_b.html

2. Office of the White House Press Secretary, Press Conference of Secretary of the Treasury George Shultz, 18 April 1973.
3. Dallek, *Nixon and Kissinger*.
4. Robert B. Oakley, interviewed by Charles Stuart Kennedy and Thomas Stern, ADST Oral History Collection.
5. Marvin Kalb and Bernard Kalb, *Kissinger* (New York: Dell Publishing, 1974), 580.
6. Edward Sheehan, 'How Kissinger Did it: Step by Step in the Middle East', *Foreign Policy*, Spring 1976.
7. David Hirst, 'Cold Holy Warrior Turns the Screw', *The Guardian*, 14 March 1972.
8. 'Le Roi Faycal, Les Juifs et Le Communisme', *Le Monde*, 11 August 1972.
9. 'The Echo of Mein Kampf in Arab Antisemitism', *Patterns of Prejudice*, Vol. 9, No. 2, July 1975, 16. Quoting *Le Temps du Niger*, Niamey, 27 November 1972.
10. Hamid H. Mutaiwa, 'Faisal and the Fidelity of History', *Mecca Cultural Club*, 1979, 63.
11. *Jerusalem Post*, 5 July 1968, quoted in 'The Protocols Among Arabs', *Patterns of Prejudice*, Vol. 9, No. 4, p.18,
12. Kalb & Kalb, *Kissinger*, 580–1.
13. Bernard Gwertzman, 'Kissinger Warns Arabs on Oil Ban', *New York Times*, 7 February 1974.
14. Henry Kissinger, 'Faisal's Complex Course', *Time*, 1 March 1982, extracted from Kissinger, *Years of Upheaval*.
15. Isa K. Sabbagh, interviewed by Charles Stuart Kennedy, ADST Oral History Collection.
16. Katrina Thomas, 'America as Alma Mater', *Aramco World*, May/June 1979, Vol. 20, No. 3.
17. Ford Fraker, 'Remembering Prince Saud Al Faisal bin Abdulaziz', Politico, 29 December 2015.
18. Memorandum of Conversation, Washington, 29 November 1973. Ford Library, National Security Adviser, Memoranda of Conversations, Box 2, 29 November 1973.

    Foreign Relations of the United States, 1969–1976, Volume

XXXVI, Energy Crisis, 1969–1974, Document 251. https://history.state.gov/historicaldocuments/frus1969-76v36/d251

19. Ibid.
20. Telegram from the Embassy in Saudi Arabia to the Department of State, Jeddah, 26 November 1973. National Archives, Nixon Presidential Materials, NSC Files, Box 630, Country Files, Middle East, Saudi Arabia, Vol. IV. Secret.

    Foreign Relations of the United States, 1969–1976, Volume XXXVI, Energy Crisis, 1969–1974, Document 246. https://history.state.gov/historicaldocuments/frus1969-76v36/d246

CHAPTER 14: CHOKED WITH OIL

1. David Lennon, 'Golda: Europe stand "Munich attitude"', *Jerusalem Post*, 12 November 1973.
2. Francine Klagsbrun, *Lioness: Golda Meir and the Nation of Israel* (New York: Schocken Books, 2017), 645.
3. Brief for the Ministry of Industry's meeting with Sheikh Yamani and M. Abdesalaam, 29 November 10.30 a.m.
4. TNA: PREM/1842. Alan Rothnie, Jeddah, to the FCO, 23 November 1973.
5. Jeddah. 'Possibility of Decrease in Oil Prices'. Wikileaks Cable: 1973STATE250751_b. Dated: 1973, December 27, 18.36. https://wikileaks.org/plusd/cables/1973STATE250751_b.html
6. 'King Faisal Clarifies Stand on Oil Weapon', interview with Faisal published in Al-Anwar, Beirut, 22 November, translation published by MEES 28 November 1973.
7. TNA: PREM/1842. Memo of meeting between Tom Boardman of Prices Commission and Yamani, 29 November 1973.
8. TNA: PREM/1842. Record of Conversation between the Foreign and Commonwealth Secretary and the Algerian and Saudi Arabian Ministers of Petroleum at the FCO, Thursday 29 November 1973. NBS 12/2.
9. Peter Walker, *Staying Power* (London: Bloomsbury, 1991), 108–9.
10. TNA: PREM/1842. Memo to Prime Minister, reporting lunch Yamani and Sir Alec Douglas-Home.

11. 11 December 1973, Lord Rothschild to the Prime Minister.
12. James Schlesinger, 'A Testing Time for America', *Fortune*, February 1976, 77.
13. Transcript of Telephone Conversation Between Secretary of State Kissinger and the White House Chief of Staff (Haig), Washington, 27 October 1973. Foreign Relations of the United States, 1969–1976, Volume XXV, Arab-Israeli Crisis and War, 1973, Document 293. https://history.state.gov/historicaldocuments/frus1969-76v25/d293
14. Note from Peter Rousel of the RNC to George H. W. Bush, 27 November 1973. National Archives, Nixon Presidential Materials, NSC Files, Box 1336, NSC Unfiled Material 1973.

    Foreign Relations of the United States, 1969–1976, Volume XXXVI, Energy Crisis, 1969–1974, Document 250. https://history.state.gov/historicaldocuments/frus1969-76v36/d250
15. Memo from Arthur Mendolia, Asst. Secretary of Defense for Installations and Logistics to Brigadier General Richard Lawson, Air Force Military Assistant to the President. 30 November 1973. Nixon Presidential Materials, NSC Files, Box 321, Subject Files, Energy Crisis, Nov 73–Feb 74.
16. Paper Prepared in the Office of the Director, Installations and Logistics, Department of Defense, 27 November 1973. Washington National Records Center, OASD/IL Files: FRC 330–85–0035, Petroleum—Arab Oil Embargo 1973–74. Confidential.

    Foreign Relations of the United States, 1969–1976, Volume XXXVI, Energy Crisis, 1969–1974, Document 249. https://history.state.gov/historicaldocuments/frus1969-76v36/d249
17. Memorandum of Conversation, Washington, Washington, 26 November 1973, 11:30 A.M., National Archives, RG 59, Central Files 1970–73, FSE 1 US. Secret; Sensitive. Drafted by Lodal.

    Foreign Relations of the United States, 1969–1976, Volume XXXVI, Energy Crisis, 1969–1974, Document 247. https://history.state.gov/historicaldocuments/frus1969-76v36/d247
18. Marilyn Berger, 'Arbs Warned by Kissinger on Oil Cutoff', *The Washington Post*, 22 November 1973, A1.
19. Telegram 4914 from The Hague, 8 November; ibid., RG 59, Central Foreign Policy Files.

20. TNA: PREM15/1768. Record of meeting by Lord Cromer; Public Records Office.
21. Glenn Frankel, 'U.S. Mulled Seizing Oil Fields in '73', *Washington Post*, 31 December 2003.
22. 'Saudi Arabian oil minister speaking in Copenhagen about the oil production', *Associated Press*, 23 November 1973.
23. A. Elizabeth Jones interviewed by Charles Stuart Kennedy, ADST Oral History Collection.
24. Edward Sheehan, 'Mastermind of Mideast Oil', *Reader's Digest*, September 1974.
25. Minutes of Washington Special Actions Group Meeting, 29 November 1973. National Archives, Nixon Presidential Materials, NSC Files, NSC Institutional Files (H–Files), Box H–117, Washington Special Action Group, WSAG Meetings Minutes, (Originals), 10/2/73–7/22/74.

    Foreign Relations of the United States, 1969–1976, Volume XXXVI, Energy Crisis, 1969–1974, Document 254. https://history.state.gov/historicaldocuments/frus1969-76v36/d254
26. Memo of Conversation, 5 December 1973. Library of Congress, Manuscript Division, Kissinger Papers, Department of State 1968–1977, Box CL 342, MemCons External, Sep 73–Feb 74.

    Foreign Relations of the United States, 1969–1976, Volume XXXVI, Energy Crisis, 1969–1974, Document 263. https://history.state.gov/historicaldocuments/frus1969-76v36/d263
27. *Der Spiegel*, 3 December 1973, interview with Yamani. Translated by MEES.
28. Bancroft, *American Perspectives of Aramco*, 134–6.
29. Telegram from the Embassy in Saudi Arabia to the Department of State, 30 December 1973. Source: Library of Congress, Manuscript Division, Kissinger Papers, Box CL 207, Geopolitical Files, Saudi Arabia, 28 Nov 73–Jan 74.

    Foreign Relations of the United States, 1969–1976, Volume XXXVI, Energy Crisis, 1969–1974, Document 275. https://history.state.gov/historicaldocuments/frus1969-76v36/d275
30. Jungers, *The Caravan Goes On*, 158.

CHAPTER 15: THE CZAR

1. Harry Maurer, 'Organizing the Gypsies', *The Nation*, 11 January 1975.
2. David Harris, 'Truckers Go to Washington', *Rolling Stone*, 25 April 1974.
3. Memo from P.L. Essley Jr. To William Simon. Dept. of the Treasury, 29 October 1973.
4. 'Love returns home "battered, bruised" ', *Rocky Mountain News*, 5 December 1973.
5. 'A Fitzgerald Hero in Washington', *Time*, 21 January 1974.
6. Edward Cowan, 'President Is Open on Gas Rationing', *New York Times*, 18 November 1973.
7. 'Mideast Oil Stops Flowing – and U.S. Feels First Pinch', *U.S. News and World Report*, 19 November 1973.
8. 'Making It Through This Winter', *CBS News*, 29 November 1973.
9. 'New Chief of Energy Programs', *New York Times*, 4 December 1973.
10. 'Simon "Tough" Says Sister', *Sentinel Star, Orlando*, 5 December 1973.
11. Evans & Novak, 'What Simon Says', *New York Post*, 12 December 1973.
12. Oliver S. Moore III, 'Fourth down for the "Vince Lombardi of energy" ', *New Times*, 8 March 1974, 9.
13. Frank Zarb Interview, for Richard Nixon Presidential Library and Museum. 2007-10-04 ZAR.
14. Simon, *A Time for Reflection*, 109.
15. 'Energy Office Flooded by Suggestions', *New York Times*, 7 January 1974.
16. Memorandum of Conversation, Riyadh, 14 December 1973, evening. National Archives, RG 59, Central Files 1970–73, POL 27 ARAB–ISR. Foreign Relations of the United States, 1969–1976, Volume XXXVI, Energy Crisis, 1969–1974, Document 267. https://history.state.gov/historicaldocuments/frus1969-76v36/d267
17. Paper prepared by William Quandt of the NSC. 14 December 1973. Nixon Presidential Materials, NSC Files, Box 1279, Saunders Files, UAR, 12/1–12/15/73. Foreign Relations of the United

States, 1969–1976, Volume XXXVI, Energy Crisis, 1969–1974, Document 266. https://history.state.gov/historicaldocuments/frus1969-76v36/d266

18. 'Memorandum of Conversation,' Washington, 1 February 1974, 8.A.M. Foreign Relations of the United States, 1969–1976, Volume XXXVI, Energy Crisis, 1969–1974, Document 294. https://history.state.gov/historicaldocuments/frus1969-76v36
19. Memorandum of Conversation, 1 February 1974. Library of Congress, Manuscript Division, Kissinger Papers, Box C1.142, Geopolitical Files, Germany FRG, Chron Files, Jan–Feb 1974. Foreign Relations of the United States, 1969–1976, Volume XXXVI, Energy Crisis, 1969–1974, Document 295. https://history.state.gov/historicaldocuments/frus1969-76v36/d295
20. Memorandum of Conversation, Riyadh, 14 December 1973, evening. National Archives, RG 59, Central Files 1970–73, POL.27 ARAB-ISR.

    Foreign Relations of the United States, 1969–1976, Volume XXXVI, Energy Crisis, 1969–1974, Document 267. https://history.state.gov/historicaldocuments/frus1969-76v36/d267
21. Dallek, *Nixon and Kissinger*, 546–8.
22. Charles W. Colson, *Born Again: The Classic True Story of One Man's Remarkable Transformation* (Grand Rapids, Michigan: Chosen Books, 1976), 197.
23. Jeddah. 'OPEC Price Increase'. Wikileaks Cable: 1973Jeddah05626_b Dated: 1973, December 21, 12.00. https://wikileaks.org/plusd/cables/1973Jeddah05626_b.html
24. Nick Renniston, *Scenes from a Year of Crisis* (Harpenden: Oldcastle Books, 2023), 23.
25. 'Oil Price Doubled by Big Producers on Persian Gulf', *New York Times*, 24 December 1973.
26. Asadollah Alam, *The Shah and I: The Confidential Diary of Iran's Royal Court* (London: I. B. Tauris & Co., 1991), 349; Telegram from the Department of State to the Embassy in Iran. Washington, 29 December 1973. National Archives, Nixon Presidential Materials, NSC Files, Box 604, Country Files – Middle East, Iran, Vol. V, May–December 1973.

Foreign Relations of the United States, 1969–1976, Volume XXVII, Iran; Iraq, 1973–1976, ed. Monica L. Belmonte (Washington: United States Government Printing Office, 2012), Document 49. https://history.state.gov/historicaldocuments/frus1969-76v27

CHAPTER 16: A HANDFUL OF DESPERADOES

1. Walker, *Staying Power*, 105–6.
2. Patrick Keatley, 'British Team Flies to Shah', *The Guardian*, 23 January 1974.
3. 'Royal Guests', *The Observer*, 27 January 1974.
4. Geoffrey Levy, 'Icy Welcome for Barber', *Daily Express*, 25 January 1974.
5. Anthony Barber, *Taking the Tide: A Memoir* (London: Michael Russell, 1996), 139.
6. 'Nixon and Faisal: If Arabs mistrust America, there's good reason', *International Herald Tribune*, 19 December 2002.
7. 'Sonny Kleinfeld, "Hey buddy, can you spare a gallon?"' *New Times*, 8 March 1974, 12–16.
8. 'More tempers exploding into gas-station violence', *Associated Press*, 21 February 1974.
9. 'In U.S. It's Almost Anything for Gasoline', *UPI*, 13 March 1974.
10. 'Energy Situation Has Its Weirder Moments', *UPI*, 1 April 1974.
11. 'It Gets to You That Long Wait', *Honolulu Star-Bulletin*, 25 January 1974.
12. Kleinfeld, 'Hey Buddy'.
13. 'Strike Cuts Meat Supply', *Columbus Herald*, 8 February 1974.
14. 'Slain trucker: no protester', *UPI*, 7 February 1974.
15. David Harris, 'Truckers Go to Washington', *Rolling Stone*, 25 April 1974.
16. Dee Jackson to the Editor, 'As Long as It Takes', *Overdrive*, June 1974.
17. 'The Second Shutdown – What Really Happened', *Overdrive*, March 1974.
18. Akins, private memoir.

19. Backchannel Message from the Ambassador to Saudi Arabia (Akins) to Secretary of State Kissinger, 5 February 1974. National Archives, Nixon Presidential Materials, NSC Files, Kissinger Office Files Box 139, Country Files, Middle East, Saudi Arabia, Dec 73–74.
    Foreign Relations of the United States, 1969–1976, Volume XXXVI, Energy Crisis, 1969–1974, Document 303. https://history.state.gov/historicaldocuments/frus1969-76v36/d303
20. Akins, private memoir.
21. FRUS 1969-1976, Volume XXXVI, Energy Crisis, 1969–1974, Document 309. https://history.state.gov/historicaldocuments/frus1969-76v36/d309

CHAPTER 17: A QUIET END

1. Telegram from the Embassy in Saudi Arabia to the Department of State. Jeddah, 16 February 1974. National Archives, Nixon Presidential Materials, NSC Files, Kissinger Office Files, Box 139, Country Files, Middle East, Saudi Arabia, February–July 1974. Foreign Relations of the United States, 1969–1976, Volume XXXVI, Energy Crisis, 1969–1974, Document 325 https://history.state.gov/historicaldocuments/frus1969-76v36/d325#fn:1.7.4.4.28.366.16.44.14
2. Hume Horan, interviewed by Charles Stuart Kennedy, ADST Oral History Collection.
3. 'Memorandum for the President's Files', Washington, 19 February 1974. 11:09 A.M. National Archives, Nixon Presidential Materials, NSC Files, Box 1028, Presidential/HAK Memcons, 1 Jan–28 Feb 1974.
    Foreign Relations of the United States, 1969–1976, Volume XXXVI, Energy Crisis, 1969–1974, Document 327 https://history.state.gov/historicaldocuments/frus1969-76v36/d327
4. Transcript of a Telephone Conversation Between Secretary of State Kissinger and President Nixon. Washington, 13 February 1974. Foreign Relations of the United States, 1969–1976, Volume XXXVI, Energy Crisis, 1969–1974, 322. https://history.state gov/historicaldocuments/frus1969-76v36/d322

5. 'Memorandum of Conversation', Washington, 9 March 1974. National Archives, Nixon Presidential Materials, NSC Files, Box 1028, Presidential/HAK MemCons, 1 March–8 May 1974.
6. 26 April meeting between Kissinger and Saqqaf. Library of Congress, Manuscript Division, Kissinger Papers, Box C1.145, Geopolitical Files, Great Britain, Chron Field, Mar–Apr 74.

   Foreign Relations of the United States, 1969–1976, Volume XXXVI, Energy Crisis, 1969–1974, ed. Linda Qaimmaqami (Washington: Office of the Historian, 2011), Document 332. https://history.state.gov/historicaldocuments/frus1969-76v36/d332
7. Jeddah. 'Saudi Petroleum Minister's position on the consumers' conference and subsequently consumer producer meetings'. Wikileaks Cable: 1974Jeddah00692_b. Dated 1974 February 11, 13.10. https://wikileaks.org/plusd/cables/1974Jeddah00692_b.html
8. Jedda. 'Joint US Saudi Economic Commissions: Saudi Enthusiasm'. Wikileaks Cable: 1974Jeddah01192_b. Dated: 1974, March 11. 11.53. https://wikileaks.org/plusd/cables/1974Jeddah01192_b.html
9. 'Seven Arab States Cancel Oil Embargo Against U.S.; Saudi Arabia Pledges to Boost Its Production Levels', *Wall Street Journal*, May 1974.
10. 'Yamani Interview with CBS Television', transcript published MEES 22 March 1974.
11. Bremer, ADST.

CHAPTER 18: NIXON IN JEDDAH

1. Abdulaziz H. Al Fahad, 'Raiders and Traders: A Poet's Lament on the End of the Bedouin Heroic Age', in Bernard Haykel, Thomas Hegghammer, Stéphane Lacroix (eds), *Saudi Arabia in Transition: Insights on Social, Political, Economic and Religious Change* (Cambridge: Cambridge University Press, 2015), 231–62.
2. Bancroft, *American Perspectives of Aramco*, 244.
3. Mohamed Heikal, *The Sphinx and the Commissar: The Rise and Fall of Soviet Influence in the Middle East* (New York: Harper & Row, 1978), 262.

4. Willard Beling (ed.), *King Faisal and the Modernization of Saudi Arabia* (London: Croom Helm, 1980), 129.
5. 'In Saudi Arabia, Sports Cars and Law of the Koran', *New York Times*, 6 April 1974.
6. Dallek, *Nixon and Kissinger*, 586.
7. James Akins personal history.
8. The Nixon Foundation, June 16, 2010. Thirty-Six Years Ago: RN Meets King Faisal.
9. Memorandum of Conversation, Jeddah June 15, 1974; Library of Congress, Manuscript Division, Kissinger Papers, Box CL 208, Geopolitical File, Saudi Arabia, 6 June–9 August 1974.
10. Akins in Jeddah to the Department of State / Saudi Arabia, 5 May 1974, 1974Jeddah02421_b
11. Akins to Jersualem / Tel Aviv embassies, 28 May 1974, 1974STATE110957_b
12. 10 July 1974. From US Embassy, Jeddah, to Department of State, 1974Jeddah03946_b
13. Henry Mitchell, 'Henry and the Prince and 1,400 Guests', *Washington Post*, 8 June 1974.
14. 'Oil-Fueled Arab Tie', *New York Times*, 10 June 1974.
15. 'Rising Oil Prices Causing Dismay', *New York Times*, 17 June 1974.
16. London Letter by Joe Roeber, *Finance Magazine*, June 1974.
17. 'McCloy Testifies He Took the Oil Companies' Case on International Talks to President Kennedy', *New York Times*, 7 February 1974.

    Multinational Corporations and United States Foreign Policy. Hearings Before the Subcommittee on Multinational Corporations of the Committee on Foreign Relations. United States Senate. 93rd Congress. First and Second Sessions on Multinational Petroleum Companies and Foreign Policy, 6 February 1974. P.79 Testimony of John McCloy, 6 February 1974.
18. 'Oil Billions for the Few – Sand for the Starving', *New York Times*, 3 April 1974.
19. Coping with the Oil Crisis, address to the National Press Club, Washington DC, Thursday 9 May.

20. William F. Buckley Firing Line, the Energy Crisis. Interview with Bill Simon, 9 December 1974.
21. 'Yamani Rejects IMF Plan', *Washington Post*, 10 May 1974.
22. International Petrodollar Crisis. Hearings before the Subcommittee on International Finance of the Committee on Banking and Currency, House of Representatives, 93rd Congress, Second Session, 17, 9 July 1974 (statement of Jack Bennett, Under Secretary of the Treasury).
23. Foreign Direct Investment, SAG's views. 22 August 1974. Horan, Jeddah.
24. Terence Smith, 'Clash over Ma'alot Disclosed by Dayan', *New York Times*, 21 May 1974.

CHAPTER 19: RIYAL POLITIK

1. 12 May 1973, Kissinger meets Abba Eban, Israeli Foreign Minister, in Washington. Memo of Conversation. National Archives, Nixon Presidential Materials, NSC Files, Kissinger Office Files Box 135, Country Files, Middle East, Rabin/Dinity Sensitive Memcons, 1973.

   Foreign Relations of the United States, 1969–1976, Volume XXV, Arab-Israeli Crisis and War, 1973, Document 55. https://history.state.gov/historicaldocuments/frus1969-76v25/d55
2. James Akins Memorandum for the File: US-Persian-Israeli cooperation, 28 August 1975, Ref: Jeddah 6009. Quoted Shawcross, *The Shah's Last Ride*, 178–9.
3. Oriana Fallaci, 'The Shah of Iran: An Interview with Mohammad Reza Pahlavi', *New Republic*, 1 December 1973.
4. 'Constructive Influence on Arab Investing Is Goal of Trip to Mideast, Simon Says', *American Banker*, 15 July 1974.
5. Senate Finance Committee Chairman Subcommittee on financial markets, December 1974.
6. Alam, *The Shah and I*, 396.
7. Moorer, *Reminiscences*, 1497.
8. Jim Akins, private memoir.
9. 'Simon Has Meeting with Saudi King on Investing In US', *UPI*, 20 July 1974.

10. Jeddah. 'Saudis Now Appear to Wish Substantive Talks on Finance'. Dated: 1974, July, 13:25 July 1974. Jeddah to State. Akins. Wikileaks Cable: 1974JIDDA04107_b. https://wikileaks.org/plusd/cables/1974JIDDA04107_b.html
11. Jeddah. 'US-Arab Economic Cooperation and the Middle East Political Relations Are Inseparable According to the Saudis'. Wikileaks Cable: 1974JIDDA04232_b. Dated 1974, July 16:20. https://wikileaks.org/plusd/cables/1974JIDDA04232_b.html
12. 'After Simon's Talks With Arabs – Hope for Lower Oil Prices', *U.S. News & World Report*, 12 August 1974.
13. April 1974 Memo, Jack Bennett at Treasury to Kissinger, Congress House Committee on Government Operations, Federal Response to OPEC, part 1, 472–3.
14. Department of State Bulletin, DO.1844, 28 October 1974, 576.
15. 'Energy: Kissinger Lays Out His Floor Plan', *Time*, 17 February 1975.
16. Memo of Conversation. Washington 3 February 1975. National Archives, RG 59, Records of Henry Kissinger, Lot 91D414, Box 10, Classified External Memoranda of Conversations, January –April 1975.

    Foreign Relations of the United States, 1969–1976, Volume XXXVII, Energy Crisis, 1974–1980, ed. Stephen G. Halpern (Washington: United States Government Printing Office, 2012), Document 39.

    https://history.state.gov/historicaldocuments/frus1969-76v37/d39
17. Michael Quint, 'His Formula: Smith Barney + Shearson = Powerhouse', *New York Times*, 28 March 1993.
18. Frank Zarb Interview for Richard Nixon Presidential Library and Museum. 2007-10-04 ZAR.
19. Memorandum of Conversation, Washington 13 October 1975. National Archives, RG 59, Central Foreign Policy Files, P820123-2170.

    Foreign Relations of the United States, 1969–1976, Volume XXXI, Foreign Economic Policy, 1973–1976, ed. Kathleen B. Rasmussen (Washington: United States Government

Printing Office, 2009), Document 235. https://history.state.gov/historicaldocuments/frus1969-76v31

20. Elizabeth Jones, ADST Oral History.

CHAPTER 20: GOD'S WILL

1. 'Du pétrole sur le tapis vert', *L'Express*, 14 October 1974, 153–4.
2. Airgram from the Embassy in Saudi Arabia to the Department of State, Jeddah, 16 December 1974. Source: National Archives, RG 84, Jeddah Embassy Files: Lot 79F80, POL 15-4, Denmark File.

   Foreign Relations of the United States, 1969–1976, Volume E–9, Part 2, Documents on the Middle East Region, 1973–1976, Document 122. https://history.state.gov/historicaldocuments/frus1969-76ve09p2/d122
3. Ford Library, National Security Adviser, Memoranda of conversations Box 4, 12 August 1974, Ford, Kissinger.
4. 'Kissinger Meets Faisal for Talks on Long Oil Pacts', *New York Times*, 16 February 1975.
5. *Business Week*, 13 January 1975.
6. Sheehan, Edward, *The Arabs, Israelis, and Kissinger: A Secret History of American Diplomacy in the Middle East* (New York: Reader's Digest Press, 1976), 164.
7. Airgram from the Ambassador to Saudi Arabia (Akins) to the Department of State, Jeddah, 13 April 1975. Washington National Records Center, OSD Files: FRC 330-78-0058, Box 70, Middle East 381, 1975.

   Foreign Relations of the United States, 1969–1976, Volume XXXVII, Energy Crisis, 1974–1980, Document 52. https://history.state.gov/historicaldocuments/frus1969-76v37
8. Oriana Fallaci, 'A Sheik Who Hates to Gamble', *New York Times*, 14 September 1975.
9. Robinson, *Yamani*, 221.
10. Jungers, *The Caravan Goes On*, 170–1.
11. James Fox, 'The Last Moments of King Faisal', *The Sunday Times*, 30 March 1975.

12. Airgram from the Ambassador to Saudi Arabia (Akins) to the Department of State, Jeddah, 13 April 1975. Washington National Records Center, OSD Files: FRC 330-78-0058, Box 70, Middle East 381, 1975.

    Foreign Relations of the United States, 1969–1976, Volume XXXVII, Energy Crisis, 1974–1980, Document 52. https://history.state.gov/historicaldocuments/frus1969-76v37
13. 'The Death of a Desert Monarch', *Time*, 7 April 1975.
14. TNA: FCO 8/2598-2600. UK ambassador report on funeral.
15. The Quran, passage 5.33–4.
16. Registry N335, 20 June 1975, from Jedda 190830Z. Priority FCO Tel No 303 of 19/6/75.
17. Jeddah, Thursday 19 June 1975. *Arab News*, Vol. 1, Issue 53. AP report.
18. Juan de Onis, 'Faisal's Killer Is Put to Death', *New York Times*, 19 June 1975.
19. Robinson, *Yamani*, 221.
20. Fallaci, 'A Sheik Who Hates to Gamble'.

CHAPTER 21: THE JACKAL

1. Ibrahim Almuhanna, *Oil Leaders: An Insider's Account of Four Decades of Saudi Arabia and OPEC's Global Energy Policy* (New York: Columbia University Press, 2022), 19.
2. *Newsweek*, December 1973.
3. Fallaci, 'A Sheik Who Hates to Gamble'.
4. Kissinger, *Years of Upheaval*, 867–77.
5. *PIW*, 29 December 1975.
6. Tehran. 'Amouzegar Attacks Yamani, Defends Oil Prices, Calls for Aid to LDC's'. Wikileaks Cable: 1974TEHRAN04153_b. Dated 1974, May 23, 11:52. https://wikileaks.org/plusd/cables/1974TEHRAN04153_b.html
7. 'Sheikh Ahmed Zaki Yamani Speaks About Carlos the Jackal', *APTV*, 2 November 1997.
8. Libya Oil Minister Mabruk, *Al Fatih*, Libyan Army Weekly.
9. Bancroft, *American Perspectives of Aramco*, 148.

10. 'Sheikh Ahmed Zaki Yamani Speaks Out About Carlos the Jackal', *AP*, 10 December 1997.
11. Account drawn from Yamani's interview on Saudi television, reports from the US embassy in Jeddah released on Wikileaks, (Jeddah. 'MINPET Yamani's Remarks on OPEC Kidnapping'. Wikileaks Cable: 1976JIDDA00100_b. Dated: 1976, January 7, 05:27. https://wikileaks.org/plusd/cables/1976JIDDA00100_b.html; and Bancroft, *American Perspectives of Aramco*, 148.
12. Berlin. 'Terrorist Attack Against OPEC HQs in Vienna'. Wikileaks Cable: 1976USBERL00129_b. Dated: 1976, January 23, 16:23. https://wikileaks.org/plusd/cables/1976USBERL00129_b.html
13. Yallop, *Tracking the Jackal*, 'Gaddafi denied', 316; 'Austrian authorities', 164.
14. Yallop, *Tracking the Jackal*, 387.

CHAPTER 22: RUNNING FOR THE STORM CELLARS

1. Letters, *The Times*, 29 November 1973.
2. Arab Oil and Gas, 16 February 1975, cited in Terzian , *OPEC*, 212.
3. A. Craig Copetas, *Metal Men: How Marc Rich Defrauded the Country, Evaded the Law, and Became the World's Most Sought-After Corporate Criminal* (New York: G. P. Putnam's Sons. 1985), 142.
4. Robinson, *Yamani*, 43.
5. Richard Norton-Smith, *On His Own Terms: A Life of Nelson Rockefeller* (New York: Random House, 2014), 698–9.
6. Akins, private memoir.
7. 'Gaddafi's last moments: "I saw the hand holding the gun and I saw it fire"', *The Guardian*, 20 October 2012.
8. William E. Mulligan papers, Saudi Aramco Publications Collection, GTM-20230816. Georgetown University Manuscripts.
9. 'Oil Profits Under Fire', *Time*, 4 February 1974.
10. Multinational Corporations and United States Foreign Policy. Hearings Before the Subcommittee on Multinational Corporations of the Committee on Foreign Relations. United States Senate. 93rd Congress. First and Second Sessions on Multinational Petroleum

Companies and Foreign Policy. 31 January; 1 and 6 February 1974, 237. Senator Percy. Testimony of George Schuler. 1 February 1974.

11. De Gaury, *Faisal*, 34.
12. 'Report Massacre of Whole Arab Town; Inhabitants of Taif put to the Sword – Mecca Appeals to the World for Vengeance', *New York Times*, 13 September 1924.
13. Mai Yamani, *Cradle of Islam: The Hijaz and the Quest for Identity in Saudi Arabia* (London: I. B. Tauris & Co., 2009), xi.
14. 'People'. *Time*, 29 December 1975.
15. Peter Kihss, 'Khalid, Quiet King and Desert Hunter', *New York Times*, June 14, 1982.
16. Roger Upton, *Arab Falconry* (Surrey: Hancock House Publishers. 2002), 111.

Image Credits

Every effort has been made to contact all copyright holders. The Publishers will be pleased to amend in future printings any errors or omissions brought to their attention. The images come from the following sources:

Ibn Saud (Kuwait, 1910), Volgi archive / Alamy; Ibn Saud's (Abd al-Aziz Ibn Saud) army on the march near Habl, W.H.I. Shakespear / Royal Geographical Society via Getty Images; J. Rives Childs and King Ibn Saud, Bettmann via Getty; Wildcat well, Beechcraft airplane, and camel, Robert Yarnall Richie Photograph Collection, DeGolyer Library, SMU; The Quincy Agreement, Bettmann via Getty; 1947 Aramco Brats Visit King Ibn Saud, unknown author, Wikimedia Commons; King Abdulaziz and Prince Faisal Travelling in a Car, unknown author, Wikimedia Commons; Arabie Saoudite, Alain Nogues / Sygma / Sygma via Getty Images; Oil Workers' Training, Pictorial Parade / Archive Photos / Getty Images; Fire At Al Aqsa Mosque, UPI / Bettmann Archive via Getty Images; Denis Michael Rohan On Trial by UPI / Bettmann Archive / Getty Images; Israeli Soldiers by Dome of the Rock, Bettman via Getty Images; The Funeral of President Abdel Nasser Gamal, Jack Garofalo / Paris Match via Getty Images; France-Diplomacy-Hussein-City Hall, by AFP via Getty Images; Libyans demanding Gaddafi's return as Revolutionary Council Leader, Genevieve Chauvel / Sygma / Sygma via Getty Images; Ahmed Zaki Yamani, Sven Simon / United Archives via Getty Images; King Faisal During Hajj, Fox Photos / Hulton Archive / Getty Images; Third Annual Robert F. Kennedy Pro-Celebrity Tennis Tournament to Benefit the RFK Foundation, Peter Simins / WWD / Penske Media via Getty Images; White House Barbershop, Washington, DC, USA, Alfred Eisenstaedt / The LIFE Picture Collection / Shutterstock; Donald Rumsfeld, as Cost of Living Council Director during Nixon's campaign news conference,

1971, Everett/Shutterstock; Nixon and Brezhnev, © CORBIS/Corbis via Getty Images; Saudi Arabia-France-King Faisal Ibn Abdul al Saud, AFP via Getty Images; Israel marks 30th anniversary of the 1973 Yom Kippur War, Ron Frenkel/GPO/Getty Images; Egypt's chief of staff, President Sadat and minister of war, Photo12/Universal Images Group via Getty Images; MIDEAST-1973 ARABISRAELI WAR, Photo by Staff/AFP via Getty Images; MIDEAST-1973 Ara- Israeli War, by Gabriel Duval/AFP via Getty Images; Henry Kissinger Leaves White House After Meeting, David Hume Kennerly/Getty Images; Photographers take pictures of Sheikh Ahmed Yamani as he leaves Kennedy airport, Nick Sorrentino/NY Daily News Archive via Getty Images; Le Shah d'Iran en famille à Saint-Moritz, James Andanson/Sygma via Getty Images; FRANCE-GASOLINE-OIL, AFP via Getty Images; Amsterdam Horses, Keystone/Hulton Archive/Getty Images; Government Plea To Save Fuel, Terry Disney/Daily Express/Hulton Archive/Getty Images; Men crossing Piazza del Duomo on a tandem bicycle in Milan, Giorgio Lotti\Mondadori via Getty Images; Oil Crisis, Werner/Ullstein Bild via Getty Images; Truck Driver Pointing At Windscreen Bullet Holes, Photo by UPI/Bettmann via Getty Images; April 1974 - Country's Fuel Shortage Led to Problems for Motorists in Finding Gas as well as Paying Much More for It, and Resulted in Theft from Cars Left Unprotected, This Father and Son, Made a Sign Warning Thieves of the Possible Consequences, Hum Images / Alamy; Presidents Anwar Sadat, Houari Boumediene, and Hafez Assad, by Henri Bureau/Sygma/Corbis/VCG via Getty Images; King Faisal and Frank Jungers in Riyadh, by Alain Nogues/Sygma/Sygma via Getty Images; Oil Embargo 17 March 1974, by Rolls Press/Popperfoto via Getty Images/Getty Images; Henry Kissinger and Wife Nancy, UPI/Bettmann Archive/Getty Images; Henry Kissinger With Golda Meir, Bettman via Getty; Nelson Bunker Hunt, Central Press/Getty Images; Richard Nixon Shaking Hands with the King of Saudi Arabia, © Wally McNamee/CORBIS/Corbis via Getty Images; William E. Simon papers, 1972-1977. Special Collections & College Archives, Skillman Library, Lafayette College; Le Roi Fahd et Sheikh Ahmed Zaki Yamani en 1975, Bernard Charlon/Gamma-Rapho via Getty Images; Economic and Energy Advisers Meeting, David Hume Kennerly/Getty Images; U.S. Secretary of State Henry Kissinger, right, is greeted on arrival at Riyadh Airport on 19 March 1975 with a hug and kiss from Saudi Petroleum and Minerals Minister Sheik Zaki Yamani. Kissinger also held talks with King Faisal, AP Photo / Max Nash via Alamy; Joan Kennedy visits Saudi Arabia, by Nancy Moran / Sports Illustrated via Getty Images; OPEC Geiseldrama in Vienna, Brandstaetter Images / Votava / Imagno via Getty Images; Funeral of King Faisal of Saudi Arabia, Claude Salhani / Sygma via Getty Images; Saudi Arabia-Jeddah, photo by AFP via Getty Images; King Khalid with a Falcon, unknown author, Wikimedia Commons.

Index